FROMMER'S

COMPREHENSIVE TRAVEL GUIDE

CANCÚN, COZUMEL & YUCATÁN '91-'92

by Marita Adair

PRENTICE
HALL
PRESS

NEW YORK • LONDON • TORONTO • SYDNEY • TOKYO • SINGAPORE

FROMMER BOOKS
Published by Prentice Hall Press
A division of Simon & Schuster Inc.
15 Columbus Circle
New York, NY 10023

PRENTICE HALL PRESS and colophons are registered trademarks of
Simon & Schuster Inc.

ISBN 0-13-337122-0
ISSN 0899-2878

Manufactured in the United States of America

CONTENTS

MAPS

A Disclaimer

Readers are advised that prices fluctuate in the course of time and travel information changes under the impact of the varied and volatile factors that affect the travel industry. The author and publisher cannot be held responsible for the experiences of the reader while traveling. Readers are invited to write the publisher with ideas, comments and suggestions for future editions. Readers should also note that the establishments described under Readers' Selections or Suggestions have not in all cases been inspected by the author and that opinions expressed are those of the individual reader(s) only and do not in any way represent the opinions of the publisher or author of this guide.

A Word About Prices

You're liable to get your first unpleasant shock in Mexico when you see "Tacos—$8,000 in a resturant menu." The wave of relief comes as you realize that the dollar sign "$" is used to indicate *pesos* in Mexico, and that your tacos actually only cost 8,000 pesos, or a few dollars. To avoid confusion I use the dollar sign *only* to indicate U.S. dollars; peso amounts are written as figures alone, or are qualified by the word *pesos*.

Sometimes Mexican establishments will quote prices in U.S. dollars, usually written "$3 Dlls."; for the peso price, then, they may write, "$8,000 m.n.," meaning "8,000 pesos, *moneda nacional*" (that is, Mexican national currency).

Note also that Mexico has a Value Added Tax, or *Impuesto de Valor Agregado*. Abbreviated *IVA* (ee-bah), the 15% tax is *already included* in most prices in Mexico: hotels, restaurants, rental cars, souvenirs, transportation tickets.

Converting Pesos to Dollars

As this book goes to press, inflation in Mexico is between 20% and 30% per year, and the same is forecast for the year to come. The peso is being devalued daily against the dollar, and even more drastic devaluations could be in store. I've quoted all prices in this book *in U.S. dollars only*.

At presstime US$1 was worth about 3,000 pesos.

YUCATÁN: AN INTRODUCTION

1. YUCATÁN'S FASCINATING HISTORY
2. PREPARING FOR YOUR TRIP

A limitless swath of emerald jungle, bounded by sand beaches of the purest white, bordered by palm trees swaying lazily in a freshening breeze, all surrounded by water so intensely blue it seems a great liquid jewel—that's the Yucatán.

But no simple description can encompass this fascinating area, the very heart of Mesoamerica, where the ancient Mayas lifted great monuments of enduring beauty above the dense carpet of vegetation, and built a civilization that reverberates in this land even today. Although the earth here is of such poor quality that only the mat of jungle grows without toil, and the population must struggle even to feed itself, the Mayas developed a rich and advanced civilization, the Spanish conquistadores built beautiful cities, and the Roman Catholic Church raised huge churches that had to be fortresses, so fiercely did the Mayas hold to their ancient religious rites. Though the coasts present the perfect picture of tropical paradise, ruthless pirates used to cruise the sea lanes here, pillaging coastal towns that were not completely walled and heavily defended.

Always there has been a spirit of adventure, of something unexpected and unusual, like the priceless sacrificial treasures drawn by archeologists from the great well at Chichén-Itzá, or the iridescent colors of a school of fish seen by a diver near the Palancar Reef off Cozumel. You feel this spirit as you drive along a flat, dead-straight Yucatecan highway, with nothing ahead for miles except the monotony of the jungle, when, all at once, a cloud of butterflies, brilliantly yellow, will block your way. And you feel it as you penetrate the jungle at Xcaret, stumble upon a miniature Maya temple, and then come across a crystal-clear natural swimming pool of limpid water, half sheltered by a cave.

Yucatán is in Mexico, and yet Yucatán and its people, the Maya, do not really look upon themselves merely as Mexicans. Yucatán is different, they will tell you. Yucatán is special. It is not simply Mexican, nor just Caribbean, not Maya nor Spanish. You will feel this special spirit when you meet the Maya, speaking Spanish and Maya, wearing traditional costumes or modern fashions, living in thatched cottages or in air-conditioned bungalows.

Whatever happens here, you're in for an adventure. As far as I'm concerned, you couldn't have picked a better place for it, whether your idea of adventure is surfing or archeology, cuisine or architecture, diving or folk art, or meeting new people. Yucatán has enough to keep you happy and adventuring for years, not just for weeks, whatever your desires may be.

Perhaps the way to start your adventure is with a summary of Yucatán's past, a story that seems more fitting in a spellbinding novel than in a history book. After that, let's go on to some less romantic, but more practical, details of planning your trip.

1. Yucatán's Fascinating History

Yucatán's history has fascinated the rest of the world since Lord Kingsborough published a study of its ruins in 1831. Just a few years later, New York lawyer John L. Stephens and artist Frederick Catherwood made several trips through Yucatán and Central America. Stephens recorded his adventures in a fascinating series of travel books, decorated by Catherwood's superb drawings, which achieved great, immediate, and lasting popularity. The books still make for wonderful reading, and are available from Dover Publications, 31 E. 2nd St., Mineola, NY 11501-3582, or through bookstores in North America and Mexico.

Ever since Stephens' adventures, foreigners have been touring the Yucatán to view its vast crumbling cities and ponder the fall of a once truly great civilization. The Maya, though they practiced human sacrifice and self-mutilation, developed mathematical theories far in advance of European thought, and perfected a calendar more accurate than the Gregorian one we use today.

Here is a summary of Maya history so you can comprehend the importance of the archeological sites you're about to visit.

THE EARLY TIMES

The years 1500 B.C. to A.D. 320, the Preclassic Period, are thought to be the time when Maya civilization began and was shaped. It may be that the Maya learned a good deal from the mysterious Olmecs, whose great monolithic head sculptures are preserved in the Parque La Venta at Villahermosa and in the Museo de Antropología in Mexico City. Or it may be that the Maya developed from wandering tribes in what is now Guatemala's vast low-lying jungle province of El Petén.

Little is known about the first thousand years of Maya culture, except that they discovered how to cultivate corn (maize), the food —to them even a religious symbol—which was to shape their lives for thousands of years, and which still influences them strongly today.

In any case, by 500 B.C. the Maya were making great strides.

The Formative Period

The time from 500 B.C. until the end of the Preclassic Period is sometimes called the Formative Period because it is when the Maya developed their calendar, their complex and beautiful system of hieroglyphic writing, and their early architecture. The Maya religion with its 166 known deities, was also being shaped in these early centuries.

While the Maya were doing these things in the yet-to-be-"discovered" New World, the following events took place in the Old World: The Second Temple was built in Jerusalem; the Roman Empire reached the height of its power and influence; Jesus carried out his ministry; Jerusalem was destroyed and the Jewish Diaspora took place; and Constantine the Great was preparing to found his new imperial capital of Constantinople, now Istanbul.

THE CLASSIC YEARS

The great years of Maya culture were from A.D. 320 to 925, called the Classic Period. When Rome was falling to the barbarians and the Dark Ages were spreading over Europe, the Maya were consolidating their cultural gains, wiping out pockets of backwardness, and connecting their ceremonial centers by means of great roads. The finest examples of Maya architecture were conceived and constructed during these years, well before the Gothic style made its appearance in Europe. You can see these supreme achievements of Maya art at Palenque (near Villahermosa), at Copán in Honduras, and at Quiriguá in Guatemala. All these sites flourished during the last part of the Classic Period, in the 700s.

The End of the Great Era

The Classic Period closes with a century of degradation and collapse, roughly equivalent to the A.D. 800s. By the early 900s, the great ceremonial centers mentioned above were abandoned, the jungle moving in to cover them after not much more than one short century of florescence. Why classic Maya culture collapsed so quickly, we don't really know. Epidemic? Earthquake? Overpopulation? A breakdown of society?

In Europe at the time of the Maya collapse, it was the Middle Ages. Charlemagne was building his empire, an Umayyad Muslim prince reigned in Spain, the Anglo-Saxon King Alfred the Great ruled England, and the iconoclastic controversy raged in the Byzantine Middle East.

INTERREGNUM

With the collapse of Maya civilization, the Mayas seem to have migrated from their historic home in Guatemala and Chiapas into the northern lowlands of the Yucatán, roughly the modern states of Yucatán and Campeche. After their arrival around A.D. 900, they spent three centuries growing into an inferior copy of their former greatness.

Puuc Architecture

The cities near Yucatán's low western hills were built in this period in the style now called Puuc ("hills"). These include Kabah, Sayil, Labná, and Xlapak. Even though Maya architecture never regained the heights achieved at Palenque or Tikal, the Puuc buildings, such as the Codz Poop at Kabah and the palaces at Sayil and Labná, are quite beautiful and impressive.

The Putún Maya

After the Puuc period in architecture, Yucatán was profoundly affected by a strong influence from mainland Mexico. Some theories now hold that a distantly related branch of the Maya people, called the Putún Maya, were the ones who came from the borders of Mexico and crowded into the Yucatán during the Interregnum, developing a civilization of their own, heavily influenced by the cultures of mainland Mexico. The Putún Maya had been traders and navigators, controlling the coastal and riverine trade routes between mainland Mexico and the classic Maya lands in Petén and Chiapas. They spoke the Maya language poorly, using many Nahuatl (Aztec) words.

QUETZALCÓATL

The legend of Quetzalcóatl, a holy man who appeared during the time of troubles at the end of the Classic Period, is one of the most important tales in Mexican history and folklore. Quetzalcóatl means "feathered serpent," but seems to have been a religious title during later Maya times. Like the young Jesus, wise and learned beyond his years, he became the high priest and leader of the Toltecs at Tula, and did a good deal to "civilize" them and stop or ameliorate the bad effects of sacrifice. He stopped human sacrifice altogether. His influence completely changed the Toltecs from a group of spartan warriors to peaceful and fabulously productive farmers, artisans, and craftspeople. But his success upset the old priests who had depended on human sacrifice for their own importance, and they called upon their ancient god of darkness, Texcatlipoca, to degrade Quetzalcóatl in the eyes of the people. One night the priests conspired to dress Quetzalcóatl in a ridiculous garb, get him drunk, and tempt him to break his vow of chastity. The next morning they offered him a mirror, and the horror of what he saw after this night of debauch drove him in shame out of his own land and into the wilderness, where he lived for 20 years. He emerged in Coatzacoalcos, in the Isthmus of Tehuantepec, constructed a boat of feathers, bade his few followers farewell, and sailed away, having promised to return in a future age. But artistic influences noted at Chichén-Itzá in the Yucatán suggest that in fact he landed there and began his "ministry" again, which may in fact have been the Itzáes invasion (see below). He died there, but the legend of his return in a future age remained.

The Itzáes

When the Putún Maya left their ships and joined the Toltecs to overrun Yucatán, the invaders became known as the Itzáes.

It is thought that the semilegendary god-man Quetzalcóatl (in Nahuatl; Kukulcán in Maya) was the leader of the invasion. With a band of Toltecs, and the support of the Putún Maya, he conquered the town, which he called Chichén-Itzá ("In the mouth of the well of the Itzá"). It became his chief city.

Uxmal was founded during this same period (around A.D. 1000), according to some authorities, by the tribe known as the Tutul Xiú. Other scholars think that the Xiú took over from some earlier builders.

The three great centers of Chichén-Itzá, Mayapán, and Uxmal lived in peace under a confederation: The Itzá ruled in Chichén-Itzá, the Cocom tribe in Mayapán, and the Xiú in Uxmal. But in 1194 the people of Mayapán overthrew the confederation, sacked Chichén-Itzá, conquered Uxmal, and captured the leaders of the Itzá and the Xiú. Held in Mayapán, the Itzá and Xiú princes reigned over, but did not rule, their former cities.

The Xiú took their revenge in 1441 when they marched from Uxmal on Mayapán, capturing the city, destroying it, and putting the Cocom rulers to death. They thereupon founded a new city at Maní. Thereafter the Maya lands suffered from a series of battles and skirmishes, and were to know no peace until it was brought forcibly by the Spanish conquistadores.

THE SPANISH CONQUISTADORES

When Hernán Cortés and his men landed in 1519 in what would become Veracruz, the Aztec empire was ruled by Moctezuma (also, misspelled, Montezuma) in great splendor. The emperor thought the strangers might be Quetzalcóatl and his followers, returning at last, in which case no resistance must be offered; on the other hand, if the strangers were not Quetzalcóatl and his followers, they might be a threat to his empire. Moctezuma tried to bribe them with gold to go away, but this only whetted their appetites. Despite the fact that Moctezuma and his ministers received the conquistadores with full pomp and glory when they reached Mexico City, Cortés pronounced the Aztec chief to be under arrest and had him tortured. Moctezuma never did reveal where he had hidden his fabulous treasure, which had been seen by a Spaniard earlier.

Actually the Spaniards were living on bravado at this point, for they were no match for the hundreds of thousands of Aztecs; but they skillfully kept things under their control until a revolt threatened Cortés' entire enterprise. He retired to the countryside, made alliances with non-Aztec tribes, and finally marched on the empire when it was governed by the last Aztec emperor, Cuauhtémoc. He was victorious; Cuauhtémoc defended himself and his people furiously, but was finally captured, tortured, and made a prisoner. He was ultimately executed.

The Spanish conquest had started out as an adventure by Cortés and his men, unauthorized by the Spanish crown or its governor in Cuba, but the conquest was not to be reversed and soon Christianity was being spread through "New Spain." Guatemala and Honduras were explored and conquered, and by 1540 the territory of New Spain included Spanish possessions from Vancouver to Panama. In the two centuries that followed, Franciscan and Augustinian friars converted great numbers of the people to Christianity, and the Spanish lords built up huge feudal estates on which the farmers were little more than serfs. The silver and gold that Cortés had sought made Spain the richest country in Europe.

THE CONQUEST OF YUCATÁN

Francisco de Montejo, the Spaniard who led the conquest of Yucatán, was actually three men. The adventure was begun by Francisco de Montejo the Elder, a member of the lesser Spanish nobility, who had petitioned the crown for the right to conquer Yucatán at his own expense in exchange for a lifetime appointment as its governor.

"El Adelantado"

The conquest of Yucatán took a full 20 years. Montejo sailed from Spain in 1527 with 400 soldiers, landed at Cozumel, then proceeded to the mainland at Xel-ha. After scouting the terrain and plumbing the depths of the Maya's wrath, he decided to relaunch his campaign from the western coast, where he could more easily receive supplies from New Spain (Mexico).

Having regrouped in Mexico, Montejo the Elder (El Adelantado, "the pioneer") conquered what is now the state of Tabasco (1530), and then pushed onward to Yucatán. At first his campaign was successful, but Maya resistance increased along with his success, and after four difficult years (1531–1535) he was forced to return to Mexico a failure, out of money and out of energy. His soldiers had found little in the way of gold, and when stories began to arrive of the vast treasures up for grabs in newly conquered Peru, they deserted the Montejo cause en masse.

"El Mozo"

Montejo's son, Francisco Montejo the Younger (El Mozo, "the lad"), had accompanied him on this expedition, and in 1540 the father turned over his cause and his hope to the son. Montejo the Younger, bringing new vigor and his cousin (another Francisco de Montejo) to the cause, was successful in firmly establishing a town at Campeche, and another at Mérida (1542), and by 1546 (the year Martin Luther died in Germany) virtually all of the peninsula was under his control.

A few weeks after the founding of Mérida, the greatest of the several Maya leaders, Ah Kukum Xiú, head of the Xiú people, offered himself as Montejo's vassal, and was baptized. As was the custom, upon being baptized he took a new Christian name. Choosing what must have been the most popular name in the entire 16th century, he became—yes!—Francisco de Montejo Xiú. With the help of Montejo's troops he then accomplished his real objective, the defeat of the Cocoms. By allying his people with the Spaniards, Xiú signed the Cocoms' death warrant—but also his own and that of the Yucatecan Maya as a free people.

The Fruits of Conquest
The population of the peninsula declined drastically in the following centuries as the result of warfare, disease, slavery, and emigration.

Fray Diego de Landa, second bishop of Yucatán, studied the Maya culture and language and, thus equipped, used this knowledge to eradicate as much of it as possible. It was he who ordered the mass destruction of the priceless Maya codices, or "painted books," at Maní in 1562, only three of which survived.

INDEPENDENCE
Yucatán, controlled directly from Spain rather than from Mexico City, struggled along under the heavy yoke of Spanish colonial administration until the era of Mexican independence. In 1810 the Mexican War of Independence began with Father Hidalgo's famous "Cry of Dolores." With the success of the revolutionary effort in 1821, Spain signed a treaty with the newly independent country of Mexico. In that same year, the Spanish governor of Yucatán resigned, and Yucatán too became an independent country. Though it decided to join in a union with Mexico two years later, this period of Yucatán sovereignty is an indication of the local spirit. That same spirit arose again in 1845 when Yucatán seceded from Mexico, unhappy with close control from Mexico City.

Rise of the Haciendas
With independence came important changes in landholding practices, and thus in the economy. Sugarcane and henequen cultivation were introduced on a large scale, and soon there arose a culture of vast landed estates, each of which employed hundreds of Maya. The trick, according to the hacienda owners, was to keep them in debt, so much debt that they could never work their way out of it, and that is precisely what the owners did.

The same Maya who provided virtual slave labor on the haciendas also served in Yucatán's armed forces which, in the light of later events, was very poor planning on the part of the oppressive hacienda owners. Having been issued weapons with which to defend independent Yucatán against attack from Mexico or the United States, the Maya instead attacked their local oppressors. Thus, in 1847, began the War of the Castes.

WAR OF THE CASTES
The first target was Valladolid, which was attacked, looted, and sacked by the rebellious Maya in the most horrible manner. It soon

became apparent to all concerned that this was a race war, and the line was drawn between the Maya on one side and those of Spanish blood on the other.

The Maya, increasing their numbers with every victory, bought more guns and ammunition from British merchants in Belize (British Honduras). By June 1848 they held virtually all of Yucatán except Mérida and Campeche—and Mérida's governor had already decided to abandon the city. Feeling sure they had won the war, the rebel fighters went off to do something equally important: plant the corn. In the meantime reinforcements arrived from Mexico, which sent this aid in exchange for Yucatán's resubmission to Mexican authority. Government troops took the offensive, and things went badly for the Maya. Many retreated to the wilds of Quintana Roo, in the southeastern reaches of the peninsula.

The Talking Crosses

Then came the Talking Crosses. Massed in southern Quintana Roo, the Maya needed inspiration in their war effort. It came in the form of a cross that "spoke." The cult was begun in 1850 by a Mayan ventriloquist and a mestizo "priest," and carried on a tradition of "talking idols" that had flourished for centuries in several places, including the sacred Maya island of Cozumel. The first appearance of the loquacious symbol was at a place that later became the town of Chan Santa Cruz, named "Little Holy Cross" in its honor. Soon several crosses were talking, inspiring the Maya in their rebellion.

This worked pretty well until about 1866, when the fighting subsided. The Yucatecan authorities seemed content to let the rebels and their talking crosses rule the southern Caribbean coast, which they did with only minor skirmishes until the late 1800s. The rebel government received arms from the British in Belize, and in return allowed the British to cut lumber in rebel territory.

The End

But at the turn of the century, Mexican troops with modern weapons penetrated the rebel territory, soon putting an end to this bizarre, if romantic, episode of Yucatecan history. The town of Chan Santa Cruz was renamed in honor of a Yucatecan governor, Felipe Carrillo Puerto, and Yucatán was finally a full and integral part of Mexico, just in time for the Mexican Revolution.

THE MEXICAN REVOLUTION

From 1877 to 1911 the prime role in the drama of Mexico was played by an emotional strongman named Porfirio Díaz. Hailed by some as a modernizer, he was a terror to his enemies and to anyone who stood in his way or challenged his absolute power. He was finally forced to step down in 1911 by Francisco Madero and the greater part of public opinion.

The fall of the Porfirist dictatorship only led to more trouble, however. The country was split among several factions, including those led by "Pancho Villa" (real name Doroteo Arango), Alvaro Obregón, Venustiano Carranza, and Emiliano Zapata. The turbulent era from the fall of Porfirio Díaz through the next 10 years is referred to as the Mexican Revolution. Drastic reforms were proposed and carried out by the leaders in this period, and the surge of vitality and progress from this exciting if turbulent time has inspired Mexicans to the present day. Succeeding presidents have invoked the spirit of the Revolution, and it is still studied and discussed.

THE 20TH CENTURY

After the turmoil of the revolution, Mexico sought stability. It came in the form of the *Partido Revolucionario Institucional (el PRI,* pronounced ell-*pree),* the country's dominant political party. With the aim of "institutionalizing the revolution," the PRI literally engulfed Mexican society, leaving little room for vigorous, independent opposition. For over half a century, the monolithic party has had control of the government, labor unions, trade organizations, and other centers of power in Mexican society.

The most outstanding Mexican president (1934–1940) of the century is without doubt General Lázaro Cárdenas. A vigorous and effective leader, Cárdenas broke up vast tracts of agricultural land and distributed parcels to small cooperative farms called *ejidos;* reorganized the labor unions along democratic lines; and provided funding for village schools. His most famous action was the expropriation of Mexico's oil industry from U.S. and European interests. The expropriated assets became Petroleros Mexicanos (Pemex), the enormous government petroleum monopoly.

The PRI has selected Mexico's president (and, in fact, virtually everyone else on the government payroll) from its own ranks after Cárdenas, the national election being only a confirmation of the choice. Among these men have been Avila Camacho, who continued many of Cárdenas' policies; Miguel Alemán, who expanded national industrial and infrastructural development; Adolfo López Mateos, who expanded the highway system and increased hydroelectric power sources; and Gustavo Díaz Ordaz, who provided credit and technical help to the agricultural sector.

In 1970, Luis Echeverría came to power, followed in 1978 by José López Portillo. During their presidencies there emerged a studied coolness in relations with the United States and an activist role in international affairs. This period also saw an increase in charges of large-scale corruption in the upper echelons of Mexican society. The corruption, though endemic to the system, may have been fostered by the river of money that began to flow into Mexican banks (and Mexican pockets) because of the precipitous rise in oil prices. As oil income skyrocketed, Mexican borrowing and spending did likewise. Virtually all bankers, economists, and politicians saw the rise in oil prices as permanent. When, in the 1980s, oil prices dropped as fast as they had risen, Mexico was left with an enormous debt to foreign banks, and serious deficiencies in its infrastructure.

MEXICO TODAY

While oil wealth was paying all the bills, Mexico neglected its agricultural and industrial sectors to concentrate on petroleum production and marketing. Once oil was no longer king, the country had the difficult and painful job of rebuilding these sectors, cutting government expenditures, taming corruption, and keeping creditors at bay. President Miguel de la Madrid Hurtado, who assumed the presidency (1982–1988), struggled with these problems, and made important progress. But the economy and society are still under tremendous economic pressure, and charges of government corruption still abound. There is much still to be done by the new president, Carlos Salinas de Gortari, who took office at the end of 1988.

MEXICAN FACTS AND FIGURES

The United Mexican States today is headed by an elected president and a bicameral legislature. It is divided into 31 states, plus the Federal District (Mexico City). The population of about 80 million is 15% descendants of the Spaniards; 60% mestizo, or mixed Spanish and Native American blood; and 25% pure Native American (descendants of the Mayas, Aztecs, and other peoples). Although Spanish is the official language, about 50 Native American languages are still spoken, mostly in the Yucatán peninsula and the mountainous region of Oaxaca. Economically, Mexico is not by any means a poor country. Only about a sixth of the economy is in agriculture. Mining, which made the Spanish colonists and their king fabulously rich, is still fairly important. Gold and silver account for some of it, and there are many other important minerals still mined, but the big industry today is oil. Mexico is also well industrialized, manufacturing textiles, food products, everything from tape cassettes to automobiles.

In short, Mexico is well into the 20th century, with all the benefits and problems that contemporary life brings, and although vast sums are spent on education and public welfare (much, much more than is spent on implements of war), a high birth rate, high unemployment, and unequal distribution of wealth show that much remains to be done.

ABOUT YUCATÁN

Contrary to popular belief, which places Yucatán in the extreme southeast of Mexico, the land of the Maya forms the far east-central part of the Republic. A look at the map reveals that the Yucatecan capital, Mérida, is north of such major population centers as Mexico City, Guadalajara, Puebla, and Veracruz. Mérida is also surprisingly close to the tip of Florida: From Mexico City to Mérida it's about 600 miles as the crow flies, and from Mérida to Miami it's a mere 675 miles.

Actually there are two Yucatáns—the peninsula and the state. The peninsula is the piece of land north of Hwy. 186, which extends from Francisco Escárcega to Chetumal, and includes part of the state of Campeche and all of the state of Yucatán, plus most of the state of Quintana Roo. The Yucatán state is a wedge-shaped entity that includes Mérida and many of the best archeological sites.

2. Preparing For Your Trip

LEGAL DOCUMENTS

You'll need a Mexican Tourist Card, issued free, available at the border, at a Mexican consulate, or at any of the Mexican tourist offices listed below. Those flying to Mexico can ask their travel agent or airline to get them a Tourist Card; most agents will do so at no extra charge.

Note: The Tourist Card is more important than a passport in Mexico, so hold on to it carefully—if you lose it, you may not be able to leave the country until you can replace it, and that bureaucratic hassle takes several days or a week at least.

To get your Tourist Card, be sure to bring along a valid birth certificate, passport, or naturalization papers (not photocopies) when you apply, and when you travel in Mexico. You'll also need this proof of citizenship to reenter the United States or Canada. Minors under the age of 18 when traveling alone must have a notarized statement of parental consent *signed by both parents* before they can get a permit. One parent entering Mexico with a minor child must have written consent from the other parent. Check with the nearest Mexican tourist office for details.

Important Note: A Mexican Tourist Card can be issued for up to 180 days, and although your stay south of the border will doubtless be less than that, you should get the card for the maximum time, just in case. When the official who fills out your card asks you how long you intend to stay, say "six months," or at least *twice* as long as you really plan to be there. Who knows? You may find the perfect stretch of beach and not want to leave, or you may have to stay for some reason, and you'll save yourself *a lot* of hassle if you don't have to renew your papers. This hint is especially important for people who take cars into Mexico.

Mexican government tourist offices abroad include those in the following cities in the United States and Canada:

Chicago: 70 East Lake St., Suite 1413, Chicago, IL 60601 (tel. 312/606-9015).
Houston: 2707 North Loop West, Suite 450, Houston, TX 77008 (tel. 713/880-5153).
Los Angeles: 10100 Santa Monica Blvd., Suite 224, Los Angeles, CA 90067 (tel. 213/203-8191).
Montréal: One Place Ville Marie, Suite 2409, Montréal, QC H3B 3M9 (tel. 514/871-1052).
New York: 405 Park Ave., 10th Floor, New York, NY 10022 (tel. 212/755-7261).
Toronto: 2 Bloor St. West, Suite 1801, Toronto, ON M4W 3E2 (tel. 416/925-0704).
Washington, D.C.: 1922 Pennsylvania Ave. NW, Washington, DC 20006 (tel. 202/726-1750).

RESERVE IN ADVANCE FOR HOLIDAYS

Those planning to be in the Yucatán on major holidays (Mexican as well as international) should definitely write ahead for hotel reservations. Christmas and New Year's are the worst for crowding. If you discover you're up against a holiday when you're almost there, plan to arrive in the resort early in the day—before noon—and see what you can find. Here's a suggestion: Write for reservations in plenty of time, saying in your letter that you'll forward a deposit upon receipt of a confirmation. Or, instead, place a telephone call or send a Fax to the hotel concerned, make the reservation, get the name of the person who takes the reservation, and then send your deposit check by registered mail, return receipt requested. Remember that the process can take a good deal of time.

If you plan to make hotel reservations from home before leaving for Yucatán, be aware that the hotel of your choice may charge as much as two or three times the current local price for a room, especially in resort areas such as Cancún. It's amazing but true: If you walk off a Mexican street into a hotel and ask the price of a double room, they may quote you $25. But if you call or write from the United States or Canada, they will happily quote you a rate of $60! Why? Because they know that if you are writing or calling for reservations, they've got your business already, so they might as well jack up the price. Not being able to compare rates easily, you won't know the difference. Though it sounds underhanded, it isn't really. Virtually all hotels throughout the world, and especially the large luxury places, charge higher or lower rates depending on who's calling, from where, and when.

IMPORTANT TELEPHONE INFORMATION

Telephoning to and from Mexico holds special complexities and perils that you must know about. Calls to and from Mexico are unusually expensive, no matter how you do it. Before you make *any* long-distance call, whether it be to, from, or within Mexico, please read "Telephones" in Chapter XIII.

Here's an example of how to dial direct from the United States to Mexico: If you have direct international dialing service, dial "011" to connect with the international network, "52" for Mexico, "5" for Mexico City (or "748" for Acapulco, "73" for Cuernavaca, or "732" for Taxco), then the local number. The local number will be seven digits for Mexico City, six digits for Cuernavaca, or five digits for Acapulco or Taxco. Thus, to call from the United States to the Secretaría de Turismo's information number in Mexico City, you would dial 011-52-5-250-0123, and be billed anywhere from $1.65 to $2.65 per minute, depending on the time of day you called.

WEATHER, CLOTHING, PACKING

Virtually every day, Yucatán is hot. During the dry season (late October through mid- or late May), the days start out hot and get hotter so that by midafternoon the only place to be is on the beach or in an air-conditioned room. April and May are definitely the hottest months of the year. But even in these months you may get a little relief from the heat in the form of a *norte*. These fast-moving storms build in the northern skies and sweep across Yucatán at dizzying speed. You may be happily baking on the beach one moment, and in the time it takes to sip a cool drink, the skies may darken, the thunderheads climb into the stratosphere, the winds pick up force, and the rains come down in buckets. As quickly as it came, the *norte* will move on, and after less than a half hour, the sun will be shining again, and the skies radiant blue. The only reminder of the storm will be a welcome coolness in the air and puddles in the streets.

During the rainy season (mid-May through mid-October), there are often daily showers, usually in the afternoon, but these bring little relief from the heat; rather, they add high humidity to the hot air. Since virtually all of Yucatán is flat jungle, there's no escaping to the mountains for a breath of cool air.

The hurricane season runs roughly from July through October. In the best of years it means more rain, cloudy days, and perhaps a lengthy *norte*, which may be more strong wind than anything. In the worst of years it unleashes a furious storm as Hurricane Gilbert did in 1988.

Lightweight, airy cotton clothing should make up most of your wardrobe. Though visitors to Cancún like to dress up in the evening, jacket-and-tie formality is almost unheard of. Instead, men wear the dressy square-tailed shirt called *guayabera*, which is not tucked into the trousers. It's cool, handsome, and on sale throughout Yucatán. Women will likewise find lots of cotton fashions on sale, in case your wardrobe has a preponderance of winter woolens.

Everyone who visits Yucatán should have a hat, plus suntan lotion, without fail. The sun is relentless, and you will be spending lots of time bathed in it, whether you want to or not, clambering up Maya temples, strolling the shopping streets, relaxing on the beach, waiting for buses or taxis, or on boats. You've got to have protection. Also bring some insect repellent. If you spend most of your time at the beach in Cancún you may not need it, but if you venture into the jungle at all (which you will), it'll come in handy, especially during the summer rainy season.

As for shoes, sandals are the footwear of choice, but you should also have sneakers or running shoes that cover your whole foot. You'll need them when you climb those temples, or stroll into the jungle for a look around. All sorts of shoes and sandals are readily available at shops throughout Yucatán.

Will you need a sweater? Believe it or not, you might. In the evening, with a sea breeze blowing, it can become cool. After a day in the sun the contrast can be striking, and you'll want a light sweater to stay warm.

TRAVELING WITH CHILDREN

With Mexico's high birth rate, small children make up a large part of the population. The Mexican government has big programs to promote children's well-being. You should check with your doctor at home, and get advice on medicines to combat diarrhea, etc. Bring a supply, just to be sure. If your child is an infant, you'll be happy to know that disposable diapers are made and sold in Mexico (one popular brand is Kleen Bebé). The price is about the same as at home, though the quality is not quite as high. Also, Gerber's baby foods are on sale in many stores. In addition to the foods you're used to, you'll see "exotic" ones such as mango and papaya! Dry cereals, powdered formulas, baby bottles, purified water—they're all available easily in the larger cities.

The one problem you may encounter is with cribs. Except for the largest and most luxurious hotels, few Mexican hotels will have cribs, so you should be prepared to manage some other way.

HEALTH

Of course, the very best ways to avoid illness or to mitigate its effects are to make sure that you're in top health and that you *don't overdo it.* Travel, strange foods, upset schedules, and overambitious sightseeing tend to take more of your energy than a normal working day, and missed meals provide less of the nutrition you need. Make sure you get three good, wholesome meals a day, get *more* rest than you normally do, don't push yourself if you're not feeling in top form, and you'll be able to fight off traveler's diarrhea.

How to Prevent Traveler's Diarrhea

Traveler's diarrhea is the name given to the pervasive diarrhea, often accompanied by fever, nausea, and vomiting, that attacks so many visitors to Mexico on their first trip. Doctors say it's not just one "bug," or factor, but a combination of different food and water, upset schedules, overtiring, and the stresses that accompany travel. I've found that I get it when I'm tired and careless about what I eat and drink. A good high-potency (or "therapeutic") vitamin supplement, and even extra vitamin C, is a help; yogurt is good for a healthy digestion, but it is not available everywhere in Mexico.

The U.S. Public Health Service recommends the following measures for prevention of traveler's diarrhea:

□ **Drink only purified water:** This means tea, coffee, and other beverages made with boiled water; canned or bottled carbonated beverages, including carbonated water; beer and wine; or water that you yourself have brought to a rolling boil or otherwise purified.

□ **Choose food carefully:** In general, avoid salads, uncooked vegetables, and unpasteurized milk or milk products (including cheese). Choose food that is freshly cooked and still hot. Peel fruit yourself. Don't eat undercooked meat, fish, or shellfish.

What to Do If You Get It

The Public Health Service does not recommend that you take any medicines as preventives. All the applicable medicines can have nasty side effects if taken for long periods of several weeks. The best way to prevent illness is to take care with food and water, get rest, and don't overdo it.

Should you get sick, there are lots of medicines available in

Mexico that can harm more than help. You should talk with your doctor before you go, and ask what medicine he or she recommends for traveler's diarrhea. If someone other than a doctor recommends a drug, be suspicious and get another opinion.

How To Get Well

Should you come down with traveler's diarrhea, the first thing to do is go to bed, stay there, and don't move on until it runs its course. Traveling with the illness only makes it last longer; you can be over it in a day or so if you take it easy. Drink lots of liquids: tea without milk or sugar, or the Mexican *té de manzanilla* (chamomille tea), is best. Eat only *pan tostada* (dry toast rusks), sold in grocery stores and *panaderías* (bakeries). Keep to this diet for at least 24 hours, and you'll be well over the worst of it. If you fool yourself into thinking that a plate of enchiladas or an alcoholic drink can't hurt, you'll be back at square one as far as the traveler's diarrhea is concerned.

The Public Health Service advises that you be especially careful to replace fluids and electrolytes (potassium, sodium, etc.) during a bout of diarrhea. Do this by drinking glasses of fruit juice (high in potassium) with honey and a pinch of salt added; and also a glass of pure water with one-quarter teaspoon of sodium bicarbonate (baking soda) added.

Bugs and Bites

Another thing you should consider is the bugs and bites. Mosquitoes and gnats are quite prevalent along the coast and in the lowlands of Yucatán. Insect repellent *(rapellante contra insectos)* is a must, and it's not always available in Mexico. Also, those sensitive to bites should pick up some antihistamine cream from a drugstore at home.

Most readers won't ever see a scorpion, but they are found in most parts of Mexico. Stings can be painful to dangerous (if you're particularly sensitive to the venom), and it's best to go to a doctor if you get stung.

THE LANGUAGE

Of course, not everyone in Yucatán speaks English (this isn't as silly as it sounds; these days English is taught in most Mexican schools), so it helps tremendously to have some basic vocabulary at your fingertips. For this, the Berlitz *Latin American Spanish for Travelers* phrase book, available at most bookstores, cannot be recommended highly enough. *The American Express Pocket Guide to Spanish* is another useful possibility.

THE WAGES OF CHANGE

On the subject of money, it might be good to put in a word about prices and inflation. Back in the halcyon days (several decades ago) when prices throughout the world changed at a rate of about 3% a year, a traveler could take an old copy of a good travel book abroad and make a mental adjustment for a small price rise. But recently the inflation rate for Mexico has been in the neighborhood of

20% to 30% per annum; some businesses (hotels and restaurants included) will hold off as long as they can, perhaps two years, and then raise prices by even more than this factor to compensate for *future* inflation! Every effort is made to provide the most accurate and up-to-date information in this book, even to the point of predicting price increases that I feel are on the way and that will arrive before the book reaches the reader's hands; but changes are inevitable and uncontrollable with inflation.

Virtually all prices in this book are quoted in U.S. dollars only. You can figure the approximate peso price by simply multiplying the U.S. dollar price by the current peso equivalent of $1. Thus, if I say that a meal costs about $10, if the exchange rate is $1 = 3,000 pesos, the meal should cost about 30,000 pesos.

Speaking of currency, don't forget that the dollar sign ($) is used by Mexicans and some other Latin Americans to denote their own national currencies, and thus a Mexican menu will have "$2,500" for a glass of orange juice and mean 2,500 pesos. To avoid confusion I will use the dollar sign in this book *only* to denote U.S. currency.

GETTING THERE AND GETTING AROUND

1. GOING BY AIR
2. TOURING YUCATÁN

Getting to Yucatán is easy and not really very expensive. The peninsula is closer to many American cities than it is to many Mexican ones: It's almost as easy, and quick, to fly from Miami to Cancún or Cozumel as it is to fly from Mexico City to those same Yucatecan resort destinations.

Air travel is the method of choice for getting to Yucatán. The Mexican railroads south and east of the Isthmus of Tehuantepec run chronically behind schedule, the trains are uncomfortable, and incidents of theft are common. Though bus routes are operated efficiently, and ticket prices are surprisingly low, it's a very long haul of some 1,500 miles (2,300 km) along the shortest route from the border (Brownsville, Texas) to Mérida. The long, hot drive is the prime reason not to come by private car, also. And as of this writing, there are no regular passenger boat or car ferry services from, say, New Orleans or Florida to the Yucatán peninsula. So you'll probably get to Yucatán by air.

1. Going By Air

Air fares to Yucatán are a bargain, and you have a virtual smörgåsbord of opportunities from which to choose.

SCHEDULED FLIGHTS

Many scheduled airlines, including Aeroméxico, American, Continental, LACSA, Mexicana, and United, operate convenient flights to Cancún, Cozumel, and Mérida from Atlanta, Chicago, Dallas/Fort Worth, Denver, Houston, Los Angeles, Miami, New Orleans, New York, Philadelphia, San Antonio, San Diego, and Washington, D.C. From many other cities there are convenient connecting flights.

Excursions and package plans are offered for any preference, from a one-week, all-expenses-included vacation to a two-month vagabond tour.

The Mexican carriers, Aeroméxico and Mexicana, are both top-flight operations with high standards. Of the two, Mexicana may have the edge on inflight service. These two companies are marketing their sunny destinations very aggressively, at very good prices for you. A travel agent can give you all the latest details, prices, and schedules at no cost.

In addition, regional carriers such as Aero Cozumel, Aero Caribe, Aeromar, and Aviacsa now offer flights to harder-to-reach places like Palenque, San Cristobal de las Casas, Cozumel, and Chetumal.

THE HALF-AND-HALF ITINERARY

In these days of airline deregulation, it's not unusual to find very low fares in effect between two American cities. You can use this to your advantage. As airfares within Mexico are surprisingly cheap, you might be able to fly to a town on the U.S. side of the border (El Paso, Texas, for example, or San Diego, California), cross the border, and catch a domestic Mexican flight from Ciudad Juárez (or Tijuana) to Cancún. This sort of planning requires a cooperative travel agent, a willingness to experiment, and a sense of adventure, but airfare savings can be substantial. If your travel agent is unfamiliar with the procedure, you might call an airline directly for a reservation to the border, then call Aeroméxico or Mexicana for a reservation on the Mexican portion of your trip.

CHARTER FLIGHTS

Besides the scheduled flights, you should be aware that dozens of charter flights depart each week from many North American cities for Yucatán, and in many cases you can get in on the low charter fares whether or not you participate in a package tour. Here's how it works:

A company that organizes package tours signs a contract with an airline (either a scheduled carrier or a charter airline) to provide a certain number of seats on a particular date. The tour company then tries to fill the seats with its tour participants, but in many cases there are empty seats. Though the company would prefer that you buy the package deal, it prefers even more strongly that the seats in the plane not go empty, so the company will sell you a seat at a very, very good price.

Price is the advantage; the disadvantage is that you cannot easily change your mind. In most cases, once you've signed up for such a flight, you must depart and return on the dates designated. If you

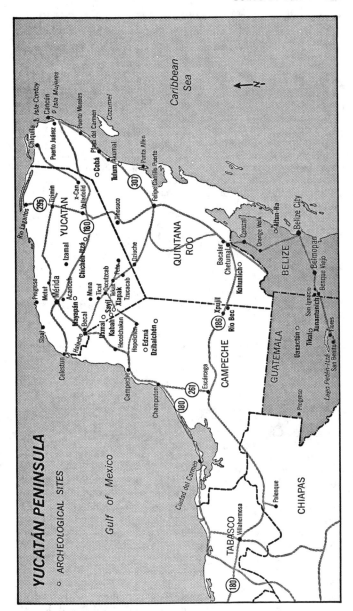

YUCATÁN PENINSULA
○ ARCHEOLOGICAL SITES

miss your flight, you cannot use your ticket on another flight. Your ticket becomes a worthless slip of paper. Let me hasten to add that tour companies that buy many seats on a regular basis (perhaps even one planeload a week) sometimes permit you to change your mind, and your travel dates, as long as you fly only on one of the company's flights.

PACKAGE TOURS

Speaking of package tour companies brings up the question of package tours: Should you take one? The answer is a resounding "yes," if the tour resembles fairly closely the itinerary you desire. You could never equal the value of the services provided by arranging your own itinerary and staying in the same hotels. Tour companies bargain for wholesale rates on flights, hotels, meals, transfers, and sightseeing tours, and they pass some of these wholesale savings on to tour participants. A luxury hotel that charges $100 a night to the individual traveler may charge a tour company only $50 for the very same room on the very same day. So package tours can provide you with the most cost-effective way to see Yucatán.

I must add that signing up for a package tour can limit you to certain cities. If, for instance, you buy a package tour to Cancún, but you want to take an overnight trip to, say, Cozumel or Mérida, you'll have to pay out of your own pocket for hotels and meals in those places. Surprisingly, a package tour is often so cheap that it remains a bargain, even if you pay some of your own off-the-route expenses.

Some tour companies will sell you only those features of a tour that you desire. For instance, you can purchase the inexpensive charter air travel for a two-week trip, and four nights' hotel lodging in Cancún. On the fifth night you must pay for your own hotel, but by then you may be on the road, visiting the ruins at Chichén-Itzá, shopping in Mérida's bustling market, or lazing on the beach in Cozumel. As tour companies tend to work with the more expensive hotels, you can often realize big savings by staying at more modest hostelries. Check with your travel agent for details of all these options. If you want to look into the details of charter flights and package tours yourself, get hold of a copy of *JAXFAX Travel Marketing Magazine,* the monthly "bible" of the charter air travel business. A travel agent may show you a current issue, or give you a past issue, or you can order a year's subscription for only $12 from the publisher, Jet Air Transport Exchange Inc., 397 Post Rd., Darien, CT 06820.

Here are some examples of package tours to **Cancún,** offered from major U.S. cities by various tour companies. All include round-trip airfare and a week's lodging, airport-to-hotel transfers, and one meal. Rates below are for one person traveling midweek in the low season. Double the price for two people sharing a room. The lowest rates shown here are for moderately priced hotels and the highest prices buy luxury accommodations. High-season rates are roughly 50 to 75% higher. *Tip:* Although package deals are higher on weekends, in summer hotels in Cancún often give huge discounts on the rates to weekend guests. Before buying a package, compare the package against arranging the air and room separately.

Atlanta	$212 to $500
Boston	$238 to $525
Chicago	$288 to $575
Dallas	$213 to $500
Los Angeles	$213 to $500
New York	$238 to $525
Philadelphia	$238 to $525
Washington, D.C.	$238 to $525

ARRIVING IN YUCATÁN

Arrival in Yucatán couldn't be easier. As you step out of the airplane and feel the warm Caribbean sun on your face, you'll know you've come to the right place.

Cancún, Cozumel, and Mérida all have attractive, modern, efficient airports. The first Mexican official you'll encounter is the Immigration officer *(Migración)*, who will stamp your Tourist Card and ask you to sign it on the back (you can save time by signing it in advance—he doesn't have to witness your signature). The official will keep one copy of the form, and you'll keep the other. Safeguard it carefully.

Next comes the Customs *(Aduana)* inspection, which is usually nothing more than spot checking. You may not even have to open your bags.

Currency exchange counters are often located within the Customs area (that is, in the same room in which you pick up your luggage). You cannot return to this room once you leave it, so decide now if you want to change some money into pesos. I suggest changing at least $50 into pesos to cover transportation, tips, and incidentals until you can get to a bank in town. If it's a holiday or a weekend, change more money because the banks will be closed. You can always change money at your hotel, but the exchange rate will be much worse than at a bank.

Rental car desks are located in the arrivals hall of each airport. You will also see a desk at which you can purchase tickets for seats in a minibus that drops passengers at any hotel or in the center of town. See the chapter on a particular destination for details and prices of this service.

THE DEPARTURE TAX

While on the subject of airports, you should be aware that Mexico levies a Departure Tax on all visitors who leave the country by air. It's roughly equivalent to $12, and is payable in either pesos or dollars at check-in and before security clearance on your return flight. You can always exchange leftover pesos for dollars in the departure lounge after you've paid the tax, cleared security, and handed in your Tourist Card.

NOW THAT YOU'RE HERE

Having arrived safely in Yucatán, let's explore the possibilities of where to go, how to get there, and what to do. Here are some examples of how to see the fascinating dominion of the Maya.

2. Touring Yucatán

ITINERARIES

Any good itinerary of Yucatán would involve the following elements:

Mérida: Spend at least overnight here; two full days to see the city would be much better. You can also use Mérida as your base for visits to Chichén-Itzá, Uxmal, Kabah, Sayil, Xlapak, Labná, and Loltún, taking organized tours or renting a car to tour on your own.

Uxmal: If you get as far as Mérida, seeing Uxmal is an absolute must! Traveling from Mérida, touring the ruins, and returning to the city will take the best part of a day. There are hotels at Uxmal where you can spend the night.

Kabah, Sayil, Labná, Xlapak, Loltún: These Maya cities, south of Uxmal, demand another full day of touring time. If you stay overnight at Uxmal, you'll save travel time from Mérida.

Campeche, Edzná, Dzibilnocac, Hochob: Campeche, capital of the state of the same name, is a pleasant city with a charming walled colonial center. It's not a necessity on your Yucatán itinerary, but you may want to stay the night here if you're en route between Palenque and Mérida. Campeche is also the most convenient place to stay for those visiting the Maya sites at Edzná and Dzibalchén (Dzibilnocac and Hochob).

Chichén-Itzá: This is another must-see, the most impressive Maya city in Yucatán. You'd be well advised to spend the night here, as there is a good range of hotels, with several in the budget category. If you take a day tour from Mérida or Cancún, you'll arrive and begin to climb pyramids at the very hottest, most crowded time of day, and you'll climb back into your bus for the two-hour return ride just when the light on the ruins is prettiest and the heat is abating. Plan to spend the night at Chichén-Itzá.

Cancún: You'll want to see this world-class resort, and perhaps use it as your base, but you needn't plan to spend all of your beach time here. There's a laid-back ambience at Playa del Carmen and on nearby Isla Mujeres, and the skindiving and snorkeling are best on Cozumel.

Isla Mujeres: Easily accessible from Cancún by city bus and ferry boat, this small island is great for a day-trip, or even for a stay of several days.

Caribbean coast: You'll certainly want to take a trip along the coast south of Cancún, certainly as far as the beautiful cove of Xel-ha and the Maya seaport of Tulum. Inland from Tulum lies the ancient city of Cobá, well worth the detour if you have the time.

Cozumel: Mexico's entry into the Caribbean islands competition, it's a skindiver's paradise.

TIME AND DISTANCE

You must become aware of the distances involved in a trip to Yucatán. For instance, a trip to Yucatán's nicest colonial city, Mérida, from the peninsula's premier resort, Cancún, involves a bus ride of five or six hours.

To help specifically in planning your trips **from Cancún,** here are some distances from that city to other Yucatecan points:

Destination from Cancún	Kilometers	Miles
Belize City	610 km	378 miles
Chetumal	390 km	242 miles
Chichén-Itzá	200 km	124 miles
Cobá	175 km	109 miles
Felipe Carrillo Puerto	230 km	143 miles
Isla Mujeres Ferry Dock (Punta Sam)	10 km	6 miles
Mérida	320 km	199 miles
Palenque, via Chetumal	895 km	555 miles
Palenque, via Mérida	940 km	583 miles
Playa del Carmen (Cozumel passenger dock)	68 km	42 miles
Puerto Morelos (Cozumel car ferry dock)	36 km	22 miles
Tulum and Xel-Ha	130 km	81 miles
Uxmal	400 km	248 miles
Valladolid	160 km	99 miles
Villahermosa, via Chetumal	1,200 km	744 miles
Villahermosa, via Mérida	1,240 km	769 miles

You can touch on all the high points of Yucatán in a week of touring by rental car, but you'll be traveling fast. Ten days is a more reasonable period to spend, and two weeks is excellent. You can easily spend three weeks and even more if you plan to explore ruined Maya cities off the beaten track, or put in several hours of beach or pool time every day.

TEN DAYS TO TWO WEEKS

Here is a sample itinerary for a visit of ten days to two weeks, starting on the day you arrive in Cancún:

Day 1, Cancún: On the day of arrival, plan to settle in, get your bearings, perhaps change some money, adjust to the heat, and try out the nearest beach.

Day 2, Cancún: Put on your bathing suit and spend the day on one of Cancún's fine beaches. In the evening, wander around the restaurants and nightspots.

Day 3, Isla Mujeres: Get an early start, and spend the day on Isla Mujeres' beaches, especially Garrafón, with its good snorkeling and diving. Perhaps stay the night.

Day 4, Cozumel: Spend a day on Cozumel, taking the passenger ferry or the shuttle flight from Playa del Carmen, or a flight from Cancún.

Day 5, Caribbean coast: Using Cancún, Playa del Carmen, or Cozumel as your base, visit Tulum, Xel-ha, and perhaps other beaches and sites along the coast between Tulum and Cancún. If you have a car, drive inland to Cobá also. By bus or hitchhiking, Cobá will take at least a full day by itself.

Day 6, Chichén-Itzá: Ride from Cancún through Valladolid and henequen country to Chichén-Itzá. Find a hotel room, have lunch, perhaps take a nap, then hike to the ruins and tour until closing time.

Day 7, Mérida: Spend the morning at the ruins of Chichén-Itzá, then ride to Mérida in the afternoon. Find a hotel and settle in.

Day 8, Mérida: Tour the city, stopping at each of the historic buildings near the Plaza Mayor, and along the Paseo de Montejo. Save some time for the market!

Day 9, Uxmal: If you're driving, you can stop at Mayapán on your way from Mérida to Uxmal. These two sites, and perhaps a quick stop in Ticul, will fill your day. Return to Mérida for the night, or stay at Uxmal.

Day 10, Kabah, etc.: Spend the day touring sites of Kabah, Sayil, Labná, Xlapak and the Grutas (caves) de Loltún. If you're absolutely fascinated by ruins and can't get enough, head for Campeche to spend the night, then spend the next day at Edzná, Dzibilnocac, and Hochob. Otherwise return to Mérida, or head back to Cancún on the southern route via Oxcutzcab and Felipe Carrillo Puerto.

Day 11, Cancún: Return to Cancún and try to get in one last visit to the beach before departure.

BEST MEANS OF TRANSPORT

Touring Yucatán is best done by car, though this presents several problems. First and foremost, rental cars in Mexico as of this writing are fairly expensive. For a week's rental of a VW Beetle, adding in the costs of unlimited mileage, insurance, tax, and gas, you might pay $300 to $370 if you arrange the rental before you leave the States. If you have several people to share the cost, if you shop around and haggle a bit, and if it's not high season, the price becomes more reasonable.

Another caution is that roads are narrow, with virtually no shoulders or rest stops—just jungle on both sides. Though daytime driving is all right, you should not drive at night. I mean this!

A way to cut the high cost of renting a car is to rent one only on certain days. For instance, touring from Mérida to Chichén-Itzá and Cancún, take the bus—or even fly. From Cancún, take the ferry to Isla Mujeres, or the bus to the ferry for Cozumel, but rent a car for a day to see Xel-ha, Tulum, and Cobá. This involves more paperwork, but if a car costs $60 or $75 per day, you don't want it sitting around unused. For more detailed information on car rentals, see Chapter XIII.

Of course, the bus is by far the most economical transport. Prices are incredibly low, less than $1 for an hour's travel. Although the buses go everywhere, you will spend a lot of time waiting at highway intersections, particularly near Uxmal, Kabah, etc., and along the Caribbean coast. Hitchhiking doesn't help too much, as traffic is usually light. If you plan to take buses exclusively, you must allow at least two weeks to see Yucatán thoroughly.

DRIVING IN MEXICO

Cardinal rule: *Never drive at night if you can avoid it.* The roads aren't good enough; the trucks and carts and pedestrians and bicycles usually have no lights; you can hit potholes, animals, rocks, dead ends, and bridges with no warning. Enough said.

Indeed, get used to the fact that people in the countryside are not good at judging the speed of an approaching car, and often panic in the middle of the road even though they could easily have reached the shoulder. It's not rude to use your horn if it may save someone from injury.

Road Signs

Here are the most common ones:

Road Repairs	**Camino en Reparación**
Keep Right	**Conserva Su Derecha**
Watch Out for Cattle, Trains	**Cuidado con el Ganado, el Tren**
Dangerous Curve	**Curva Peligrosa**
Earthquake Zone	**Derrumbes**
Slow	**Despacio**
Caved-in roadbed	**Deslave**
Detour	**Desviación**
Slow Down	**Disminuya Su Velocidad**
Highway Junction	**Entronque**
School (Zone)	**Escuela**
Loose Gravel	**Grava Suelta**
Men Working	**Hombres Trabajando**
Road Closed	**No Hay Paso**
Danger	**Peligro**
Narrow Bridge	**Puente Angosto**
Continuous White Line	**Raya Continua**
Road Under Construction	**Tramo en Reparacio**
One-lane Road 100 Meters Ahead	**Un Solo Carril 100 m**
School Zone	**Zona Escolar**

Also *Topes,* or a sign with a drawing of a row of little bumps on it, means that there's a row of speed bumps across the road placed there by the authorities to slow you down through towns or villages. Slow down when coming to a village whether you see the sign or not—sometimes they install the bumps but not the sign!

Kilometer stones on main highways register the distance from local population centers. There is always a shortage of directional signs, so check quite frequently that you are going on the right road.

Credentials

Whether you rent a car or drive your personal car from the States, you must carry your **vehicle permits** in the car at all times. Rules for entering Mexico in your own car are covered in detail in *Frommer's Mexico on $35 a Day*. In general, though, they include an insurance requirement and pollution control restrictions for driving in certain Mexican cities.

The Green Patrols

The Mexican government sponsors an admirable service whereby green, radio-equipped, repair trucks manned by uniformed, English-speaking officers patrol the major highways during daylight hours to aid motorists with troubles. Minor repairs and adjustments should be free of charge, although you pay for parts and materials if you have need of these "Green Angels."

Minor Accidents

Most motorists think it best to drive away from minor accidents if possible. You are at a distinct disadvantage without fluent Spanish when it comes to describing your version of what happened. Sometimes the other descriptions border on mythology, and you may end up spending days (perhaps from a jail cell) straightening out things that were not even your fault. In fact, fault often has nothing to do with it.

Maintenance

Able mechanics are readily available all over Mexico. However, it's a good idea to perform a general check of your oil and tire pressure before starting out each day. Regarding the tire pressure, Mexican service stations generally have air to fill tires, but no gauge to check the pressure. If you don't carry your own gauge you'll have to find a tire repair shop to do the job. A combination gauge/air compressor sold at automotive stores in the United States is a handy gadget to have along. It plugs into the car cigarrette lighter, making tire maintenance a simple procedure. *Note:* Not that many Mexican cars comply, but Mexican law requires that every car have **seat belts** and a **fire extinguisher.** Rental cars should have these.

Parking

I use pay parking lots in cities, especially at night, to avoid annoyances such as broken antennas, swiped emblems, or break-ins. Never leave anything within view inside your locked car on the street (day or night), for Mexico has thieves like every place. Another good reason to use pay parking lots is that you avoid parking violations, and when a cop in Mexico finds you parked illegally, and knows you may ignore a ticket, he'll take out his pliers and screwdriver and remove your license plate and take it to the station house. Then you must go there to pay the fine and retrieve the tag. When pay lots are not available, dozens of small boys will surround you as you stop, wanting to "watch your car for you." Pick the leader of the group, let him know you want him to guard it, and give him a peso or two when you leave. Kids may be very curious about the car and may look in, crawl underneath, or even climb on top, but they rarely do any damage.

Mexican Roads

Most Mexican roads, although quite sufficient, are not up to northern standards of smoothness, hardness, width of curve or grade of hill, or safety marking. You will have to get used to the spirited Latin methods, which tend to depend more on flair and good reflexes than on system and prudence. Be prepared for new procedures, as when a truck flips on his left-turn signal when there's not a crossroad for miles. He's probably telling you that the road is clear ahead for you to pass—after all, he's in a position to see better than you are. How do you tell that's what he means, and not that he intends to pull over on the left-hand shoulder? Hard to say.

Getting Gas

Along with Mexico's economic difficulties has come a return to highway robbery at the pumps. Though many service station attendants are honest and above-board, a surprising number are not. Here's what to do when you have to fuel up:

Drive up to the pump and get close enough so that you will be able to watch the pump run as your tank is being filled. Check that the pump is turned back to zero, go to your fuel filler cap and unlock it yourself, and watch the pump and the attendant as the gas goes in. By the way, it's good to ask for a specific peso amount rather than saying "full." This is because the attendants tend to overfill, splashing gas on the car and anything within range.

As there are always lines at the gas pumps, attendants often finish fueling one vehicle, turn the pump back quickly (or don't turn it back at all), and start on another vehicle. You've got to be looking at the pump when the fueling is finished, because it may show the amount for only a few seconds. This "quick draw" from car to car is another good reason to ask for a certain peso amount of gas. If you've asked for 20,000 pesos' worth, the attendant can't charge you 21,000 for it.

Once the fueling is complete, *then* you can let the attendant check your oil, or radiator, or put air in the tires. Do only one thing at a time, be with him as he does it, and don't let him rush you. Get into these habits, or it'll cost you.

If you get oil, make sure that the can that is tipped into your engine is a full one. If in doubt, have the attendant check the dipstick again after the oil has supposedly been put in.

Check your change, and don't let them rush you. Check that your locking gas cap is back in place.

Note: Don't depart from a major town or city except with a full or near-full tank of gas. Yucatán is a big area, and service stations are not quite as frequent as in other countries. It's wise to keep the gas tank pretty full at all times.

All gasoline in Mexico is sold by the government-owned **Pemex** (Petroleras Mexicanas) company. Nova (81 octane) costs about 80¢ per gallon. Nova is leaded gasoline (*con plomo*), and comes from the blue pump; Extra is a high-octane unleaded (*sin plomo*) gasoline, from the silver pump, but you will rarely find it available in the Yucatán; the red pump is for diesel fuel, which costs about 60¢ a gallon. In Mexico fuel and oil are sold by the liter, so, a liter being slightly more than a quart, 40 liters equal about 10½ gallons.

No credit cards are accepted for gas purchases, so be prepared to pay in cash.

CANCÚN: THE MEGA-RESORT

A view of Cancún from the air reveals a vast country-club layout: wide tree-lined streets, golf courses, emerald lawns, yachts at anchor. But not too long ago this huge and phenomenally successful resort was nothing more than unbroken jungle, wide unpopulated beaches, and crystalline blue water.

The Mexican government, having seen how successful Acapulco was in luring foreign visitors (and their dollars) south of the border, decided to build a brand-new world-class resort from scratch. Government planners fed data about various sites into a computer, and out popped the magic word: Cancún.

Plans for the resort were ambitious, and thoroughly Mexican in their audacity. The resort's "Touristic Zone," where most of the development would take place, was to be a 14-mile-long spit of sand called Isla Cancún, just off the coast near the sleepy village of Puerto Juárez. To house the workers (and later the resort's service personnel), a modern planned town for 70,000 people would be built on the mainland at the northern end of the sand spit. The southern end of the sand spit would be connected to the mainland by a causeway. On the mainland where the causeway came ashore would be an international airport capable of taking wide-body jets.

That was the dream, and it all came true in an astoundingly short period of time. Crowds of sunseekers flocked to Cancún as soon as the airport was finished and the first hotels opened, and the flocks have now turned to a flood. The influx has changed the whole vacation travel pattern in Yucatán. Whereas most visitors used to begin their Yucatecan adventure in Mérida, most now head for Cancún first.

What makes Cancún the perfect site for a resort? The land is the beautiful Yucatecan jungle, the long sand spit is perfect for seaside hotels, and the beaches are covered in a very fine sand that has been called "air-conditioned" by its ingenious promoters. Maya ruins at Tulum, Chichén-Itzá, and Cobá are a short drive away, and for a change of scene the older resorts of Isla Mujeres and Cozumel are close at hand. The Caribbean waters are incredibly blue and limpid, temperatures (both air and water) are just right, and the coral reefs and tropical climate guarantee brilliant underwater life, good snorkeling, and fine scuba-diving.

GETTING AROUND

There's plenty of transport available, no matter where you're going.

From the Airport

Special minibuses run from Cancún's international airport to the hotels and into town for $2 per person. As of this writing, minibus service is one way only, and you'll have to hire a taxi for $8 to $16 to get back to the airport.

By Bus

Out in the Zona Turística, you'll find the buses handy for getting from one hotel or beach to another, and for getting into town. At certain times of the day when the work shift changes at the hotels, the buses may be filled to capacity with workers coming from or going to their jobs.

In town, almost everything's within easy walking distance. The only places you need take buses to are the beaches near the luxury hotels in the Zona Turística, and to Puerto Juárez/Punta Sam for ferries to Isla Mujeres. City buses will trundle you from your in-town hotel to the beaches of the Zona Turística for a ridiculously low fare. These "Ruta 1-Hoteles" buses operate every 15 minutes or so along the Avenida Tulum, Ciudad Cancún's main street, all the way to Punta Nizuc at the far end of the Zona Turística.

As for Puerto Juárez/Punta Sam, catch a Ruta 8 (to Puerto Juárez and Punta Sam) bus along Cancún's main street, Avenida Tulum, and the bus will take you straight to the ferry docks for less than 25¢. A taxi costs around $3.

By Taxi

The city officials have instituted an authorized table of taxi fares, but in any case it's best to make a deal on a fare in advance. From Ciudad Cancún out to, say, the Hotel Camino Real should cost $4 or less; a short ride between two of the big hotels, around $2; from Ciudad Cancún to the airport, $16.

By Moped

You'll see lots of moped (motorbike) rental places in Cancún, particularly in the Zona Hotelera. Fees for a day's rental can run around $25. The lowest rates come from the guys who have set up shop on a piece of sidewalk: no phone, no desk, no address, just a few mopeds and a folding chair. Highest rates are from legitimate agencies with a phone number you can call in case of emergency or breakdown. They usually have newer bikes in better repair.

When you rent, try to get a discount if it looks like business is slow. You will have to pay the estimated rental in advance, and perhaps leave your driver's license as security for the moped. You should receive a crash helmet and a lock and chain with the rental.

Mopeds are a dangerous way to cruise around the Zona Hotelera, and they're not really good for trips to and from town. Riding in the roadway itself pits you against hundreds of would-be Latin Grand Prix racers in beat-up Datsuns—not a cheery prospect.

By Calesa

An alternative to the expensive car and dangerous moped is the *calesa,* which in Cancún means a little two- or four-person horseless carriage. But the *calesa* is unwieldy and no match for the race-car scene on the Paseo Kukulkán. These antique-style putt-putts rent for $14 to $18 per hour, up to $50 for a full day until 6pm. These prices, for two- and four-seat models respectively, include gas, mileage, tax, and insurance. Rent one in the parking lot next to the Plaza Caracol shopping mall, between the Viva and Krystal hotels (no phone).

ORIENTATION

Here's the layout. Ciudad Cancún, the new town on the mainland, has banks, travel and airline agencies, car rental firms, restaurants, hotels, and shops, all within an area about nine blocks square. The main thoroughfare is Avenida Tulum. Heading south, Avenida Tulum becomes the highway to the airport, Tulum, and Chetumal; heading north, it joins the Mérida–Puerto Juárez highway.

The Zona Hotelera, or Zona Turística, stretches along the former Isla Cancún (Cancún Island), a sandy strip 14 miles long, shaped like a "7." Now joined by bridges to the mainland at north and south, it is an island no longer. Cancún's international airport is just inland from the base of the "7."

A Note on Addresses

One would think the city planners of Ciudad Cancún, starting with a clean slate, would have laid out a street-numbering system that was simple and easy to use, but such has not been the case. Addresses are given by the number of the building lot and by the *manzana* or *super-manzana* (city block). Some streets have signs with names on, although the establishments along the street may refer to the street only by its number, as Retorno 3, etc. In short, it is very difficult to find a place in Ciudad Cancún just by the numbers. Luckily, the city is still relatively small and the downtown section can easily be covered on foot. I've tried to be very specific in my directions to recommended establishments. Your best companion in confusing Cancún is the map in this book.

FAST FACTS

The information below covers not only the location of banks, etc., but also transportation to and from Cancún. (See also Chapter II.)

Airlines:

Mexicana Airlines' downtown ticket office is at Avenida Cobá 39 (tel. 988/4-1423, 4-1444, or 4-1265 or at the airport 4-2740). Hours are 9am to 5pm daily. Mexicana has nonstop flights between Baltimore/Washington, Chicago, Dallas/Fort Worth, Guadalajara, Los Angeles, Mexico City, Miami, Philadelphia, and Tampa/St. Petersburg.

Aeroméxico's downtown office is at Avenida Cobá 80 (tel. 988/4-3571, 4-1186, or at the airport 4-2728 or 4-2639). It's open 8am to 6:30pm except Sunday when the hours are 9am to 5pm. There are nonstop flights from Mexico City, Campeche, Houston, Mérida, New York, and Tijuana.

Aero Cozumel and **Aero Caribe,** Avenida Tulum 99 at Uxmal (tel. 988/4-2000, 4-2111, or at the airport 4-3683), are regional carriers that fly to Cozumel, Chetumal, Mérida, Oaxaca, Veracruz, and Ciudad del Carmen.

American (tel. 988/4-2947 and 4-2651 at the airport) has nonstop flights from Dallas/Fort Worth and Raleigh/Durham.

Continental (tel. 988/4-2540 at the airport), flies nonstop from Houston, New Orleans, and New York.

United (tel. 988/4-2528 at the airport) has numerous connecting flights from the United States.

Banks: Most are downtown along the Avenida Tulum, open from 9:30am to 1:30pm, Monday through Friday. There are also a few *casas de cambio* (exchange houses). In addition, you may find downtown merchants particularly eager to change cash dollars, sometimes at very advantageous rates. In Cancún it's important to shop around for a good exchange rate. Many places, particularly hotels, will offer you absolutely terrible rates of exchange.

Buses (Intercity): The **Autotransportes del Caribe** buses are located in a raunchy bus station across the street from the pleasant Hotel Plaza Caribe. The **ADO** bus company, next door, has created a slightly better environment. Both are in downtown Ciudad Cancún at the intersection of Avenidas Tulum and Uxmal. Autotransportes del Caribe originates one bus a day to Playa del Carmen at 9:30am. Buy your ticket a day in advance. Five *de paso* buses ply this route beginning at 8am. ADO offers seven buses a day to Playa del Carmen, the first at 12:30am and the last at 5:30pm. If you have a

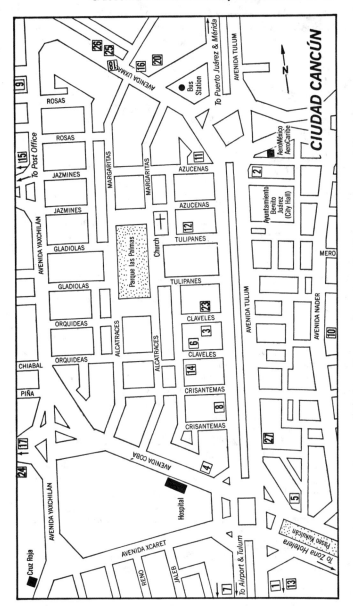

long wait at the station, escape across the street to the Hotel Plaza Caribe for blessed air conditioning and reasonably priced sandwiches and soft drinks.

Consulates: The U.S. Consular Agent (tel. 988/4-2411) is in the office of Intercaribe Real Estate, Avenida Cobá 30, next to La Dolce Vita Restaurant, a block off Avenida Tulum going toward the Zona Hotelera. The agent's hours are Monday through Friday from 9am to 2pm; the office is open from 3 to 4pm on those days. In an emergency, call the U.S. Consulate in Mérida (tel. 99/25-5011 or 25-5409).

Medical Care: Cruz Roja (Red Cross; tel. 4-1616), good for first aid, is on Avenida Labná near the intersection with Avenida Xcaret next to the Colegio LaSalle. For more serious ailments, head for the **IMSS** (Mexican Social Security Institute) Hospital General de Zona (tel. 4-1108 or 4-1907), on Avenida Cobá at Avenida Tulum. "Urgencias" means "Emergencies."

Post Office: The main post office (tel. 4-1418) is at the intersection of Avenidas Sunyaxchen and Xel-Ha, open 8am to 7pm Monday through Friday and on Saturday from 9am to 1pm. Stamps can be bought at newsstands as well.

Rental Cars: If you plan to visit other cities and beaches, plus major Maya ruins, the way to do it is to rent the cheapest car, a VW Beetle, for a week at the unlimited-mileage rate. Total cost for the week, including gas, insurance, rental fee, and IVA tax, might be $362, which comes out to $51.68 per day. Several companies offer this weekly unlimited-mileage rate.

Tourist Information: The **State Tourism Office** is centrally located downtown on the east side of Avenida Tulum between the Ayuntamiento Benito Juárez building and Comermex Bank, both of which are between Avenidas Cobá and Uxmal (tel. 4-8073). Office hours, more or less, are 9am to 9pm Monday through Sunday. Among the information on hand is a list of hotels with rates, addresses, and telephone numbers and ferry schedules. Should this office be unreachable, try calling or going to the **Federal Tourism Office** at Avenida Naves in the Fonatur building (tel. 4-3238 or 4-3438). Hours there are 8am to 3:30pm Monday through Friday.

Pick up a copy of the monthly pocket-sized publication called *Cancún Tips*. It's handed out for free at the airport when you arrive, and is available downtown in several places. It's got lots of useful information, as well as fine maps. The publication sponsors information offices in several locations, stocked with well-informed personnel, brochures, and a collection of restaurant menus for browsing. The scheme is designed to benefit the publication's advertisers, of course, and its own affiliated businesses such as the Captain's Cove Restaurant, Tropical Cruiser, time-share condos like the Royal Mayan and Vacation Clubs International, and another helpful publication *Cancún Scene;* but these people and their booklets are very helpful nonetheless.

1. Where to Stay

Despite its reputation for glamor, Cancún actually has a full range of accommodations, from the sybaritic high-rise right on the beach to tiny pensions. Prices, likewise, go from $500 per night right down to $20 per night and below. And luckily for the visitor, there are no gaps in this vast range. No matter how much you plan to spend on a room, you'll find a place that's exactly right for you.

Though your chosen hotel may have rooms at your price, you must make sure they also have a room reserved in your name. It is not much of a problem during the summer, which is off-season, when lots of rooms are available. But in December, January, and February, rooms in many hotels can be in short supply. If you plan to stay at a hotel costing, say, $50 or more per night, you can have your travel agent make the reservation at no extra charge to you. As for the less expensive places, you'll have to make reservations yourself, by mail—allow lots of time!—or by phone.

Pricing Details: Cancún, like other Mexican resorts, has a two-season price structure. December through April is the busy season, when prices are higher; during holiday periods (Christmas, New Year's, Easter) surcharges are added to the already high winter prices. You may get a slight reduction from the regular winter rates during the "mini-off-season" from January 2 through 21. True off-season is the warm period from May through November, when prices (especially in the most expensive hotels) are 25% to 40% lower than during the winter. Note also that the 15% Value-Added Tax (*Impuesto de Valor Agregado,* or *IVA,* pronounced *"ee-*bah") has already been included in the prices quoted below.

As Cancún is a planned resort aimed directly at the package-tour market, most of the larger hotels have similar services. In any hotel charging $90 or more for a double room in winter ($65 in summer), you can expect to find several restaurants and bars, a swimming pool with a swim-up bar, a beachfront location, air conditioning, color cable TV with satellite dish to receive U.S. programs, a balcony or terrace with water view from each room, and perhaps a self-serve "pay as you go" refrigerator bar in each room.

In the past few years, Cancún's popularity with sunseekers has accelerated beyond all previous limits, and the resort is undergoing yet another building boom, and with it Cancún has finally come of age. The once empty beaches between the Club Med and Hotel Sheraton have given birth to miles of grand, sophisticated, high-rise hotels, each one architecturally unique. Many of the existing hotels have rushed to complete large new sections of rooms to meet the demand, and new grand hotels are sprouting like mushrooms along the beaches of Isla Cancún. Prior to this explosion of building, hoteliers could name their price and get it. At this writing competition has finally reached the luxurious hotel zone. New hotels are offering low promotional rates and established hotels don't seem to be increasing high-season rates as outlandishly as in the past. The tourist is the winner. Take time to compare package rates and use this guide to read about the hotel offered in the package you are considering.

Construction is underway or nearing completion on a number of new hotels: the Conrad International Regina Cancún, Camino Real Caribe, Marriott, Melia Turquesa, Melia Cancún, Hilton, and

Fiesta Americana Coral Beach. As these hotels are finished and ready for visitors, Cancún's number of hotel rooms will increase by several thousand. Even so, there's plenty of room left on Isla Cancún for yet more luxurious resorts, and demand for space on Cancún's "air-conditioned" sand shows no signs of slackening any time soon.

Here, then, are the best of Cancún's hotels, those that were open to visitors on my last inspection visit.

TOP HOTELS

At the pinnacle of Cancún's lodging structure are these luxurious places, ready to provide every service and comfort you might desire on a beach resort vacation. Prices begin at $160 double in winter.

Camino Real Cancún, Box 14, Cancún, Q. Roo 77500 (tel. 988/3-0100; toll free 800/228-3000 in U.S.), right at the tip of Punta Cancún, is among this resort's most appealing places to stay. Though it has a choice location, a lavish country-club layout, and dramatic architecture that inspired many other buildings at Cancún, it is not an enormous hotel. There are 381 rooms, including the new luxurious 18-story Royale Beach Club. The rooms are elegantly outfitted with pink breccia-marble floors, tropical high-backed raffia easy chairs, servi-bar drinks refrigerators, and drapes and spreads in light, soft pastel colors. On each lanai terrace, a hammock is already hung and waiting. Rooms in the new 87-room Royale Beach Club have truly elegant use of Mexican touches such as lacquered armoires and chests from Olinalá, Guerrero, couches festooned in purple, pink, and yellow pillows, or a color theme around deep purple and turquoise. Junior suites (all corner rooms with expansive glass views) have swivel TVs, large dining tables with four chairs, and hot tubs on the balconies. Royale Beach Club guests receive a complimentary continental breakfast daily in the Beach Club lobby as well as complimentary cocktails and snacks there each evening.

On the lush grounds spilling over with tropical verdure, swimming and paddling possibilities include a beautiful freshwater pool, a private saltwater lagoon with sea turtles and tropical fish, and a more or less private surf beach. The hotel has its own sailing pier and water sports center for sailboard and boat rentals and other water sports, and also three of its own tennis courts. There's a bar for every mood: a swim-up bar in the pool, a lobby bar for people-watching, and another for gazing at the Caribbean. As for restaurants, you can choose from La Brisa at the edge of the sea, Calypso for Caribbean fare, Azulejos with Mexican specialties for any meal any time, or the Snack Shack by the pool. The beachside Aquarius Disco swings into action along with its tanned patrons at 10:30pm. The price for all this luxury? Package deals give you the best value, but if you come on your own, you'll pay $215 to $224 double in winter, $145 to $155 double in summer. The rate for a deluxe room in the low season at the Royal Beach Club is $190 single or double and in high

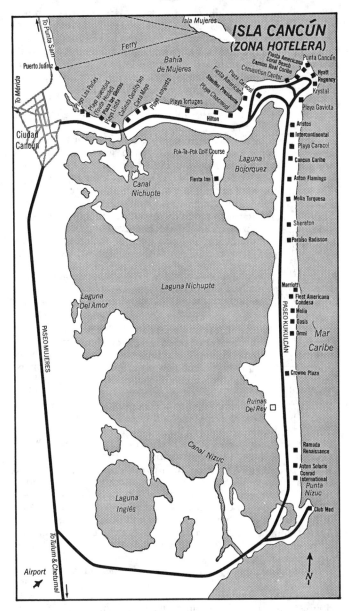

season $253. Suites run $350 in low season and $500 a night in the high season.

Cancún Sheraton Resort, Paseo Kukulcán, Cancún, Q. Roo 77500 (tel. 988/3-1988; toll free 800/325-3535 in U.S.), three

Maya step-pyramid buildings on their own vast stretch of surf beach south of Punta Cancún, is certainly lavish. In the main lobby are expanses of green tiles and a dramatic stainless steel sculpture of birds in flight, plus comfy bamboo furniture and wood accents to go with the tile. Including the new V-shaped tower section, the resort has 748 luxurious rooms and suites, with views of the Caribbean (to the east) or of the lagoon (to the west); if you choose one of the suites, you'll find a private whirlpool bath waiting. Tower guests enjoy the services of a personal butler who attends to a variety of tasks from shoe shines to snack service.

Emerald lawns extend in every direction from the main buildings, hammocks hang in a shady palm grove, and a small reconstructed Maya ruin crowns a craggy limestone hillock. Both adults and kids are busy at basketball hoops, mini-golf, aerobics, and shuffleboard, or at the playground or fitness center. There are six lighted tennis courts and two swimming pools (one indoors). For sustenance, the Sheraton offers several restaurants and bars, including a lobby bar with music for dancing. The Yan Kin Grill is perched above the beach, airy and open to the sea breezes; La Gaviota is the fancy dining room, with a pianist each evening. La Duna is the venue for a variety of special feasts, including an international buffet, a Mexican fiesta, an Italian food festival, and a lavish Sunday brunch. In the Towers you'll find the restaurant Cardinale with homemade Italian pastas, El Oriente if your tastes turn to Oriental fare, and the cozy La Fonda for a romantic Mexican meal. Besides Daphney's Video Bar with its multilevel dance floors, there are five more bars on the premises. One of them, in the tower lobby, exudes romance and sophistication with cozy bamboo seating, dim lighting, and soft piano music in the evenings. For the evenings, Tabano's Disco is open from 9pm to 4am. For a room in the midst of all these possibilities, the price is $175 to $275 double in winter, $115 to $250 double in summer. Tower rooms run $215 to $275 single or double in winter and $145 to $250 in summer.

There's a luxurious South Seas feel to the new **Sierra Inter-Continental Hotel,** Paseo Kukulcán, Zona Hotelera, Cancún, Q. Roo 77500 (tel. 988/5-0755; toll free 800/327-0200 in U.S. and Canada). Lots of potted palms dot the interior along with rattan furniture, brass, hot pink and purple area rugs, and wood louvered doors in the guest rooms. The hotel has its own marina and lagoon in front along with both lagoon-view and ocean-view pools, two lighted tennis courts, three restaurants, a nightclub, healthclub, and ice machine on every floor. The standard rooms all have balconies, sitting area, combination bathtub/shower, hair dryers, minibars, and ceiling fans. Master suites have standard amenities and lots of extras like Berber carpet, large living/dining area, and a kitchen with its own private entry (for all those catered parties you'll no doubt be throwing). In the junior suites, the living and sleeping areas are divided by a handsome dresser/TV console, and there's a separate bathtub and shower. In short, there's lots of attention to detail here. High-season rates begin around $200 single or double for ocean-front rooms. Ocean-view and lagoon-view rooms cost less. Off-season cost of an ocean-front room runs $140 and less for ocean-view or lagoon-view rooms.

For the moment at least, Cancún's largest hotel is the **Hotel Oasis,** Paseo Kukulcán 2.5, Apdo. Postal 1081, Cancún Q. Roo 77500 (tel. 988/5-0752 or 5-0867; toll free 800/446-2747 in U.S.). It has been open over a year, but the sprawling 1,170-room resort won't be entirely finished until the suite/convention area is completed at the end of 1990. By then there'll be 10 restaurants, 3 swim-up bars, and 8 interlocking pools. Four separate two-story buildings are anchored by a mock pyramid that holds the suites and convention center all surrounded by grassy lawns. The whole effect is one of a palm-studded private country club. Rooms have balconies facing either the lagoon, interior grounds, or ocean. For all this luxury, standard rates for one or two people run between $161 and $184 in season and $130 for the same rooms the rest of the year.

Hyatt Regency Cancún, Box 1201, Cancún, Q. Roo 77500 (tel. 988/3-0966; toll free 800/228-9000 in U.S.), at Punta Cancún, is handsome but unremarkable from the outside. When you enter the hotel you'll find yourself at the bottom of a vast and lofty cylindrical court, the walls of which are festooned with greenery. The 300 guest rooms are entered from walkways overlooking the central space; once in your room, you'll head straight for the balcony to take in the sea view—every room has it, and views from rooms on the upper floors are particularly fine. When you inspect your quarters, you'll find attractive bamboo furniture and deep, rich colors in the drapes and bedspreads, plus a color television. The list of service here is long: ice machines on every floor, movies on closed-circuit TV, a nursery to look after the children, a telex station, several bars, an Italian restaurant called Scampi, and another restaurant, Arrecifes, specializing in steaks and seafood. The Seafood Market Restaurant is by the pool. The location at Punta Cancún puts you at the center of the action, within walking distance of the convention center, and many nightclubs, restaurants, and shops. The beach here is perhaps not as commodious as at other locations, but you needn't go far to find a better one. Rooms, single or double, cost $215 in winter, $155 in summer. Note that there are two Hyatt hotels in Cancún.

Hyatt Cancún Caribe, Paseo Kukulcán, Cancún, Q. Roo 77500 (tel. 988/3-0044; toll free 800/228-9000 in U.S.), is the other Hyatt hotel in this resort, south of Punta Cancún. Because of its dramatic crescent shape, all rooms in this 202-room hotel face the sparkling Caribbean, and have terraces on which to enjoy the view. Between the hotel and the beach is a pool complex built to resemble a Maya village—a very, very posh one! A replica of chac-mool gazes out to sea, like any sunbather. Though the other Hyatt is generally thought to be the snazzier place, the Cancún Caribe has recently renovated its lobby and restaurant. Prices here are almost the same as those at its sister establishment mentioned above.

Fiesta Americana Cancún, Paseo Kukulcán, Cancún, Q. Roo 77500 (tel. 988/3-1400; toll-free 800/223-2332 in U.S.) started an architectural trend. Instead of the up-to-the-minute architecture found in most Cancún buildings, the five-story Americana is built to resemble the charming jumble of an Old World city street. Balconies and windows of different styles are placed at random on the façade, and a ground-floor arcade simulates a row of shops. It echoes the charm of another time and place. All services are provided in the 286 guest rooms, including in-room movies and self-serve bar, Caribbean views, and purified water. The decor is semitropical, with bamboo furniture including striking arched "sunburst" headboards on the beds. The beach here is surf, but there's a veritable system of swimming pools (lots for kids), with one pool large enough to boast its own little island. The hotel's collection of restaurants is more eclectic, however. For formal dinners, try the fancy Condesa del Mar, with pastel colors, lace tablecloths, silver candelabra, and French cuisine. The Chula Vista is the place for a buffet breakfast, then lunch and dinner; occasionally they serve up barbecued steaks and chops, and grilled seafood on the terrace. At poolside the Palapa Chac-Mool provides charcoal-grilled seafood and steak fajitas as well as drinks each afternoon. Another bar, the Loco Coco, is open on that little island in the swimming pool. The Lobby Bar is open most of the day, with jazz or mariachi entertainment in the evenings between 8 and 11pm. Finally, Friday Lopez, open from 6pm to 3am, is the singles bar, with two bands and a flashing video screen. Besides all these entertainments, the Fiesta Americana's location is ideal: right across the street from the Mayfair Galleria shopping mall, which adjoins other beautiful shopping arcades. Room rates in winter are $210 single or double; in summer, $146.

Fiesta Americana Plaza Cancún and Villas, Paseo Kukulcán Km 11, Cancún, Q. Roo 77500 (tel. 988/3-1022; toll free 800/223-2332 in U.S.), is Fiesta Americana's four Cancún hostelries, and it is just as interesting, beautiful, and imaginative as the first. From a distance the hotel appears to be a large complex of pink Spanish colonial villas, which indeed it is. It goes on for blocks along the Paseo Kukulcán, so it may be no surprise to learn that there are actually 638 guest rooms here: 261 in the villas, and 377 in the "Towers." If the original Fiesta Americana gives the impression of an Italian Mediterranean village, the Plaza Cancún and Villas makes you think you've landed in a brand new Spanish colonial country club; the grounds are that well kept. Rooms are decorated to a tropical inspiration, with the appropriate bamboo furniture and tranquil colors. Each room has a servi-bar and a balcony or terrace. The hotel's restaurants include La Palapa, where they lay out the breakfast buffet and later serve fresh seafood lunches; La Terraza, where the cuisine is Italian; and La Place Vendôme, where the fare and ambience are continental. Drinks are available in La Plaza, the lobby bar with live entertainment (and a happy hour each afternoon), as well as in the restaurants. If you like the feeling of being in a villa community, this is the spot for you. Rates for a single or double room are $220 in winter, $146 in summer.

Krystal Cancún, Paseo Kukulcán, Cancún, Q. Roo 77500 (tel. 988/3-1133; toll free 800/231-9860 in U.S.), is right on Punta Cancún with the Camino Real and Hyatt Regency, near the convention center, many shops, restaurants, and clubs. The Krystal has lots of luscious, cool marble used in its decoration, and striking textile "pictures" hanging on the walls of its public spaces. The 320 guest rooms in two buildings have luxury appointments, with bamboo furniture, leaf-pattern drapes and spreads in earthy tones, two double beds, servi-bar, and water views. Should you decide to rent one of the presidential suites, you'll get your own private pool. A long swimming pool complex comes complete with waterfall and seven Ionic columns overlooking the Caribbean and a beach of limestone boulders and creamy sand (fairly safe swimming here). The pool complex has a built-in optical illusion: The waterfall cascades toward the sea, and from certain positions it appears that the pool and the ocean are joined. You have your choice of two hotel tennis courts, a racquetball court, and a fitness club with whirlpool, sauna, and massage facilities. The Krystal's four restaurants and five bars include Bogart's, a chic dining room with a Moroccan "Casablanca" theme; the Aquamarina, good for breakfast, lunch, snacks, or dinner; Raratonga, specializing in seafood; and the luxurious Hacienda El Mortero, an honest-to-goodness replica of a colonial hacienda. In addition, there's room service 24 hours a day. For nightlife, head for Christine, one of the most popular discos in town, or the Lobby Bar, with music for dancing each evening. For all this, and the convenient location, you pay $184 to $207 single or double in winter, $127 in summer.

Stouffer Presidente Cancún, Paseo Kukulcán 7, Cancún, Q. Roo 77500 (tel. 988/3-0200; toll free 800/472-2427 in U.S.), is elegant and spacious without being spread out. Modern in design, with lavish marble and wicker accents, the 283-room Presidente has undergone a major facelift and expansion, and provides all of the things you'd expect: restaurants, bars, a good nightclub, two landscaped swimming pools with a waterfall, a more or less private and fairly safe beach, water sports facilities, lighted tennis courts, two nonsmoking floors, and air-conditioned rooms with king-size beds, satellite TV, and private balconies. Rates at the Presidente are $160 to $185 double in winter, $145 double in summer. Coming from Ciudad Cancún, you'll reach the Presidente before you get to Punta Cancún.

At the **Holiday Inn Crowne Plaza,** Paseo Kukulcán, Zona Hotelera, Cancún, Q. Roo 77500 (tel. 988/5-1022; toll free 800/465-4329 through Holiday Inn in U.S.), you'll find 366 rooms and suites, two tennis courts, four pools (one indoor), health club, two nonsmoking floors, and four restaurants. The circular entry rises from the street level revealing a dramatic hot-pink sculpture. Inside the architecture is just as futuristic, with soaring buttresses and a glass-covered atrium that requires neck craning to see completely. Sea breezes sweep through the totally open lobby. Outside, the oceanside pool is filled to the brim and its edge seems to disappear into the sea. Standard single and double rates in high season start at $180. Other times the rate drops roughly $40.

Villas Tacul, Paseo Kukulcán (reservations: 1008 77 Sunshine Strip, Harlingen, TX 78550 (tel. 512/428-0217), is unique among Cancún hostelries. Here you find a private compound wonderfully landscaped with tropical flowers and shrubs. Accommodations are in private villas with two to five bedrooms. Facilities include a quiet stretch of beach and a lagoon-like swimming pool. You can have breakfast prepared for you in your villa each morning. For other meals, you visit independent restaurants nearby. Rates depend on the size of the villa (how many bedrooms) and the number of guests, but start at $310 double in winter and $145 in summer, continental breakfast and tax included.

EXPENSIVE HOTELS

Not as well known as the top hotels, yet in most respects just as comfortable and well located, the following hotels charge from $135 to $250 for a double in winter.

Hotel Beach Club Cancún, Paseo Kukulcán, Cancún, Q. Roo 77500 (tel. 988/31177), is not a hotel, not a condominium complex, not an apartment building, but a little bit of each. From the outside, it looks like a smaller but handsome and comfortable hotel, with a fine stretch of beach, swimming pools, health club, tennis courts, and the other diversions important to daily life in Cancún. In the lobby, it resembles a hotel, with shops, restaurants, and several bars (including that Cancún essential, a swim-up pool bar). But in the guest rooms, it resembles an apartment building, for each has a water view, whirlpool bath, kitchenette with refrigerator, color TV, and balcony. You can choose from four sizes of accommodations: Standard rooms are the size of other hotels' junior suites, and rent for $135 double; studios have two double beds in the bedroom, and a separate living room/kitchenette, for a few dollars more; two-bedroom apartments have separate living and dining rooms and two baths for $210; and duplex penthouses have an upstairs master bedroom with private bath and large terrace, plus a downstairs bedroom with bath, a living room, and kitchenette, all for $250. The Beach Club Cancún is just south of the Sheraton.

Built high on the island bedrock, the **Ramada Renaissance,** Paseo Kukulcán Km. 20.5, Cancún, Q. Roo 77500 (tel. 988/5-0096, 5-0661; toll free 800/272-6232 in U.S.), makes great use of its lofty setting. Vast expanses of glass allow sea views from the interior public areas. Interconnecting pools face the ocean and a breezy dining room overlooks the pool, beach, and ocean as does the Café Marco Polo, the hotel's luxury restaurant. Each of the 226 guest rooms has a large terrace with either a lagoon or ocean view. Winter rates run $175 to $224 single or double, but the rest of the year costs $110 to $121. Ask about summer weekend discounts.

Casa Maya Hotel, Paseo Kukulcán, Cancún, Q. Roo 77500 (tel. 988/3-0555), is huge, dramatic, and imposing, a cross between a modern high-rise hotel and a Maya pyramid. It's a popular lodging place for tour groups, with the bustle and activity that groups bring. The 356 rooms are more like junior suites, each with its balcony, color cable TV featuring U.S. stations, and tropical decor. You can swim in the hotel's own huge pool, or on its beach, or play tennis on its own courts. Prices summer and winter at the Casa Maya are $140 for a standard room, $190 for a suite.

Aston Flamingo Cancún, Paseo Kukulcán, Cancún, Q. Roo 77500 (tel. 988/3-1544), seems to have been inspired by the dramatic slope-sided architecture of the Camino Real. But the Flamingo is considerably smaller, with 162 guest rooms forming a quadrangle or courtyard in which you'll find the swimming pool. During the winter season, you usually pay $165. Rates in summer are $130 single or double.

Calinda Cancún Beach, Paseo Kukulcán, Cancún, Q. Roo 77500 (tel. 988/3-1600; toll free 800/221-2222 in U.S.), just beyond the first bridge when coming out from Ciudad Cancún, has 280 guest rooms, two-thirds of them facing the Caribbean, the others looking across the boulevard to the lagoon. Each room has either two double beds or one king-size bed, a servi-bar refrigerator, and color cable television with a satellite dish hookup. Modern patterned drapes and bedspreads in muted colors grace the rooms, which have a nice feel to them. The same decorative themes are carried through in the public rooms, including the mezzanine-level lobby and lobby bar, and the dramatic sunken dining room at pool level. Speaking of the pool, it's surrounded by thatched umbrellas and a traditional palapa bar. The pool has a swim-up bar, as every good Cancún hotel pool must, named Moana. The Seagull Restaurant is the place for breakfast overlooking the hotel grounds, or for a long romantic dinner. The beach is among Cancún's better and safer ones. Prices for the luxury rooms are $140 to $160 single or double in winter, $92 to $115 in summer. You can expect, and enjoy, all of the normal Cancún luxury hotel services here.

MODERATELY PRICED HOTELS

As I mentioned above, Cancún accommodations run the full price gamut. The following hotels are comfortable in every way, and luxurious in many ways, yet they cost substantially less than those described above—between $104 and $185 double in winter. Locations and facilities are still extremely good. You can't go wrong at any of these choices.

A good place to hold the line on costs and still enjoy a touch of class is the new **Paraiso Radisson,** Paseo Kukulcán, Hotel Zone, Cancún, Q. Roo 77500 (tel. 988/50233; toll free 800/228-9822 in U.S.). With its flying T-shaped architecture, and without balconies in the 300 rooms and suites, the Radisson may be the least dramatic of its sophisticated neighbors. But it doesn't lack for action or clients—it's a popular hotel. The comfortable rooms have all the required basics: air conditioning, minibar, and color TV. There's an oval-shaped pool, good beach, three restaurants, poolside bar, and a lobby bar with good entertainment nightly. Rooms for one person run from $115 to $184 mid-December through Easter week and other times cost from $80 to $130. Ask about their good package rates and super-saver weekend deals.

For golf lovers (or anyone else for that matter) who'd rather spend more on entertainment than on the room, an excellent choice is the new 120-room **Fiesta Inn Golf,** Paseo Pok-ta-Pok, Lote 21-22, Cancún, Q. Roo 77500 (tel. 988/3-2200; toll free through Fiesta Americana Hotels in U.S. 800/223-2332). It's across the Laguna Bojorquez from the main hotel zone, and almost adjacent to Cancún's 18-hole golf course. The stylish, comfortable rooms all have balconies or private terraces facing a large inner lawn and swimming pool. It's a five-minute walk to the golf course where hotel guests receive a 25% discount for a round of golf. Winter rates are $115 single or double, but drop to $70 the rest of the year.

Miramar Misión, Paseo Kukulcán, Cancún, Q. Roo 77500 (tel. 988/3-1755), is the Cancún incarnation of a popular Mexican hotel chain. This is a moderate-sized (225-room) hotel that has an ingenious setting and design so that each room has views of both the Caribbean and the lagoon from its lanai terrace. Guest rooms are smallish but very comfortable, with dark bamboo furniture offset by sun-yellow cushions and bedspreads. The private bathrooms have polished limestone vanities and incandescent bulbs. In the public spaces throughout the hotel you will find lots of dark wood, cream-beige stucco, red tile, and sun-yellow accents. A big swimming pool is right next to the beach (be sure to pay attention to the signs warning about undertow). As for the hotel's restaurants, they include the Batacha, with live music for dancing until very late; and a buffet breakfast in the less formal Khan-Nab for the morning after. Rates here are $110 to $120 in winter, $75 to $98 in summer.

Best Western Playa Blanca Hotel and Marina, Box 107, Cancún, Q. Roo 77500 (tel. 988/3-0344; toll free 800/528-1234 in U.S.), has the distinction of being among the "older" hotels in Cancún. As no building here is very old, that means simply that the Playa Blanca's courtyard gardens have had time to mature. You'll love the greenery. Guest rooms have all the comforts and services found at the more expensive places, and guests can avail themselves of a similar list of recreational opportunities, including lighted tennis court, nice swimming pool, several restaurants and bars, and a night spot that provides the setting for various theme evenings: "Pirates' Night," "Mexican Fiesta," "Seafood Bar," and the like. With 161 rooms and suites, the Playa Blanca is not big and not small, but very pleasant, and priced at $115 single or double, $127 triple in winter, about 40% less in summer.

Best Western Aquamarina Beach, P.O. Box 751, Paseo Kukulcán Km. 4, Cancún, Q. Roo 77500 (tel. 988/3-1344; toll free 800/528-1234 in U.S.), is only a few steps from the beach, a series of modern white six-story buildings holding 200 guest rooms done with upbeat modern textiles and equipped with all the services, from rattan furniture and color satellite TV to telephone and air conditioning. There's even a safe deposit box in each room. The hotel's swimming and wading pools are supplemented by a whirlpool. Restaurant, snack bar, lobby bar, and coffee shop keep you happy, and other establishments allow you to rent a car, buy a souvenir or bathing suit, find a newspaper, or book a flight. The Aquamarina Beach is on the northern beach of Isla Cancún's "7" shape, which means safer sea swimming. Rates are reasonable, at $104 double in winter, $81 double in summer.

Cancún Viva, Paseo Kukulcán Km 3.8, Cancún, Q. Roo 77500 (tel. 988/3-0800; in Mexico City 5/553-5444), member of a Mexican chain, is right next door to the Fiesta Americana Cancún and has a blockhouse look from the street side. But on the ocean side you'll find a small but pretty patio garden and a beach that is fairly safe for swimming as the surf breaks farther out. There's white stucco everywhere, along with clean white laminate and polished floors of tawny limestone. All of the rooms face the sea, and have private balconies so you can enjoy the view. The 210 rooms at the Viva have all the little luxuries, from color cable TV through refrigerator (162 rooms), and 64 rooms have kitchenettes as well. Most rooms have two double beds, but some have twins. The hotel has a pair of its own lighted tennis courts, a swimming pool for adults and another for the kids, and water sports equipment and its own marina. For dining, the Viva offers three restaurants with Mexican themes, Delicatessen, La Guacamaya, and La Terraza, as well as bars in the lobby, at poolside, and on the beach. The price for a room, single or double, is $115 ($123 triple) in winter; $90 single or double, $95 triple in summer. You may be able to bargain for a slight discount during the "mini-off-season" of early to mid-January, when occupancy is lower.

Club Verano Beat, Paseo Kukulcán, Cancún, Q. Roo 77500 (tel. 988/3-0772), has architecture inspired by the Camino Real, with the swimming pool in a courtyard surrounded by the rooms and by nice (if small) gardens. Rustic thatch here and there adds a Yucatecan touch. Rooms, as usual, are air-conditioned and have balconies, and cost $116 double in winter, $58 in summer.

Condominiums are readily available for rent in Cancún in the luxury price range. These modern units give you bedroom, kitchen facilities, daily maid service, and locations close to many sports facilities and dining and dancing establishments. Among the popular condo complexes are the **Royal Caribbean, Club International,** and **Royal Mayan Beach Club.** Daily prices depend on the building, the unit, and the facilities of course, but range from $120 for a one-bedroom condo to $260 for a two-bedroom unit with water view. For brochures, information, and reservations, contact Vacation Club Rentals, Inc., P.O. Box 18225, San Antonio, TX 78218 (tel. toll free 800/531-7211 in the U.S. and Canada).

A BUDGET HOTEL

Yes, the expensive Hotel Zone does have an economy hotel that holds prices at $55 in summer and at $80 in winter. The **Hotel Aristos Cancún,** Paseo Kukulkán, Box 450, Cancún Q. Roo 77500 (tel. 988/3-0011; toll free 800/527-4786 in U.S.), on Playa Choc Mool, is one of Cancún's first hotels. Its darkish, two-story motel-type architecture of the 1970s doesn't beckon like its glamorous high-rise neighbors in the Zona Hotelera. But so what if the exterior isn't jazzy; it's what's inside that counts. All 244 comfortable, air-conditioned rooms face either the Caribbean or the Paseo Kukulkán and lagoon. Rooms with the best views (and no noise from the Paseo) are on the Caribbean side. There's a nice wide stretch of beach one level below the pool and lobby, a marina with water sports equipment, two lighted tennis courts, and a babysitting service as well as one restaurant and several bars. The large pool is surrounded by plants, lounge chairs, and a poolside restaurant and bar.

CIUDAD CANCÚN

All of the aforementioned hotels are located in the Zona Turistica, or Zona Hotelera, along Paseo Kukulcán on Isla Cancún. There are almost as many hotels located on the mainland, in Ciudad Cancún. Although the town can boast no five-star places, and few hotels have views of the water, the guest rooms are comfortable, air-conditioned, and surprisingly lower in price than beachfront rooms.

Moderately Priced Hotels

The in-town hotels with prices of $54 to $100 in winter, are not on the beach, but most of the better ones have vans to shuttle guests to and from the beaches. Other facilities may be comparable to Isla Cancún hotels: restaurants and bars, discothèques, health clubs. A bonus is the easy walk to all of the independent shops, banks, restaurants, and nightspots in town.

Hotel América, Box 600, Cancún, Q. Roo 77500 (tel. 988/4-1500), on Avenida Tulum near the intersection with Brisa, is fairly large, quite comfortable, and fully equipped with a nice big swimming pool, central air conditioning, a restaurant, coffee shop, and several bars. Except for the absence of the surf, you'd think you were on Isla Cancún. You can be on the beach in minutes by shuttle van to the hotel's own beach club and marina. The América is among the more expensive places downtown, charging $100 single or double in winter, about $40 less in summer.

The **Hotel Plaza del Sol,** Avenida Yaxchilán 31, Cancún, Q. Roo 77500 (tel. 988/4-3888), near the intersection with Avenida Sunyaxchén, is part of a shopping and office complex. But I hasten to add that it is not engulfed in city hubbub. In fact, the hotel is a charming oasis in the midst of a busy resort city. The 87 rooms, furnished with Mexican touches in textiles and pale earth tones, each have two double beds, wall-to-wall carpeting, central air conditioning, telephone, and piped-in music; some have color television. A small swimming pool takes care of that urge for a quick dip and a free four-times-a-day shuttle van can whisk you to the hotel's beach club at the Hotel Maya Caribe. Other services include a restaurant, coffee shop, lobby bar, pool bar, travel agency, and shopping arcade; there are at least a dozen other restaurants within a few minutes' walk. Winter rates are $60 single and $70 double. In summer rates drop to a more reasonable $46 for one or two persons.

Hotel-Suites Caribe Internacional, Avenida Yaxchilán 36, Cancún, Q. Roo 77500 (tel. 988/4-3999), at the corner with Avenida Sunyaxchén, has 80 rooms, junior and master suites, a swimming pool, snack bar, lobby bar, and guarded parking lot. Each room has a balcony overlooking the grassy traffic circle and the town. The hotel is modern, comfortable, and well located, but perhaps its biggest attraction is that you can rent as much space, for as many persons, as you like. In winter, one or two people pay $54 and $87 in a junior suite; three people in a junior suite costs $100; five persons in a master suite costs $147, or $29.40 per person. In summer subtract 30% from these prices.

For big families, the place is the **Hotel Hacienda Cancún,** Avenida Sunyaxchén 39-40, at Avenida Yaxchilán, Cancún, Q. Roo 77500 (tel. 988/4-3672 or Fax 4-1208). The building gives a whole new dimension to the word *stucco,* but some of the rooms can hold up to six persons, for $90 total. Other rates are $50 single or double, $60 triple; continental breakfast is included in these rates. Off-season rates are roughly 40% less. The hotel has its own parking lot, swimming pool, and restaurant.

Budget Hotels

It is truly astounding that a visiting couple can spend the night in this billion-dollar resort for as little as $20 per night, but so it is. For $20 to $61 in winter, you can get a double room with one or two beds (perhaps two double beds), private bath, ceiling fan, and perhaps even an air conditioner. The room may have little other furniture—a telephone, table and chair, perhaps, and a place to hang your clothes (but no hangers!)—and the hotel will have few other services. You won't find a swimming pool, or whirlpool, or shuttle vans to the beach, or nightclub. In the very cheapest hotels, the management gets away with cleaning the rooms only every other day or so. But if you're traveling on a budget, the chance to see Cancún at these prices is an indisputable bargain.

Here are Cancún's budget hotels, grouped by area so you can walk from one to the next, inspecting rooms, until you find one you like.

On and Off Avenida Tulum

Parador Hotel, Avenida Tulum 26, Cancún, Q. Roo 77500 (tel. 988/4-1922 or 4-1043), is in a convenient location right on Avenida Tulum between the city hall and the Aeroméxico office. The entry, lobby, and modest public rooms are laid out on an odd asymmetrical plan, but the three stories of guest rooms (66 in all) are arranged along two long, narrow garden courtyards leading back to the swimming pool (with separate kiddie pool) and grassy sunning area at the back. The air-conditioned guest rooms are modern, with two double beds, nice tile bathrooms with showers, color cable television, and plastic carafes of drinking water. The staff is very friendly and helpful, the location good, and the prices very inexpensive: $30 single or double in the busy winter season. You can get a discount during the summer months. The hotel has its own restaurant and bar.

Just off Avenida Tulum, entered from Calle Claveles 37, Cancún Q. Roo 77500, is the **Antillano Hotel** (tel. 988/4-1532 or 4-1244). Modern wood-and-stucco in design, the Antillano has air-conditioned rooms that overlook the busy Avenida Tulum and also the side streets. It's decidedly a bit fancier than its neighbors, and includes a swimming pool. Consider that when you study the prices: $40 single, $45 double, $49 triple in season. Rates are 40% less in summer.

Plaza Caribe, Avenidas Tulum and Uxmal, Cancún, Q. Roo 77500, facing the bus station (tel. 988/3-1252), is obviously modern in design. Inside, you'll find a tidy, nicely furnished, air-conditioned hostelry charging moderate prices in winter, and lower prices in summer. The 200 rooms have all the Mexican comforts, including two double beds in each, and rent for $61 single or double in high season, about $50 off season. You can enjoy a swimming pool, gardens, two bars, and a cafeteria-restaurant. The noise from the nearby bus station is not really obtrusive.

The seafood restaurant chain of Soberanis has both a restaurant and a hotel in Cancún. The 50-room **Hotel Soberanis,** P.O. Box 421, Cancún, Q. Roo 77500, Cobá 5, near the corner with Avenida Tulum (tel. 988/4-3080 or 4-1858), has two double beds to a room, and some with little balconies, but the views aren't much. All rooms are air-conditioned and TV-equipped, of course, and are priced at $53 single or double with one double or two twin beds in high season and $30 single or double in low season.

Novotel en Cancún, Avenida Tulum at Azucenas, P.O. Box 70, Cancún, Q. Roo 77500 (tel. 988/4-2999), near the intersection with Avenida Uxmal, is a convenient choice near the bus station and Aeroméxico offices, as well as the banks, restaurants, and shopping to be found along the Avenida Tulum. Though modern, it has enough traditional touches such as white stucco walls, metalwork, and colorful craft decorations to give it a truly Mexican spirit. The 40 rooms are arranged around an enclosed interior court with plants and sitting areas. Each of the small guest rooms has a tiled bathroom with shower, a color television set, an air conditioner, a tiny balcony (and I mean tiny!) and a colonial-style decor of chunky dark wood pieces. Off to one side on the ground floor of the courtyard is the pleasant dining room, and in another corner is the bar. There's a travel agency off the entrance hallway. The Novotel is often booked solid at winter-season prices of $20 single or double with a fan, or $33 with air conditioning.

Carrillo's, for which the official address is Retorno 3, Supermanzana 22 Cancún, Q. Roo 77500 (tel. 988/4-1227), is on a side street called Calle Claveles that meets Avenida Tulum at two places (Claveles forms a loop). Look for the intersection of Claveles and Tulum that's right across from the Banco Nacional de México and its large statues of Tula's Atlantean men. Now that you're there, you'll find Carrillo's to be one of the strangest places in Cancún. Although a few of the hotel's rooms are older and more standard, most are finished—walls and ceiling—in a nubbly white stucco that gives the entire place a troglodytic quality. Add plywood vanities, tile showers, and individual air conditioning units and you have the standard room at Carrillo's, which rents for $38 single or double in high season and $30 for two other months. Besides the two-story hotel, Carrillo's building houses a seafood restaurant.

The **Hotel Cancún Handall,** at the intersection of Avenidas Tulum and Cobá, Cancún, Q. Roo 77500 (tel. 988/4-1122 or 4-1976), opened in 1980. Two wings of two floors each hold a variety of single rooms, doubles, and suites, and a pool awaits your pleasure outside. Most of the 50 modern rooms have two double beds, and cost $36 single or double, and $51 triple.

On and Off Avenida Yaxchilán

Avenida Yaxchilán, west of and parallel to Avenida Tulum, also has a good selection of hotels in all price ranges.

Suites Albatros, Avenida Yaxchilán 154 at Venado, Super-manzana 20, Cancún, Q. Roo 77500 (tel. 988/4-2242), is a nice little complex of modern rental efficiency apartments facing the Red Cross station. If you walk south on Avenida Yaxchilán away from the center of the commercial district (ask for directions to *Cruz Roja*), you will eventually come to the Cruz Roja (Red Cross) station and telephone company tower on the right-hand side of the avenue, and Suites Albatros on the left. Find suite no. 8, which serves as the office, and ask to see a suite. You'll be shown an attractive modern accommodation with two double beds, air conditioning, a little dining table, a hotplate, a refrigerator, a kitchen sink, plates, cups, glasses, and utensils. In back is a place to hang wet bathing suits and laundry. The price is $25 double daily in season, about $21 off-season. It's quiet here, with friendly management, and the cooking facilities keep your breakfast and lunch bills low.

The **Suites Residencial "Flamboyanes,"** Avenida Carlos J. Nader, no. 101-103, Super-manzana 3, Cancún, Q. Roo 77500, just off Avenida Cobá (tel. 988/4-1503; for reservations in Mérida, call 992/7-2498 or go to Prolongación 30 no. 78), is a different and delightful place. There are 22 suites in a number of attractive two-story buildings surrounded by grass and trees, and equipped with a private swimming pool. All suites are air-conditioned and include a bedroom, a living room with couches to sleep two more people, fully equipped kitchen with dining area, bathroom, and terrace/porch. Off-season suite for one or two persons costs $26 to $35, plus $5 for each additional person. The daily rate goes down for extended stays, of course. Remember that you are renting an *apartment* here, and not just a hotel room.

---

2. Where to Dine

Dining in Cancún gives you the chance to sample many varieties of Mexican cuisine. In addition to the familiar tacos and enchiladas, you'll find restaurants specializing in seafood, steaks, and the indigenous Maya cuisine of Yucatán.

Cancún restaurant prices are higher than in places like Mérida, which do not draw resort crowds, but even so, you'll probably find your dinner tab here much lower than at home. Many restaurants provide entertainment during your meal. The show might be a rope-twirling *charro* (Mexican cowboy), a guitarist or two, or even a mariachi band. For the moderate price of dinner, you'll often get an entire night's entertainment.

ON ISLA CANCÚN

The Zona Turística has lots of lavish restaurants, many of them operated by nearby hotels. Some appeal to a fun-loving, upbeat beachcomber crowd, others to those looking for a more sedate dining experience, yet others cater to visitors who like dinner and a show. Here are some examples.

Across from the Convention Center in the Zona Hotelera are two restaurants under the same roof and management: the Mauna Loa and Beef Eaters Angus Steak House, Avenida Kukulcán, Km. 9 (tel. 3-0191 or 3-0693). The **Mauna Loa** is Polynesian from the swiveling hips to Polynesian food. For good measure there's Chinese food too. While patrons dine around the circular dance floor, there are two different and extravagant shows featuring dances of Tahiti, Hawaii, Samoa, the Philippines, and New Zealand nightly at 7 and 9pm. Prices range from $32 to $45 per person depending on the menu selected and include an open bar for two hours and the show. When the last show is over, there's disco dancing to tunes from Cuba, Colombia, Mexico, and the United States. Open from 6:30pm to 2am.

At the **Beef Eaters Angus Steak House** guests dine in a quieter atmosphere in a window-filled dining room overlooking the Nichupte Lagoon. And the menu is definitely aimed at north-of-the-border patrons. The 10 different cuts of beef are all imported from the United States "so people will have confidence in what they are eating," I was told. A 7-ounce steak runs $15 and one twice that size costs around $28, and both come with baked potato or mesquite-flavored fries or a basket of vegetables. Besides steaks the menu offers corn beef and pastrami, 6-ounce "monster burgers" with fries for $7, and an elaborate unlimited salad bar for about the same price. There's even Swenson's Ice Cream. How's that for catering to foreign tastes! Open from noon to 11pm daily.

Carlos 'n' Charlie's, Paseo Kukulcán just a bit east of the Hotel Casa Maya on the lagoon side of the road (no phone), is Cancún's branch of the well-known Mexican restaurant chain. The mood here is decidedly upbeat and fun-loving, as you will be able to tell the minute you enter the rambling restaurant-bar-disco-marina complex. A sign proclaims that the place is "Open from 11:59am" to "Members and Nonmembers Only," with lunch served from noon to 5pm, dinner from 6pm to midnight. After dinner, dancing continues on the terrace. The decor is early junkyard, with that special Carlos Anderson inspiration. A sign here says, "We don't speak English, but we promise not to laugh at your Spanish." The menu (on a wooden board) starts with black bean soup and other favorites, then continues the jocular theme with chicken ("Peep") prepared on the grill, or barbecued, or various other ways; beef ("Moo") charcoal-grilled, or with lime butter, or pepper, or mushrooms, or à la Tampiqueña, or as Stroganoff; fish ("Splash") and seafood take up a prominent and large part of the menu, of course. For desserts, the

Carlos specialty is called Pemex, after the Mexican national oil company: vanilla ice cream topped with Kahlúa and xtabentun, and definitely high-octane. If this is too much for you, have the key lime pie. For your jolly meal at Carlos 'n' Charlie's expect to pay $15 to $25 per person, all included, which includes drinks, tips, and dancing.

Senior Frogs, Avenida Kukulkán next to Carlos 'n' Charlie's (no phone), will get you smiling in no time at this addition to the popular Anderson lineup of restaurants. A stuffed bear holds the menu as you enter, but attention is quickly diverted to the jaunty life-size papier-mâché frog and lively music. Soon paper streamers will dangle from you just as they do the bear, the frog, rafters, and other patrons. Shuffle through the sawdust-filled floor for a seat near the band (after 10:30pm), the oyster bar, or the lagoon. The menu runs the gamut from hamburgers and fries, to pastas, to oysters, to tacos or quesadillas, all between $3.50 and $6. There's a cover charge of $2 after 8pm for those who don't order dinner. Live music starts at 10:30pm and goes until 2am. Open daily from noon until 2am.

Calypso, the Hotel Camino Real's elegant street-entry restaurant (tel. 3-0100), serves up the diverse cuisines of the Caribbean that combine influences of Spain, France, Africa, and East India. But the Calypso goes beyond the usual by using stars to reflect either low or high calories and cholesterol content. You might start out with a hot appetizer of shrimp and oysters over green fettuccini topped with creamy herb sauce ($12), fork on to roasted quail in a raspberry vinaigrette ($8), or Dominican chicken breast with watercress and oyster sabayon ($11). Open from 6pm to midnight daily.

On my last visit the **Captain's Cove** (tel. 5-0016) was packing them in on several levels of dining facing big open windows overlooking the lagoon and Royal Yacht Club Marina. You'll find it at the far end of the Zona Hotelera not far from the Omni Hotel. It's open at breakfast with an all-you-can-eat buffet for around $6. Lunch and dinner entrees of steak and seafood run $9 to $20 plus tax and tip. Desserts are moderately priced at $3.50 to $5 and there's a menu catering especially to children. From the dock here you can also sign up for a lobster dinner cruise from 4:30 to 7:30pm for around $45. To save the cost of a $6 taxi from downtown Cancún, take the local bus. Open from 8am to 11pm daily.

For a breakfast with great atmosphere and food try **La Bamba,** Avenida Kukulcán, Langosta Shopping Center (tel. 3-0669). It's between the Hotel Casa Maya and Puerto Linda. With a background of classical music, dine under three grand palapa-topped domes while gazing on the sea and beach through giant shuttered windows open to cool morning breezes. While sea gulls preen and bathe in a small tidal pool, and joggers huff past, begin a $5.70 feast made up of a tall glass of fresh orange juice, a basket of fresh croissants and lightly sweet rolls, unlimited coffee, and a choice from the menu. Among the selections are French toast made from homemade raisin nut loaf, or apple and nut crêpes. The Popeye omelet comes with spinach and lots of chunky pieces of shrimp, fresh fried potato chips, and two fruit skewers. La Bamba is open for lunch and dinner too and serves entrees between $7 and $15. Friday nights ladies receive free drinks while there's disco dancing on the terrace. If you'd like to try for a free lunch or dinner, come with a group of six or more. The one who can sing a whole verse of La Bamba gets lunch or dinner on the house. For other deals, ask about the La Bamba breakfast and Isla Mujeres cruise special that takes off from the dock by the restaurant, or Margarita Mondays where those potent drinks are $1 all day, or the 20% discount on all meals on Saturday and half-price drinks daily from 4 to 6pm. In season La Bamba is open from 7am to 11pm and may be closed at lunch during the low season.

The **Bombay Bicycle Club Restaurant and Video Bar,** Avenida Kukulkán, Km. 6 (no phone), is a Hotel Zone eatery determined to try harder. It grabs attention with appealing perks such as an all-you-can-eat ribs and chicken breast for $8.50, lobster tail for $9.95, free salad bar with an order of shrimp, fish, or rib eye, enormous margaritas and daiquiries for under $3, and ice tea with free refills. There's an all-you-can-eat breakfast for around $5. For that you can linger over unlimited coffee, multiple trips to the fruit bar, an orange juice, and as much as you want from the regular menu. The only drawback is that when the restaurant is full, the air conditioning doesn't keep the place cool. Open 7am to 11pm daily.

In Plaza Caracol Shopping Mall

During your time shopping in the Plaza Caracol Shopping Center near the Convention Center, you'll probably get hungry. When you do, don't despair, as the shopping complex holds several good places for lunch or dinner.

For something different, drop in at **Karl's Keller** (tel. 3-1104). The decor is Bavarian, the air conditioning is arctic, and the menu is in German, English, and Spanish. For starters have Gulaschsuppe (goulash soup, almost a meal in itself) or Bohnensuppe (bean soup), go on to familiar items such as Bratwurst and Wiener Schnitzel, and finish up with Apfelstrudel or Linzertorte, and your bill will come to $16 to $18 per person, tax included. You can dine quite nicely for just over half that amount if you like. Open from 8am to 11pm every day.

IN CUIDAD CANCÚN

Most of Cancún's independent restaurants (the ones not connected to large hotels) are downtown, in Ciudad Cancún. Virtually everyone who stays at one of the large hotels on Isla Cancún makes the trek downtown at least once during their stay. When you go, here are some places to look for:

Among the most pleasant and elegant small downtown restaurants is **La Dolce Vita,** Avenida Cobá 87, near Avenida Nader (tel. 4-1384), open each evening for dinner. A small sunken sidewalk terrace dining area here is supplemented with larger interior rooms, all done in soft, pleasing colors. The Italian menu is fine, full, and very tempting. Appetizers include pâté of quail liver and snails in puff pastry. There's always seafood soup. You can order pastas such as tortellini in cream, manicotti of lobster in white wine sauce, or rigatoni Mexican style (with chorizo, mushrooms, and chives) as an appetizer for half price, or as a main course for full price. Other main courses include tournedos of beef, veal saltimbocca, scampi, sea conch, calamari, and various fish. Desserts are the Italian favorites. The cost per person for a dinner here can be $18, or it can be $30 or slightly more, depending on your preferences. Make reservations, as La Dolce Vita is often busy. Open from 5 to 11pm daily.

You may feel transported to Italy at **Don Giovani,** Cobá, at Nube a block and a half off Tulum going toward the Hotel Zone (tel. 4-5063). It's across from the restaurant La Dolce Vita. A large maroon and yellow sign announces the restaurant. Once inside you'll find Italy typically re-created with red and white checked tablecloths, fresh carnations, maroon walls, and low-hanging green-shaded lights suspended above each table. It all creates a cozy atmosphere for dining. A meal might start with an appetizer of fried squid (calamari) with tartar and garlic sauce. For the main course you might choose pasta Giovani, combining shrimp, squid, tomato, cream, and basil; lasagna; or grilled lobster with lemon and pesto sauce. Pastas are made fresh daily and all meals are served with fresh round loaves of bread topped with a light garlic sauce. That's lunch or dinner for around $25 if you tackle soup through dessert, or closer to $8 for an entree alone. If you stop in at breakfast, baked goodies take center stage including an assortment of fresh croissants for $3.50 with a choice of several fillings. A plate of fruit costs under $2. They promise breakfast in 10 minutes or you don't pay. By the way, no matter how stuffed you are, the incredibly tempting bakery shop in front will waken tastebuds all over again. Open daily from 7am to 11pm; closed Sunday in the low season.

Another Italian place is **Augustus Caesar,** Calle Claveles (tel. 4-1261), a small, cozy place with the feel of a fairly fancy trattoria in an Italian hilltop town, except that there's a small garden dining area as well. White stucco, carved wood, fancy tables in the old style, and a very full menu of Italian dishes (especially seafood) with a Cancún accent are the draw here, not to mention careful and attentive service. Your dinner can be as simple as spaghetti with seafood, or a traditional favorite such as scaloppine alla marsala, or as fancy as an entire lobster, followed by a flaming pineapple dessert, and the bill will be somewhere between $8 and $25 (the latter for lobster). If you linger at the entrance, looking at the menu, when you arrive, a waiter may hand you a card good for a free postprandial drink. Augustus Caesar is open every day for lunch and dinner. There's a branch in the Zona Turística in the Costa Blanca shopping center.

There are many Italian and Mexican restaurants in Cancún, but only one restaurant specializing in fondue. That's **La Fondue,** Avenida Tulum 200 at Calle Agua (tel. 4-1697), two blocks south of the Hotel América in the Plaza Mexico shopping complex at street level. A set-price menu allows you to have a five-course meal such as this for less than $20 per person: hearts of palm, or avocado stuffed with shrimp; onion soup; salad; a fondue of beef, cheese, chicken, or fish; and a dessert such as chocolate fondue or chocolate mousse. The attractive restaurant is light and pleasant, and slightly fancy without formality; the management is authentically *franco-*

québecoise. Dinner is served every day from 5pm to midnight. During the busy winter season, La Fondue is also open for lunch from 11am to 3pm.

A lot of Mexican-style fun awaits you at **Mi Ranchito,** Avenida Tulum 15 and 16, 1-B (tel. 4-7814), in front of the Banco del Atlántico near the intersection with Avenida Cobá. If you linger at the sidewalk menu as you pass by, the welcoming hostess will no doubt offer you a little card good for a free drink with dinner. And linger you will, especially in the evenings, if only to listen to the mariachi band, and to figure out exactly what Mi Ranchito is. Sure, there are brick archways and white walls, and lots of wooden tables crowded with the happy and the hungry. But then there are piñatas, balloons, and serapes hanging from the ceiling, at night three bands battling one another, an open grill laden with shish kebabs, shrimp kebabs, T-bone steaks, filets of fish, chickens, and more. One part of the restaurant is a sidewalk café, another is an oyster bar, and yet others are cozy corners. Breakfast can cost $3 or $4, lunch or dinner about $10 to $20 per person, all included. It's lively and popular, and open from 8am to midnight for breakfast, lunch, and dinner seven days a week.

SEAFOOD

There always seems to be a line for dinner at the **Restaurant El Pescador,** Tulipanes 5, off of Avenida Tulum (tel. 4-2673). Fresh seafood excellently prepared and moderately priced (for Cancún) is the drawing card. You can sit on the rustic porch at streetside, in an interior dining room, or upstairs, and feast on cocktails of shrimp, conch, lobster, fish, or octopus for $3 to $6, and main fish courses priced between $7 and $15. The specialty here is Créole cuisine, such as Créole-style shrimp (camarones alla criolla), or charcoal-broiled lobster, but these cost more. Open for lunch and dinner; closed Monday.

The **Restaurant El Pirata,** Azucenas 19 off Avenida Tulum (tel. 4-1338), has the proper nautical motif, long dinner hours (4 to midnight, seven days a week), and seafood prices that are moderate for Cancún. For a dinner based on grilled filet of fish, expect to spend about $8 or $9, half again as much for fancy items such as a brochette of shrimp and steak.

The local incarnation of the Soberanis seafood restaurant group is at Avenida Cobá 5 and 7, in the **Hotel Soberanis** (tel. 4-1125). The patio dining area is shaded by large awnings, and although you're not far from Avenida Tulum here, it's fairly quiet. Service is attentive, and prices are moderate considering the general range of prices in Cancún for seafood. Fish entrees are a moderate $5 to $10, and are the best things to have. Soberanis opens about 9 in the morning (good for breakfast), and closes at 11pm or midnight.

YUCATECAN SPECIALTIES

The first **Restaurant Los Almendros** was located deep in the Maya heartland at Ticul. Then a branch opened in Mérida, and now one has been opened in Cancún (tel. 4-0807). Los Almendros specializes in Maya cooking, and the big restaurant on Avenida Bonampak at Calle Saíl (or Sayil), near Intersuites Cancún, is meant to look something like a large Maya palapa inside. Get in a cab, and for about $2 the driver will take you south on Avenida Tulum, past the Hotel América and toward the airport, and will turn left onto Avenida Bonampak. The restaurant is a few blocks down, on the left-hand side. The menu here has explanations of all the dishes (in English too), and you'll see lime soup; roast venison with radishes, onions, and sour oranges (tzic de venado); and the house specialty, which is grilled pork served with onions, chiles, and beans (pocchuc). The combinado yucateco is a sampler with small portions of four typically Yucatecan main courses. Wine and beer are served. You can lunch or dine at Los Almendros for about $10 per person, or even less. Open daily from 11am to 11pm.

The **Restaurant Papagayo,** Claveles 31, off Avenida Tulum (no phone), has a lush tropical-garden layout complete with straw-thatched palapa. It's a proper setting for Yucatecan dishes such as lime soup or tikinchik, but the menu goes beyond Yucatecan specialties to more familiar fare. Expect to spend $7 to $15 for a full lunch or dinner; breakfast is served as well. Closed Sunday.

DINING WITH ENTERTAINMENT

A place that was booming on my last visit was **Perico's,** Avenida Yaxchilán 71, at Calle Marañón (tel. 4-3152). Made of sticks to resemble a large Maya house, Perico's has a Guodalupe Posada and Pancho Villa theme. The restaurant features steaks, Cancún seafood, some continental dishes, and the more traditional Mexican dishes for very moderate rates. You should be able to choose whatever you like from the menu (except lobster) and still get out for no more than about $10 to $16 per person. Open noon to 2am.

Across the street from the aforementioned Carrillo's Hotel is **Chocko's & Tere,** at Calle Claveles 13 (tel. 4-1394), a ramshackle, semi-open-air collection of brightly lit dining rooms where the noise level is high, but the fun level is even higher. Something is always going on here between 1:30 and 11pm to liven up the already lively crowd. The food seems to be of second interest here, and the service is, well, casual and very good natured. But you can have soup, main course, dessert, and a bottle of beer, tax and tip included, for $15 to $20 per person. And don't forget all that free entertainment.

PIZZA

Is there no place to get a good, inexpensive (under $4) meal in Cancún? There is. At **Pizza Rolandi,** Avenida Cobá 12, between Tulum and Nader (tel. 4-4047), you can get the basic cheese-and-tomato pizza for just over $2, which, with a drink, will satisfy your hunger very pleasantly. The super-special pizza costs $14 and Italian specialties like spaghetti and cannelloni cost about $4.50. Italian desserts are offered. Pizza Rolandi is usually crowded, its outdoor patio tables busy with the hungry, thirsty (beer is served), thrifty set. By the way, a few of the drink prices tend to be somewhat high.

Open Monday through Saturday from 1pm to midnight and on Sunday from 4 to 11pm.

For Breakfast

The popular **Restaurant Pop,** famous in Mérida for a number of years now, has a branch in Cancún at Avenida Tulum 26 (tel. 4-1991), near the corner of Avenida Uxmal and the Hotel Parador. As in Mérida the fare tends to the light, simple, and delicious rather than the elaborate and expensive. Breakfast or a light lunch can be had in the cool comfort of Pop's air-conditioned dining room for $2.50 to $4; a more substantial dinner should be in the range of $4 to $6. Wine and beer are served. Open daily from 8am to 10:30pm except Sunday.

---

3. What to See and Do

You've come for the sun and the sea, and Cancún has them in abundance. Locals boast that this resort has over 240 completely sunny days per year. For the most part, the other 125 days are partly sunny, with few days of rain or heavy overcast.

THE BEACHES

Yucatán's native rock is a limestone made up of microscopic star-shaped plankton fossils named disco-aster. When the bedrock breaks down into sand, it yields grains of a brilliant whiteness with polished surfaces. The polish and the whiteness resist heat absorption, so even under the blazing noonday sun, Cancún's "air-conditioned" sand remains cool under foot.

As for the water, it is the lucent blue Caribbean, famed for its coral and multicolor marine life. With the air-conditioned sand, it completes an unbeatable combination.

All beaches in Mexico are public. Strictly speaking, there is no such thing as a private beach from which you (or anyone else) can be excluded. In practice, one can feel self-conscious walking in a bathing suit through a posh hotel lobby on the way to the beach—especially if one is not a guest at the hotel. The hotel has the right to usher you out of the lobby (although this never happens), but not the right to chase you from the "hotel's" beach. Feel free to swim where you like.

When swimming on eastern beaches (those between Punta Cancún and the Club Mediterranée), you must be cautious of deadly undertow and rip tides. These treacherous currents can grab swimmers without warning and rush them out to sea. It's best to swim where the surf breaks well before it reaches the beach; or where there is a vigilant lifeguard; or where signs indicate safe swimming. Sometimes you can recognize a rip tide area because the water is oddly discolored, and waves reach the shore earlier than on other portions of the beach.

If you should be so unlucky as to be swept out to sea, take these measures: First, don't panic. You'll get back to shore if you follow the rules. Second, swim at a normal speed in a direction parallel to the shore. This will get you out of the current. Once outside the current, you can swim into shore. You'll be tired, but you'll make it. If you try to swim directly toward shore against the current, you'll soon be exhausted and unable to continue.

This danger is not nearly as great on north-facing beaches, those between Ciudad Cancún and Punta Cancún.

Having warned you of the danger, here's a tip: The deserted beaches are those farthest south from Punta Cancún. Take a Ruta 1 or Ruta 2 bus south along Paseo Kukulcán, and get off at an undeveloped stretch of the road. Right over the dunes to the east is the beach. But please, please be careful about that undertow.

You should also get to know Cancún's weather-watch water safety pennant system, and make sure to check the flag at any beach or hotel before entering the water. Here's how it goes:

White	= Excellent
Green	= Normal conditions (safe)
Yellow	= Changeable, uncertain (use caution)
Black or Red	= Unsafe! Use the swimming pool instead

Here in the Caribbean, a storm can come up and conditions can change from safe to unsafe in a matter of minutes, so be on guard: If you see dark clouds heading your way, make your way to shore and wait until the storm passes and the green flag is displayed again.

WATER SPORTS

Cancún has them all, from sailing and sailboarding through scuba-diving and snorkeling to such exotica as jet-skiing and parasailing. Most hotels on Isla Cancún have their own water sports facilities where you can rent all the necessary equipment and sign up for paid lessons.

YACHT EXCURSIONS

Yacht excursions are a favorite pastime here. Modern motor yachts, trimarans, even oldtime sloops take swimmers, sunners, and snorkelers out the limpid waters, often dropping anchor at Isla Mujeres' Garrafón Beach for lunch and snorkeling around the coral reef. Trips tend to leave at 9:30 or 10am, last for five hours, include lunch (and sometimes drinks), and cost $25 to $35 per person.

The **Corsario** (tel. 3-0200), an "18th-century pirate sloop," leaves from the marina next to the Stouffer El Presidente at 10am and returns at 4pm.

The glass-bottom trimaran **Manta** (tel. 3-1676 or 3-0348) departs the marina next to the Club Caribe Cancún, and several readers have written to recommend it as a fine experience.

The motor yacht **Tropical** (tel. 3-1488) will take you from the

Playa Langosta Dock to Isla Mujeres and Garrafón on a cruise from 9am to 3:15pm daily.

Another motor yacht with an all-day excursion to Isla Mujeres is the **SSS Stela,** Avenida Bonampak 63, Depto. 103 (tel. 4-2882 or 4-3095). The itinerary goes like this: You depart the dock near Pepe's Restaurant in the Zona Hotelera and sail to Isla Mujeres. Before reaching Garrafón beach, continental breakfast is served. There's time for swimming and snorkeling before heading out for the other side of the island and a private beach club, Nauti-Beach, for lunch and shopping. Soft drinks and alcoholic beverages are included in the price.

The new two-decker **Aqua II** (tel. 4-1057 or 4-3194) is one of several boats going to Isla Mujeres from the Playa Linda Dock near the Hotels Calinda and Maya. Every day except Wednesday it leaves at 9:30am and returns at 3:30pm. Coffee and pastries are served followed by an open bar on both trips.

RUINAS EL REY

Cancún has its own Maya ruins. Though they're unimpressive compared to Tulum, Cobá, or Chichén-Itzá, the Ruinas El Rey are still of interest.

The ruins are about 13 miles from town, at the southern reaches of the Zona Hotelera, almost to Punta Nizuc. Look for the Royal Mayan Beach Club on the left (east), and then the ruins on the right (west). Admission is free daily from 8am to 5pm; write your name in the register after you pass through the gate.

This was a small ceremonial center and settlement for Maya fishermen built very early in the history of Maya culture, then abandoned, and later resettled near the end of the Postclassic Period, not long before the arrival of the conquistadores. The platforms of numerous small temples are visible amid the banana plants, papayas, and wildflowers.

BULLFIGHTS

Cancún has its own small bullring near the northern (town) end of Paseo Kukulcán. Any Wednesday at 3:30pm during the winter tourist season you can witness this Spanish spectacle. There are usually four bulls. Tickets, from any travel agency in Cancún, cost $25.

FARTHER AFIELD

Day-long excursions, or perhaps even an overnight stay, are easy using Cancún as a base. The Maya ruins at Tulum should be your first goal, then perhaps the *caleta* (cove) of Xel-ha, and later to nearby Isla Mujeres. By driving fast or catching the buses right, one can get to Chichén-Itzá, explore the ruins, and return in a day, but it's much better to make a trip of several days and include Mérida and Uxmal on the same trip. If you plan to go south to the island of Cozumel, think of staying on the island at least one night. See upcoming chapters for transportation details and further information on all of these destinations.

4. Evening Entertainment

Just as the creators and developers of Cancún have gone to great lengths to provide visitors with things to do during the day, they also have put a lot of thought into keeping you amused at night —and into the wee morning hours. Most of the late nightlife is in the large hotels and posh clubs of the Zona Turística. Downtown Ciudad Cancún has its dinner-with-entertainment restaurants and a few small clubs (described above), but it is the large hotels that can sponsor the truly glittery action. Also, the Ballet Folklorico is staged in the Zona Turística, in the convention center at Punta Cancún.

The range of nighttime pursuits also includes moonlight cruises on some of the charter yachts described above, and, of course, clubs and discos.

CLUBS AND DISCOS

All the big hotels have night places, either a supper club with live entertainment, or a nightclub with bands for dancing, or a disco. Expect to pay a cover charge of about $5 to $16 per person, or to be subject to a minimum drink bill, which comes out to about the same thing.

Note that the minimum is often not really a minimum: If the minimum is $6 and drinks are $4, you'll actually have to spend $8 (plus tax and tips) to fulfill the minimum.

Clubs and discos tend to open around 10:30pm, and to swing until 3 or 4am.

SPECIAL EVENTS AT YOUR HOTEL

Most of the large hotels sponsor special culinary and show nights for their guests, particularly a Mexican Fiesta night with a lavish Mexican buffet, mariachis, and general fun and good times. Ask for details, or refer to the hotel descriptions above to find a hotel near you with a festival to your liking.

THE BALLET FOLKLORICO

Dinner and a show here includes a table d'hôte dinner at 7pm, followed at 8:30 by a show with more than 30 dancers and musicians. Though hardly equivalent to the extravaganza staged in Mexico City's Palacio de Bellas Artes, you may consider it worth the price of $32. That price includes one drink.

Shows are staged in the Convention Center auditorium (tel. 3-0199) every evening at 7:30 except Sunday.

ISLA MUJERES: LAID-BACK AND LAZY

1. WHERE TO STAY
2. WHERE TO DINE
3. WHAT TO SEE AND DO

There are two versions of how Isla Mujeres got its name. The more popular one states that pirates used the island as a place to park their women while they were off buccaneering on the Spanish Main. The other account attributes the name to conquistador Francisco Hernández de Córdoba, who was reportedly struck by the large number of female terracotta figurines he found in temples on the island.

Although the more prosaic version is probably correct (aren't they always?), incurable romantics such as myself continue to nurse the forlorn hope that the tale about pirates and their women might have some vestige of authenticity.

Modern Isla Mujeres has happily displayed a healthy immunity toward the latter-day pirate whose prey is American green rather than Spanish gold: There is one moderately priced upscale hotel, and a satisfying number of facilities for budget travelers and even beachcombers.

GET THERE EARLY

In the busy seasons, June to August and December through February, Isla Mujeres can literally fill up with overnight visitors. Making reservations at the island's small hotels does not always go smoothly and reliably, so the best thing you can do is to get to the island as early in the day as possible. You may even have to stay a night in Cancún so that you can arise early for the first ferry. Check-out time in most hotels is 1 or 2pm. Plan to arrive no later than that in February, July, and August.

GETTING TO ISLA MUJERES

The island's position at the heart of the Mexican Caribbean's resort area and its location just a few miles from the mainland make it easily accessible.

From Mérida

Buses leave from the bus station several times a day, and you can travel either first or second class depending on the bus. Your destination is Puerto Juárez, from which you take a ferryboat to the island. You can also fly from Mérida to Cancún, and proceed from there (see below).

From Cozumel

AeroCozumel operates daily flights between Cozumel and Cancún; contact them for schedules and rates at 2-0503 or 2-0928 in Cozumel, 4-1231 in Cancún. You must then take a ferry to Playa del Carmen, then a bus to Puerto Juárez, then another ferry to Isla Mujeres (see below, and also Chapter V).

From Cancún

Passenger boats from mainland Cancún go to Isla Mujeres from **Puerto Juárez** and the passenger/car ferry leaves from **Punta Sam** farther down the same road. To get to either port, take any Ruta 8 city bus from Avenida Tulum.

From Puerto Juárez

Scheduled Puerto Juárez passenger boats run the 40-minute trip seven times daily to and from Cancún and Isla Mujeres at a cost of about 75¢. Nonscheduled, free-lance boatmen, using small fishing boats, ferry passengers between scheduled times for around 55¢. There is no ticket office; pay as you board. In bad weather the schedule will vary. A helpful tourism office at the dock is open until 6pm daily with information about hotels, the price of taxis to downtown Cancún (around $2.50) or the Cancún airport ($13), and ferry schedules in Cancún, Isla Mujeres, Playa del Carmen, and Cozumel.

Puerto Juárez Passenger Ferry

Cancún to Isla	Isla Mujeres to Cancún
8:30am	6:30am
9:30	7:30
10:30	8:30
11:30	9:30
	11:30
1:30pm	1:30pm
3:30	3:30
5:30	5:30
7:15	

From Punta Sam

If you are taking a vehicle to Isla Mujeres, you'll use the **Punta Sam** port just a little farther on past Puerto Juárez. The ferry runs the 40-minute trip daily all year except in bad weather. Cars should arrive an hour in advance of the ferry departure to register for a place in line and pay the $1.50 to $2 fee. Foot passengers pay about 35¢ each.

Punta Sam Car Ferry

Cancún to Isla	Isla Mujeres to Cancún
7:15am	6:00am
9:45	8:00
Noon	11:00
2:30pm	1:15pm
5:15	4:00
7:45	6:30
10:00	9:00

ORIENTATION

Isla Mujeres is about 5 miles long and 2½ miles wide. The ferry docks right at the center of town, within walking distance to all hotels except (if your luggage is heavy) the Hotel Del Prado. If your gear is light, the Del Prado is easily reached on foot. The street running along the waterfront is Rueda Medina, commonly called the *malecon.*

FAST FACTS

The Post Office, telegraph office, and market (Mercado Municipal) are all in a row on Calle Guerrero, an inland street at the north edge of town, which, like most streets in the town, is unmarked by signs.

---

1. Where to Stay

Isla Mujeres was hard hit, but by no means demolished, by Hurricane Gilbert; the result is a much spruced-up island. Most hotels sport fresh paint or at the very least a scrubbed and tidy appearance. In an effort to make up for revenue lost after the storm, many hotel owners have increased prices in excess of what their lodgings are worth. The island that was once the budget travelers' delight can still be easy on the budget, but not to the extent as in years past. Besides working around relatively high prices, you'll have to consider Isla Mujerers' high season, from December 1 through the end of May, that runs a bit longer than either Cancún or Cozumel and Mexico's Pacific Coast; and some hotels extend it to August 1.

TOP HOTELS

Hotel del Prado, Islote El Yunquei, Punta Norte, Isla Mujeres, Q. Roo 77400 (tel. 988/2-0029 or 2-0017), has a dramatic situation, perched on its own tiny islet at the northern tip of Isla Mujeres, surrounded by jagged coral and creamy sand splashed by the pellucid waters of the Caribbean. The sound of the surf reaches every one of the 101 guest rooms, all of which have air conditioning and FM radio. Though the hotel is not huge or fancy, it does have two restaurants and two bars, a swimming pool, and facilities for fishing, scuba-diving, snorkeling, and surfing. A few of the rooms have ocean-view balconies. Prices for this secluded resort are $125 single or double in winter and $110 in summer. A buffet breakfast here costs about $15.

At the **Hotel Nautibeach,** Avenida Rueda Medina, Isla Mujeres, Q. Roo 77400 (tel. 988/2-0259 or Fax 2-0487), 24 units of a 35-unit condominium complex are for rent on Coco Beach, the island's most beautiful stretch of sand. All units are spacious apartments with air conditioning, two bedrooms, kitchen/living room combination furnished with *equipales* furniture and a huge circular glass dining table. Each has either a terrace or balcony facing the Caribbean, positioned just right for sunset. There's a restaurant (see description under "Where to Dine"), and pool. Prices are high for Isla, but on the other hand this is the island's best-planned and most comfortably furnished hotel. In high season two people can rent a two-bedroom apartment for $75 daily or in low season it drops to $55. Four people renting the same space pay $95 in season and $75 in the off months.

MODERATELY PRICED AND BUDGET HOTELS

All of the island's other lodging places are less expensive; most are less than half the price of "the big place." Quality of housekeeping seems to be on a rollercoaster, however: If a hotel fills up, the manager tends to sit back, fire the housekeeping staff, put off repairs, and take it easy. When business drops off, he gets back to work. That's life in these island towns.

The **Hotel Perla del Caribe,** Avenida Madero 2 at Guerrero, Isla Mujeres, Q. Roo 77400 (tel. 988/2-0444), is one of the island's newer hotels, situated right on the eastern open-surf beach called Playa Norte. All of the 94 rooms have sea views, little balconies, fans, and private baths, and many have air conditioning. In the lobby is a television lounge and restaurant, and outside is a small swimming pool, sunning patio, and the beach itself. The base price is $30 single or double for a room on the landward side, or $40 double for a room overlooking the beach; rooms with air conditioners cost a few dollars more. In the heights of the busy winter season these rates may double; in summer, they will certainly be lower, and you may be able to afford a sea-view room on your daily budget.

The **Hotel NaBalam,** Zazil Ha 118, Isla Mujeres, Q. Roo (tel. 988/20446 or 20279 or Fax 2-0011), a new 12-"suite," two-story, hotel near the Hotel Del Prado on Coco Beach, is a fine addition to the island's lodging lineup. Eight more units were in progress when I was there and may be finished by the time you arrive. The lower six units all have terraces on the beach. Three upper units have balconies, and three others do not. What they call suites are really spacious rooms and each comes with two double beds, table and chairs, refrigerator, and ceiling fan. A small restaurant for breakfast and snacks was nearly finished when I was there; light meals may be served as well. High-season rates are $55 single or double for rooms with a terrace or balcony. Those without are about $5 less. Rates are reduced about 50% in low season.

A half block from NaBalam, the **Hotel Cabañas Maria del Mar,** Avenida Carlos Lazo 11, Isla Mujeres, Q. Roo 77400 (tel. 988/2-0179 or Fax 2-0213), is another good choice on Playa Coco. You'll know you are there by the 3-foot-high clay Maya band in the lobby. Twenty-five nicely outfitted rooms are in a three-story building on the beach. All have either two double beds or two single beds, air conditioning, refrigerators, and balconies with both beach and ocean views. In season expect to pay $60 single or double and $25 to $30 during the off season. Fourteen single-story cabañas with ceiling fans, but without air conditioning, cost a little less. Prices include a continental breakfast at **Buho's** next door. Ask about the 50% discount on the daily price of a motor scooter the hotel sometimes offers its guests.

The **Hotel Rocamar** (tel. 988/2-0101) is perched on the higher ground at the opposite side of town from the ferry dock, and thus has a commanding view of the sea. Everything's done in nautical style here, with every conch shell ever opened in the restaurant going to line the garden walkways; ropes and hawsers are employed as trim; even the bathroom sinks are mounted in Lucite tops, and the Lucite is chock full of small seashells. The sea breezes keep the rooms cool, assisted by ceiling fans. Although definitely among the most well-used rooms on the island, the Rocamar's collection of *quartos* has the breeze and the view. Prices are $26 single, $28 double in winter. If they're not busy, you can make a deal for a lower price.

The **Hotel Posada del Mar,** Avenida Rueda Marina 15, Isla Mujeres 77400, Q. Roo (988/20300 or Fax 20266), is an attractively furnished, long-established hotel on the *malecon* three blocks north of the ferry pier. The 42 air-conditioned rooms are in a large garden palm grove in either a three-story hotel-type building, all with terraces or balconies, or in one-story two-bedroom bungalow units. For the spacious quality of the rooms and location, this is among the best buys on the island. A wide stretch of Playa Coco is just across the street. While not as private as Coco gets if you keep walking north, it's still an appealing portion of sánd. The hotel has a pool, and casual palapa-style restaurant. High-season rates are $45 for all rooms. In the off season bungalows go for around $20, first-floor rooms with terrace for $25, and second- and third-floor rooms with balcony for $30.

The **Hotel Berny,** Avenida Juárez and Abasolo, Isla Mujeres, Q. Roo 77400 (tel. 988/2-0025), is a modern stucco building with handsome red-tile floors and an interior court with a pretty swimming pool. Each room has one queen-size bed and one single bed, plus either a ceiling fan or an air conditioner; some have a balcony with sea views, and all are fairly well used despite the hotel's modern

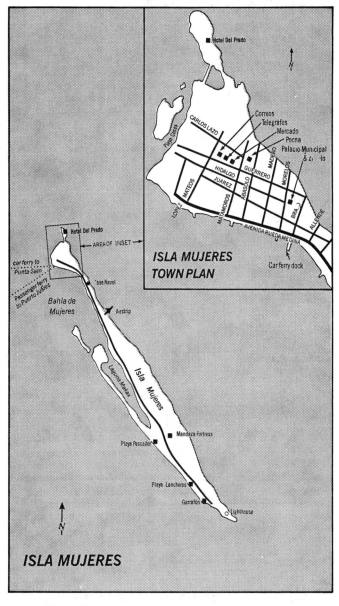

ISLA MUJERES
TOWN PLAN

ISLA MUJERES

aspect. The tradition here is to include a continental breakfast in the room prices, which are $25 single or double, and $17 in the off season.

The **Hotel Belmar,** Avenida Hidalgo between Madero and

Abasolo, Isla Mujeres, Q. Roo 77400 (tel. 988/2-0430 or Fax 2-0429), above the Pizza Rolandi restaurant, is operated by the same people who serve up those wood-oven pizzas. The 60 rooms are tidy and appealing, though simple. With air conditioning, a room goes for about $40 double in winter, around $21 at other times of the year. The Belmar is adding color televisions with parabolic antennae and the price per room will probably go up.

The **Hotel Osorio,** Avenida Madero near the corner with Avenida Juárez, Isla Mujeres, Q. Roo 77400 (tel. 988/2-0018), is noted for the friendliness of its staff and the cleanliness of its rooms, as well as for its very reasonable prices. For a room with private bath and fan, two persons pay $25 in high winter season, a little less than half that much in summer. Note that the Osorio does not have rooms with a sea view. Nothing in town is more than five minutes walk from the beach, however.

Virtually across the street, the **Hotel Martinez,** Avenida Madero 14, Isla Mujeres, Q. Roo 77400 (tel. 988/2-0154), two blocks from the ferry dock (turn left as you debark, go two blocks, and turn right), has been around for years and years, and satisfied guests keep returning because here the basics are dependably observed: Rooms are clean, sheets and towels are white (although perhaps a bit frayed here and there), and little extras such as soap are provided. Prices are fair, at $17 single or double per day, ceiling fans (but no air conditioning) included.

The new 4-suite **Hotel Mesón Bucanero,** Juárez 13 at Hidalgo 11, Isla Mujeres, Q. Roo, 77400 (tel. 988/2-0126), is above the Restaurant Mesón Bucanero and adds much needed rooms in Isla where demand often exceeds supply. Each "suite," using the term loosely, has a double or two double beds with a small separate living room area. The drawback to these otherwise nice accommodations is the lack of air conditioning and small windows. Ceiling fans are helpful, but you may still find it a little on the stuffy side. Each room has a large bathroom with a tub. Keep this one in mind if all others are full, since for the same price elsewhere you won't feel so claustrophobic. Rates in off-season are around $25 and double that in winter.

---

2. Where to Dine

In concert with Isla Mujeres' laid-back atmosphere, there are few fancy restaurants on the island. However, a good selection of comfortable, attractive, and serviceable places are here to keep visitors happy. The specialty is seafood, of course, but you can also get good steaks, pizza, light snacks, and even vegetarian dishes.

The restaurant **Chez Megaley,** fronting Coco Beach at the Hotel Nautibeach, gets the award for the restaurant with the mostest-view, decor, and food in the central village area. Slip into a matching equipales chair and table under a grand palapa inside, or outside on the beachside porch. It's a great location for sunset. Tables are festooned in royal blue, with blue-tinted blown glasses for water and drinks. A huge flower arrangement decorates the restaurant center. Prices are high, so get ready, but I think you'll enjoy your meal. For example, the mixed brochette of shrimp, tender steak, and lobster with rice and vegetables costs around $10. Other choices might be New York–cut steak or pepper steak for around $13, lobster salad for $8, grilled lobster for $18, or a hamburger and fries for $6.

Among Isla Mujeres' most dependable old standbys is the **Restaurant Gomar,** which has two outdoor tables on Avenida Hidalgo and about 16 indoors (tel. 2-0142). Decor is modern, warm, and nice, with lots of natural wood and Saltillo serape tablecloths. In general, prices here are among the highest on the avenida, but this means that meat, fish, or shrimp meals come to about $4.50 to $8, complete. Service is the best in town. Open daily from 7am to 11pm.

The **Restaurant La Peña,** behind (east of) the town square bandstand, near the water tower at Calle Guerrero 5 (no phone), gives you a choice on where to hang out: streetside porch, interior room, or seaside terrace. You get an even greater choice of what to eat, from pizzas (two sizes, many varieties, $3.25 to $4.50) through seafood to mole poblano and Chinese. Prices are low to moderate; drinks are served (happy hour from 6 to 7pm).

Right next door is the **Restaurant Galeria Sergio,** Guerrero 3-A Sur (no phone), which welcomes you with ersatz Roman decor —fake columns, wrought-iron furniture—and traditional Mexican music. It's a popular spot for sipping drinks and peoplewatching, but the food and prices aren't bad either: Substantial breakfast specials can be had for $2.20 to $3.55, Mexican antojitos (traditional dishes) for about the same. Dinner main courses of meat and fish are pricier, up to $8 for lobster, but still very good values. Open between 6pm and midnight.

Pizza Rolandi, Avenida Hidalgo between Madero and Abasolo (tel. 2-0429), the chain that saves the day with dependably good, reasonably priced food in otherwise expensive resorts, comes through in Isla Mujeres as well. The attractive dining rooms, open Tuesday through Sunday from 1pm to midnight and Monday from 6pm to midnight, are the scene for consumption of pizzas, pastas, and calzones cooked right here in a wood oven. As in Cancún, you can easily dine for $4 to $6 here, but watch out for the drink prices.

Facing Pizza Rolandi across the street is the **Mesón del Bucanero,** Juárez 13 and Hidalgo 11 (tel. 2-0236), with a comely decor of wood, palm trees, and other pirate-friendly design elements. You can come here for breakfast, lunch, or dinner any day of the week—or of the year, for that matter—and get eggs prepared various ways for only about $3, various Mexican treats such as enchiladas or tacos for about $3. The Bucanero will remind you of those frenetically upbeat restaurants along Cancún's Avenida Tulum, but here in laid-back Isla Mujeres the mood is more mellow.

Near the Hotel del Prado, on Playa Coco, the palapa-topped **Restaurant Bar Buho,** Avenida Carlos Lazo 1 (tel. 2-0213 or 2-0301), is an inviting place to start the day watching shell hunters, joggers, and walkers on this terrific beach. You can stay and gaze for hours without rushing. Besides its great location, Buho's offers inexpensive meals. The fare is the usual fish, sandwiches, and antojitos. Grilled shrimp in garlic is $6.50, delicious eggs *motoleño* style are a little less than $2, and a cup of coffee is only 35¢. If you become a regular and do some friendly nudging, you may be able to get them to serve brewed coffee instead of the instant variety. Margaritas cost around $1. Open from 7am to 11pm in season but the hours are shortened slightly in the off season; closed Monday. By the way, Buhos was adding rooms over the restaurant when I was there, so you may find it a reasonable place to stay as well as eat by the time you visit.

NEAR THE FERRY DOCK

Down on the waterfront drive called Avenida Rueda Medina are two good choices for those days (or times of day) when you *simply must* get away from the oppressive heat into blissfully cool air. In other words, both are air-conditioned.

Mirtita's Restaurant and Bar, facing the ferry dock on Avenida Rueda Medina (tel. 2-0157), resembles mightily a State-side lunchroom. Behind its brick façade you'll discover a long lunch counter, red booths, and little tables with cloths protected by glass tops. A sign says *Cervezas y preparados unicamente dos por persona con alimentos,* which translates as "Two drinks or beers only, per person, with meals only." This rule helps Mirtita's to avoid becoming more a tavern than a restaurant. And a restaurant it surely is. The menu lists fish filet, steak and french fries, seafood salads, shrimp cocktails, onion and lemon soup, club sandwiches, fried chicken, and other appetite-satisfiers. Come any day, for any meal, and expect to spend from $4 to $5 or $6 for a full lunch or dinner, less for a good breakfast.

The **Restaurant-Bar Villa del Mar,** Avenida Rueda Medina 1 Sur (tel. 2-0031), across from the ferry dock, is a bit fancier inside, with air conditioning and more the feeling of a sit-down restaurant. Prices are still good, though, and the menu is extensive. A full lunch or dinner with a main course of meat or fish might cost $4.50 to $7. If you just want a plate of tacos and a soft drink, plan on spending about $3.50 to $4. Open daily for all three meals.

---

3. What to See and Do

Isla Mujeres is a sun and sea haven with all the attractions: snorkeling, swimming, fishing, or just plain relaxing.

SEEING THE ISLAND ON A SCOOTER

Renting a "moto," the local sobriquet for motorized bikes and scooters, for a couple of hours or full day, is the best and most leisurely way to see the island. Numerous agencies rent them. If you don't want to fool with gears and shifts, rent a fully automatic one for around $16 per day or $4 per hour. Semiautomatic scooters cost about the same per day and around $3.25 per hour. They come with seats for one person or some large enough for two. Take some time to get familiar with how the scooters work and on the road be careful as you approach a couple of blind corners and hills where visibility is poor. There's only one main road, with a couple of offshoots.

THE BEACHES

There are three beaches, one in town called **Playa Cocoteros** (Coco for short) extending around the northern tip of the island to your left as you get off the boat, another at **Garrafón National Park** about 3 miles south (although it was severely eroded by Hurricane Gilbert), and **Playa Langosta** along the Caribbean edge of the Laguna Makax.

SWIMMING

The wide Playa Coco is the best swimming beach, with Playa Langosta second. Coco beach is easily reached on foot from the village. Local buses go to Playa Langosta as far as the El Paraiso restaurant on the beach. It's a public beach with several rather high-priced palapa-style restaurants. Consider bringing your own refreshments. By the way, most of the beachside restaurants along here have pens with a couple of turtles and a nurse shark or two. The marine animals are easily visible in the clear water and it costs nothing to see them. If a local swimmer holds them for view and picture taking, then a tip is expected. *Note:* There are no lifeguards on duty in Isla Mujeres. The system of flags to signify safety of water conditions that you may have noticed in Cancún and Cozumel isn't in use here either.

SNORKELING

Garrafón is by far the easiest and most popular of the snorkeling locations, but you'll need a taxi (around $2) to get there as there are no buses that go that far. Or it's about an hour and a half walk from town. Snorkeling lanes are marked off with ropes so swimmers will neither damage the coral nor be hurt by it. Another excellent location is around the **lighthouse** in the Bahia de Mujeres (bay) opposite downtown, where the water is about 6 feet deep. Boatmen will take you for around $10 per person if you have your own snorkeling equipment, or $5 more if you use theirs. Alex Betancourt, a resident snorkeling afficionado, believes that the reef by the Hotel del Prado is better than Garrafón, but cautions that it's not for beginners or weak swimmers because of the strong surf. The jagged reefs on the windward side of the island are good too, he says, but you need to know how to get in and out; otherwise the surf pushes you against the coral. For these two, hire a local to go with you who *knows* these waters. The point by the southern lighthouse and below the ruined Maya temple is too dangerous, which you would instant-

Side Trip to Isla Contoy

If at all possible, a sidetrip to Isla Contoy, a National Wildlife Reserve set aside in 1981, should be included in your plans. It's 19 miles by boat from Isla Mujeres. The pristine uninhabited island, an odd-shaped 3¾ miles long, is covered in lush vegetation and harbors 70 species of birds as well as a host of marine and animal life. Ten of the identified species nest on the island including pelicans, brown boobies, frigates, egret, tern, and cormorant. Flocks of flamingos arrive in April. June, July, and August are good months to plan an overnight trip to witness turtles nesting. Most excursions troll for fish, which will be your lunch, anchor to snorkel enroute, and leisurely skirt the island for close viewing of the birds without disturbing the habitat. After arrival, there's time to snorkel, laze on the gorgeous beach, or walk in search of birds. A modern visitor's center has excellent displays in Spanish, English, and French explaining the climate, wildlife, and geology of the island. One way, the trip takes a minimum of an hour and a half, more if the waves are choppy.

Due to the tightknit boatmen's cooperative, prices for this excursion are the same—$35—no matter whom you ask. You can join others for this trip by buying a ticket directly at the cooperative, **Sociedad Cooperativa Turistica,** on Avenida Rueda Medina, next to Mexico Divers and Brisas restaurant. Or you can buy a ticket at one of several travel agencies such as **La Isleña,** on Morelos at Juarez (tel. 2-0036). Cost for the overnight excursion will be higher than the day trip. I highly recommend the services of boat owner Ricardo Gaitan. Ask for him at the cooperative or write to him directly at P.O. Box 42, Isla Mujeres, Q. Roo 77400. He speaks English and his large boat, the **Estrella del Norte,** comfortably holds 16 passengers. He is the only one offering the overnight Isla Contoy trip.

Three types of boats go to Contoy. Medium-size boats have two motors and hold 10 passengers. Large boats have a toilet and hold 16 people, and small boats have one motor and seat 8 or 9 people. Boat captains should respect the cooperative's regulations regarding capacity and should have enough life jackets to go around. Some of these boats have a sun cover; others do not. If you spend the night on the island, be sure to take along mosquito repellent. An inflatable mattress wouldn't be a bad idea, although bedding is provided.

ly conclude upon seeing the waves crashing against the island bedrock. *Note:* No matter where you snorkel, remember coral cuts like a knife.

FISHING

To arrange a day of fishing, which costs around $200, ask at the boatmen's cooperative or the travel agency mentioned under Isla Contoy. The cost can be shared with four to six others. All year you'll find bonito, mackerel, kingfish, and amberjack. Sailfish and sharks (hammerhead, bull, nurse, lemon, and tiger sharks) are in good supply in April and May. In winter there's usually a good supply of large grouper and jewelfish.

MAYA RUIN

Just beyond the lighthouse at the southern end of the island is a pile of stones that once formed a small Maya pyramid before Hurricane Gilbert. Believed to have been an observatory built to the moon goddess Ix-Chel, it's now reduced to a rocky heap. The location is still worth seeing on a lofty bluff overlooking the sea. If you are at Garrafón National Park and want to walk, it's not too far. When you see the lighthouse, turn toward it down the rocky path. Although there's no need for a guide, the lighthouse keeper's children will gladly give a breathless rendition of the legends of the ruins—all for a small tip of course. And the keeper himself has an assortment of cold drinks, snacks, and hammocks for sale.

PIRATE'S FORTRESS

The **Fortress of Mundaca** is about 2½ miles in the same direction as Garrafón, off about ⅓ mile to your left. The fortress was built by the pirate Mundaca Marecheaga who in the early 19th century arrived at Isla Mujeres and proceeded to set up a blissful paradise while making money from selling slaves to Cuba and Belize. The fortress is set in a pretty, shady spot, and is a nice trip if you are suffering from too much sun.

SHOPPING

Shopping is a leisurely activity, nothing of the hard-sell you find in Cancún or Acapulco. Most visitors find that prices are more reasonable in Isla Mujeres too. You'll find silver, Saltillo serapes and Oaxaca rugs, pottery, and blown glassware in abundance as well as a couple of stores with quality folk art.

COZUMEL: DIVER'S PARADISE

In Mexico's Caribbean resort area, if Cancún is the jet-set's port of call and Isla Mujeres belongs to the beachcombers, Cozumel, 44 miles south of Cancún, is a little bit of both. More remote than either of the other two resorts, this island (pop. 30,000) becomes more of a world unto itself, a place where people come to get away from the day-tripping atmosphere of Isla Mujeres or the megadevelopment feeling of Cancún, a place to take each day as it comes for a week or more without moving very far from the hotel or the beach. There is actually little reason to leave the island as all the necessaries for a good vacation are here: excellent snorkeling and scuba places, sailing and water sports, fancy hotels and modest hotels, elegant restaurants and taco shops, even a Maya ruin or two. If, after a while, you do get restless, the ancient Maya city of Tulum and the lagoon of Xel-ha provide convenient and exciting goals for excursions.

Many visitors complain about Cozumel's price structure, which seems high for what you get. But if you're diving at Palancar Reef, it all seems worth it.

GETTING TO AND FROM COZUMEL

There are scheduled daily flights from Cancún as well as the United States and Mérida plus charter flights to and from the ruins of Chichén Itzá. Buses from Cancún go to Playa del Carmen where there are frequent passenger ferries to Cozumel. A car ferry leaves six times a week from Puerto Morelos.

By Air

Cozumel's airport is near downtown. **Aero Transportes** vans at the airport provide transportation to the town proper for $1.20 and to either the north or south hotel zone for $1.60. For the return, you'll have to take a taxi for around $1.60.

American (tel. 987/2-0988 or 2-0899) flies direct from Dallas/Fort Worth and Raleigh/Durham. **Continental** (tel. 987/5-0576 or 2-0487) has flights from Houston. **Mexicana,** Melgar Sur 17 (tel. 987/2-0157, 2-0263, or 2-0405 at the airport) flies from Dallas/Fort Worth, Miami, Los Angeles, and Mérida. **Aero Cozumel** (tel. 987/2-0928, 2-0503, or Fax 987/2-0500 in Cozumel and tel. 4-2862 in Cancún) has direct flights to and from Mérida and Chetumal and six flights daily to and from Cancún at 8 and 10am, noon, 2, 4, and 6pm, as well as four daily flights on a 27-seat shuttle plane to Playa del Carmen (no phone) at 9 and 11am and 3 and 5pm. The shuttle to Cozumel from Playa is 20 minutes later than these.

By Ferry

There are four passenger ferries running to and from Cozumel and Playa del Carmen. *Mexico I* is the modern water jet that makes the trip in 25 to 30 minutes compared to 40 to 45 on the *Mexico II, Xelha,* and *Cozumeleño.* Mexico I and II cost $5 one way and are enclosed vessels with cushioned seats and video entertainment. Cozumeleño and Xelha, open-air vessels with canopies, cost $2.50. Both companies have ticket booths at the main pier. Be prepared for sea sickness on windy days.

Ferry Schedule
Cozumel/Playa del Carmen

Mexico I and *II*	*Xelha* and *Cozumeleño*
4:00am	4:00am
6:30	6:30
8:00	9:00
9:00	
11:00	
1:30pm	1:00pm
3:30	6:30
4:00	8:00
5:30	
6:30	

ORIENTATION

Cozumel lies some 12 miles out in the Caribbean from Playa del Carmen. The island is roughly 28 miles long and 11 miles wide. Its only town is San Miguel de Cozumel, usually just called Cozumel. And it's Mexico's largest Caribbean Island but it's only 3% developed. By 1993, however, new construction is expected to add 2,000 more hotel rooms in the area beyond the Hotel Stouffer President and near the Palancar Reef.

San Miguel's main waterfront street is called Avenida Rafael Melgar, running along the western shore of the island. Passenger ferries dock right in the center, near the main plaza. Car ferries dock south of town near the hotels Sol Caribe, La Ceiba, Stouffer Presidente and Fiesta Inn.

The town is laid out on a grid, with avenidas running north and south, calles running east and west. The exception is Avenida Juárez, which runs right from the passenger ferry dock through the main square and inland. Juárez divides the town into northern and southern halves.

Heading inland from the dock along Juárez, you'll find that the avenidas you cross are numbered by fives for some reason: "5a Avenida," "10a Avenida," "15a Avenida." If you turn left and head north, you'll discover that calles are numbered even: 2a Norte, 4a Norte, 6a Norte. Turning right from Juárez heads you south, where the streets are numbered odd: 1a Sur (also called Adolfo Salas), 3a Sur, 5a Sur. The scheme is more systematic than it is practical.

The northern part of the island has no paved roads. It's scattered with small Mayan sites, badly ruined, from the age when "Cuzamil" was a land sacred to the moon goddess Ixchel. The sites are best visited by jeep or boat.

North and south of town are many hotels, moderate to expensive in price; many cater to divers. Beyond the hotels to the south is **Chancanab National Park,** centered on the beautiful lagoon of the same name. Beyond Chancanab is Playa Palancar, and, offshore, the Palancar Reef (*arrecife*). At the southern tip of the island is Punta Celarain, which bears a lighthouse.

The eastern, seaward shore of the island is mostly surf beach, beautiful for walking but dangerous for swimming. There is safe swimming in a few coves.

GETTING AROUND

In the town itself, everything is within walking distance. Though there is limited bus service along Avenida Rafael Melgar from north of town as far south as Palancar, you may find yourself taking taxis in Cozumel. From town to Playa San Francisco, figure it will cost you $7 to $9.50. For exploring the island, you should consider renting a car or a moped (motorbike).

Car rentals are as expensive here as in other parts of Mexico. See "Car Rentals" in Chapter XIII, for specifics.

As for motorbikes, it seems as though every shop, garage, restaurant, street cleaner, and mortician in Cozumel are also in the business of renting them. Terms and prices vary from place to place: One renter may only rent by the day or half day; another may rent you a moped for a minimum three-hour period. One may charge $6 for three hours, most will charge $25 for a full day (8am to 5pm); sometimes the rental period is from noon to noon the next day.

As part of your bargaining, carefully inspect the actual moped you'll be renting. Early in the morning, with most of the bikes waiting there to be rented, you can choose one on which all the gizmos are in good shape: horn, light, starter, seat, mirror. Later in the day you'll get the clunker on which everything is broken *and you'll pay the same full price for it.* Rent early.

One final note: Be aware that riding a moped is like sunbathing. No matter how much you cover up, your head, neck, hands,

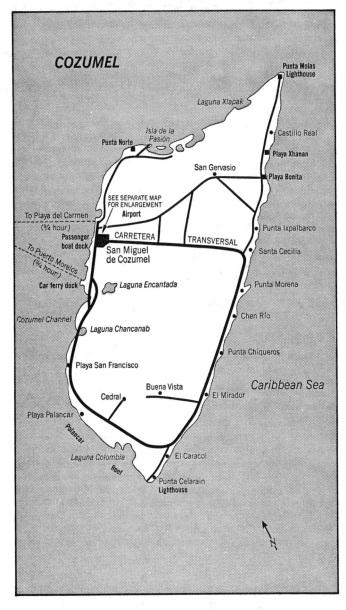

and perhaps legs will be exposed to hours and hours of intense sun. Protect yourself. There's a tendency to forget that riding in the sun all day is like lying on the beach all day.

Here's a price comparison to keep in mind: A couple renting

two mopeds for a day will pay $50. Car rental for a day may total $54. Hiring a taxi for two hours of chauffeured riding costs about $18.

FAST FACTS

Carnival: Cozumel's most colorful fiesta begins the Thursday before Ash Wednesday with daytime street dancing and nighttime parades on Thursday, Saturday, and Monday, with Monday being the best.

Diving: A day costs between $36 and $45 and includes two tanks. There's a new decompression chamber on the island.

Fishing: The best months are April through September when the catch will be blue and white marlin, sailfish, swordfish, dolfin-fish, wahoo, tuna, and red snapper. A half day of fishing costs $250.

Medical Care: Cozumel has a number of English-speaking American and Mexican doctors in residence. Your hotel or the police can help you contact one.

Post Office (Correos), Calle 7 Sur, Avenida Rafael Melgar, is at the southern edge of town.

Taxis: charges should be no more than $1.60 from the town center to the farthest hotels or to and from the airport.

Telephone: There's a long-distance office on the main plaza.

Tourist Office: You will find it on the second floor of the commercial building facing the central plaza.

---

1. Where to Stay

These days Cozumel has a good selection of hotels in all price ranges. In summer there is usually little trouble finding a room. In the high-season months of December, January, February, and March, it's good to call or write ahead for reservations. Prices are higher in those months as well.

TOP HOTELS

All of the top hotels are south of town, two near the car ferry dock (2½ miles south of the main square), and one 4 miles south near Chancanab Lagoon. Prices given below are the in-season rates for the winter. You'll pay a surcharge of 15% to 20% if you come for the Christmas and New Year's holiday period. You can expect substantial reductions if you come in summer (mid-April through August), and even greater reductions in the autumn (September to mid-December).

The **Stouffer Presidente Cozumel,** Km 6½, Cozumel, Q. Roo 77600 (tel. 987/2-0322, or toll free 800/472-2427 in U.S., or 905/395-0333 in Mexico City), is right on the beach near Chancanab Lagoon, with 189 air-conditioned rooms, two restaurants, two bars, swimming pool and tennis courts, and many facilities for water sports. Staff members are friendly and helpful. The hotel is surrounded by shady palms, and has safe swimming in its own artificial cove. As with other properties in the Presidente chain, prices are quite reasonable for what you get, and represent excellent value. To stay in this modern but unobtrusive hotel in one of the best locations on the island costs $165 for a standard double, $187 for a double with a view.

The **Hotel Sol Caribe Cozumel,** Apdo. 259, Cozumel, Q. Roo 77600 (tel. 987/2-0700, or toll free 800/223-2332 in U.S.), on the landward side of the road just north of the car ferry dock, is the island's second-largest hotel, with 220 rooms on 10 floors. The entrance is dramatic, beneath a vast thatched canopy, surrounded by tropical greenery, with rocks and replicas of Maya statuary here and there, giving you the impression that you're entering some mysterious Maya ruin. Lush big-leafed plants and trees are spread throughout the hotel grounds, providing deep shade by the huge swimming pool (which has its own swim-up bar), and to the very edge of the three lighted tennis courts. All rooms have ocean views, air conditioning, a self-service bar, room service, and piped-in music. The hotel's own beach cove, with facilities for water sports, is just across the road. For sustenance, the Sol Caribe provides an upscale restaurant called La Gaviota ("The Seagull"), a coffee shop named La Casa del Pescador, a lobby bar, that bar right in the pool, and a snack bar at the beach. As virtually the entire clientele here is North American, rates are quoted in U.S. dollars: $185 double during the winter season, about 40% less in summer. The Sol Caribe is a Fiesta Americana hotel, operated by Posadas de México.

Just before the Sol Caribe is the new **Casa del Mar** (tel. 987/2-1665 or 2-1000; reservations in the U.S. at 8117 Preston Rd., Suite 170, Lockbox No. 4, Dallas, TX 75225; tel. toll free 800/777-5873 in U.S.). The triangular building of three floors holds 106 simple and very tasteful rooms around a plantfilled courtyard. Each room has a telephone, cable television, and air conditioning; corner rooms are particularly large. What they call "bungalows" are two-floor, two-room units capable of sleeping four. There is a nice-size pool, as well as a cabaña bar, hot tub, and underwater equipment for your use. A tennis court is in the works. In the high season singles and doubles pay $86. Rates drop $20 other months.

Just across from the Sol Caribe, on the beach side of the road, is **La Ceiba Beach Hotel,** Apdo. Postal 284, Cozumel, Q. Roo 77600 (tel. 987/2-0065 or 2-0815, or toll free 800/777-5873 in U.S.). Named for the lofty and majestic tree, sacred to the Maya, which grows in the tropics, La Ceiba advertises itself as "the intimate resort" and stresses the friendliness of its staff. The 115 rooms have all the comforts, of course, including tubs and showers, air conditioning, color TV, and balconies overlooking the Caribbean. The swimming pool is only steps from the beach. The hotel has its own tennis court, but the emphasis here is on water sports, particularly scuba diving. If that's your passion, be sure to ask about the special dive packages when you call for reservations. These include five or seven nights' lodging, with or without breakfast and dinner each day, unlimited use of tanks during your stay, boat trips to Palancar Reef, a night dive, and a few other treats. Renting a room by the day in winter costs $115 single or double. Room prices are about $20 lower in summer.

EXPENSIVE HOTELS

The history of tourism on Cozumel began with a few simple hotels right in town. As the trade developed, fancier hotels were built along the small beaches on the northern shore. Today these hotels are among the older ones on the island, but they've been suitably maintained, and they provide alternatives to the much larger, newer hotels that command the highest prices.

Hotels north of town seem not to be quite so interested in attracting a diving clientele as do those south of town. Rather, these places appeal to vacationers looking for a comfortable room in a smaller hotel with a swimming pool, near the beach. The beaches north of town tend to be tiny little coves surrounded by the jagged coral that makes up Cozumel's bedrock. Here's the rundown, starting with the northernmost hotel and heading south.

The plush renovation of the 188-room **Hotel Melia Mayan Plaza** leaves the impression of a completely new top-quality hotel. It's at the end of the paved northern shore road, Apdo Postal 9, Cozumel Q. Roo 77600 (tel. 987/2-0072, or toll free 800/336-3542 in U.S.). The low-key, elegant lobby, with pale gray marble floors and rose and pale green accents, is a welcome respite on arrival. It's such a comfortable lobby, with a small bar at one end, that guests frequently congregate among the inviting couch groupings. The spacious and beautifully furnished rooms all have ocean view with either a balcony or patio. Some of the standard rooms are right on the beach. For lazing there are two nice pools and one of the longest stretches of beach on the island. Two tennis courts are on the grounds. If you want a nice, quiet and secluded getaway removed from traffic (what little there is in Cozumel) and town, this is the place. Winter rates for two people in a standard room run $140; summer rates are $87 single and $100 double.

The new 163-all-suite **Hotel Plaza Las Glorias** has the best of both of Cozumel's worlds: It's within walking distance of town and has most of the top-notch amenities of resort neighbors farther out on the island. It's on Avenida R. Melgar, Km 1.5, Cozumel Q. Roo 77600 (tel. 987/2-2000, or toll free 800/342-2644 in U.S.). Beyond the expansive comfortable lobby is the pool, multilevel deck, and sea. The large, beautifully furnished rooms all have separate living areas and balconies with ocean views, TV with U.S. channels, and minibars. The two-story, two-bedroom duplex rooms are good buys especially for two couples or families traveling together. Standard rooms in high season cost $135 to $145. Other months the rates drop to $105. Duplex suites run $200 in winter and $150 off season. Ask about other low-season discounts.

The **Hotel El Cozumeleño,** Apdo. 53, Cozumel, Q. Roo 77600 (tel. 987/2-0050 or 2-0149), is located right on Santa Pilar beach, one of the largest stretches of coral-free sand in the area. The glassed-in dining room looks out onto the Caribbean, as do all of the 100 air-conditioned guest rooms. There's a very nice palm-shaded swimming pool, with poolside palapa bar. Prices here are quite reasonable for what you get: $125 double in winter.

The motel-style **Cabañas del Caribe,** Apdo. 9, Cozumel, Q.

Roo 77600 (tel. 987/2-0017 or 2-0072), has 57 rooms facing the Caribbean and Santa Pilar beach, but in many cases the view of the sea is blocked by palm trees. Rooms have the standard comforts—private bath, air conditioning, etc.—and cost $95 double in winter. Summer rates are half that. They have a pool.

A Special Plan

The **Club Cozumel Caribe,** Apdo. 43, Cozumel, Q. Roo 77600 (tel. 987/0-0000, or toll free 800/327-2254 in U.S.), is the largest hotel on Cozumel, with 260 rooms. Many are in the older nine-floor "tower" section; others are more modern junior suites. The hotel operates on an all-inclusive plan; you pay one price and receive everything the hotel has to offer: drinks, meals, tennis, water sports, and lodging. You must stay a minimum of three nights, and you may take advantage of special reduced rates for longer stays. The land-only base price in the winter season is $496 per person, for three days, double occupancy. For seven days the price is $868 per person. In summer, the seven-day package is $700 per person, per week. Call for details of current offerings and reservations.

MODERATELY PRICED HOTELS

North of Town

Several hotels north of town have locations that are not quite as choice, rooms that are not so luxurious, and no toll-free reservations numbers, but they do have prices that are refreshingly moderate. Here they are, in order of preference:

Similar in price and comforts is the **Hotel Mara,** Apdo. 7, Cozumel, Q. Roo 77600 (tel. 987/2-0300), where each of the 48 rooms, on four floors, has its own balcony where you can watch the sunset. All rooms have an individual air conditioner and private bath, and cost $89 double in winter. The Mara has a nice swimming pool surrounded by lounge chairs for sunning, a restaurant and a bar, a dock for water sports, and a sandy "beach" held up by a retaining wall. It's an excellent place to get value for your money.

On a diminutive stretch of beach, the 60-room **Hotel Playa Azul,** Apdo. Postal 31, Cozumel, Q. Roo 77600 (tel. 987/2-0033, or toll free 800/826-6842 in U.S. and Canada), is one of the smaller hotels in the northern Hotel Zone, and one of the most economical. Here you'll want to be specific about your choice of rooms. Those on the beach with balconies or patios facing the ocean are preferable to the bungalows (too grandly called villas) that have patios facing pebbled walkways, the street, and somewhat unkempt gardens. The only pool is on the street side at the far end of the complex in the bungalow area. Both the pool and bungalows were being refurbished on my last inspection, but it could be a while before the pool is ready. The low rates, fresh paint, and all new up-to-date furnishings give the Agua Azul the edge necessary to compete with pricier neighbors. And the price is hard to beat for a beachside hotel. High-season rates for two people sharing a room go from $79 for a garden-view room to $90 in an ocean-view junior suite and $110 for a large master suite facing the ocean. The rest of the year these rates drop at least $20 in each category.

South of Town

Because the beaches tend to lie north of town, hostelries to the south cater mostly to the diving set. After all, you don't require a beach if you're going to dive from a boat. However, this does not mean that you must be a diver to enjoy your stay at one of these places. Each one has either a swimming pool, or a tiny cove, or a dock, or all three. You'll be able to swim, sun, and relax at any of these hotels. If you intend to dive, remember to bring proof of your diver's certification.

The **Hotel Barracuda,** Apdo. 163, Cozumel, Q. Roo 77600 (tel. 987/2-0002), is at Avenida Rafael Melgar Prolongación Sur No. 628, about six blocks south of town. It's the closest diver's hotel to town; you can easily walk the distance. Though it has no swimming pool, the Barracuda does have a little artificial cove in which to swim. A room here costs $75 double, breakfast included ($60 double without breakfast), and comes with a sea view, balcony, air conditioning, fan, and refrigerator. Summer rates are 50% less. The 40-room Barracuda is a favorite with divers, and has been so for years.

The **Galápago Inn,** Apdo. 289, Cozumel, Q. Roo (tel. 987/2-0663, or Aqua-Sub Tours toll free 800/847-5708 in U.S. except Texas, and 713/783-3305 in Texas), is a mile south of the main square. Homey, shady, done in colonial style with white stucco and red brick accents, the inn is usually peopled by divers who have signed up for one of the several money-saving package deals. If you come on your own, you can get a room with balcony, air conditioner, fan, and private bath, plus three meals each day, for $85 double. The inn has its own pretty swimming pool, and a bit of beach.

La Perla Beach Hotel, Apdo. 309, Cozumel, Q. Roo 77600 (tel. 987/2-0188 or 2-0819), has 23 nouveau-rustic rooms on three floors overlooking the water, a small beach, and a swimming pool raised above beach level. The atmosphere here is of and for scuba-divers, who pay $80 double (cash) or $86 double (credit card) for an air-conditioned room in winter. You're still not all that far from the town here, though you'll probably want to ride rather than walk the distance.

For a combination of economy plus trendy comfort the new **Fiesta Inn** may fit the bill. It's south of town on the Costera Sur, Km. 1.7, Cozumel, Q. Roo 77600 (tel. 987/2-2899, or toll free 800/223-2332 through Fiesta Americana Hotels in U.S.). Most of the 178 nicely furnished rooms face the inner grounds and enormous swimming pool. The beach, reached by an underground tunnel, is across the Costera and has its own small pier. There's one tennis court, a lovely restaurant and bar, and ice machines on every floor. All rooms have balconies, color TV with U.S. channels, and a tub/shower combination. Rates during the winter high season are $130 single or double, but during the low season they drop to $83.

The **Hotel Villablanca,** Apdo. 230, Cozumel, Q. Roo 77600

(tel. 987/2-0730 or 2-0865, or Fax 2-0865), has only 24 rooms, but each one is different—some have Roman tubs, TV, and refrigerator. All are air-conditioned. For $60 double in winter you get a room, plus use of the tennis court, swimming pool, and the beach dock across the road. Off-season rates drop 35%. There's a restaurant as well.

In Town

A few blocks from the square at Avenida Rafael Melgar no. 25, Cozumel, Q. Roo 77600, on the corner of Calle 3 Sur, is the new **Hotel Bahía** (tel. 987/2-1387). Atmosphere in the guest rooms comes from stucco, wood, and red tile. The layout is almost like a suite with a sitting area, kitchenette, and double bed. Only three rooms don't have kitchenettes; these are reserved for single travelers. Very few of the 25 rooms have ocean views and balconies, but all have televisions with cable hookups as well as air conditioning. All this comfort costs $55 single, $60 double.

Facing the main plaza in San Miguel is the **Meson San Miguel,** Avenida Juárez 2, Cozumel, Q. Roo 77600 (tel. 987/2-0233 or 2-0323). Though it has no beachfront, and few rooms with any view of the sea, and no divers' ambience, it does offer 97 comfortable, carpeted, air-conditioned rooms with bath and phone for only $50 double, plus use of the hotel's large swimming pool. There's a nice restaurant, and virtually any other restaurant in town is just a few minutes' walk from the hotel's front door.

BUDGET HOTELS

Virtually all of the island's low-priced hostelries are right in the town of San Miguel itself. Some are frequented by the diving crowd, but all welcome any visitor. Prices given below are the normal winter high-season rates, which may go down somewhat in summer, but not by much.

Right downtown in a mini-mall of shops is the **Hotel Suites Bazar Colonial,** Avenida 5 Sur no. 9, Apdo. 286 (tel. 987/2-0542). Prices at this nice, new 28-room hostelry seem reasonable at $45 double in the junior suites, and $40 double in the master suites. You get a nicely appointed studio or one-bedroom apartment, with complete kitchenette, for the cost. It's certainly one of the few hotels on the island to have an elevator, which serves its four floors. Rooms are quiet, and air-conditioned.

A good value can be had at the new **Hotel Safari Inn,** Apdo. 41 (tel. 987/2-0101), behind the Aqua Dive Shop five minutes south of the dock. For $35 double, you get working air conditioning, huge rooms, firm king-size beds, a built-in sofa, and tiled floors and private bath. Natural colors and stucco pervade the interior of this three-tier establishment.

Another good choice is also a newer place, but this one is north of the plaza. (As both places become more established, the prices will no doubt increase.) **Hotel Flamingo** (tel. 987/2-1264), on Calle 6 Norte no. 81, offers simple, quiet, large rooms with fan and private bath for $20 double, $25 triple. Their 21 rooms are arranged on three floors also.

---

2. Where to Dine

Cozumel is well provided with places to dine, but one must be careful in choosing a place because "resort food" is a problem here, as it is in most seaside resorts. Proprietors think that hungry customers will show up whether the food is good or not, and they're not far from wrong. A number of places sometimes rise above this level of thinking, though, and here they are:

Best all-around is a restaurant suitable for breakfast, lunch, dinner, or just a late-night dish of ice cream. The **Restaurant Las Palmeras** (tel. 2-0532) is only a few steps from the zócalo at the corner of Avenidas Juárez and Rafael Melgar, very near the ferry dock. Las Palmeras is open to the four winds, although tables are shaded from the sun. Though always busy, service here is nonetheless fairly efficient and prices are moderate. A light lunch of enchiladas suizas will be only about $3.75. Dinner can be light as lunch, or can run to seafood at $7 to $8 per plate.

On the central plaza at the corner of Avenida Juárez and 5a Avenida Norte is the restaurant that's included in many tour packages as a special treat: **Morgan's** (tel. 2-0584). Inside this wooden building you'll find low lighting, beautifully set tables, and gracious waiters. In short, it's lovely for a special evening out. Start with a Caesar salad or French onion soup. Try the baked fish filet with green pepper, onion, tomato, and achiote for $14.50 or the coq au vin for the same price. Fine desserts are $4.50 to $11, and international coffees are $4.50. A full meal with drinks will run you $25 per person. Open for lunch from 10:30am to 3pm and for dinner from 5:30 to 11pm.

If you're in the mood for a romantic dinner with a sunset view, try the **Café del Puerto** (tel. 2-0316), across from the passenger boat ferry to Playa del Carmen. After being drawn in by solicitous waiters, ascend the spiral staircase to the main dining room or continue to a higher mezzanine level of tables overlooking the rest of the dining room. Start with a soup for $3.10, proceed to shrimp in oyster sauce perhaps (add another $16 to the total), and finish with banana flambé for $6.50. Also on the menu are prime rib ($7) and a number of pasta dishes (averaging $11). Open daily from 5 to 11pm.

Cozumel, heavily populated with North Americans, finally has two unabashedly North American restaurants. Called **The Sports Page** (tel. 2-1199), one features a satellite TV antenna on the roof to snag all the Stateside network sports action, and displays team pennants and T-shirts on the walls. It's air-conditioned. It serves burgers ($4.50 to $6). Its prices are in dollars. In short, though Mexican-owned, it is very American. Hours are every day from 9am to 11:30pm. A similar establishment is **Carlos 'n' Charlie's** on the water, north of the zócalo. Prices are quoted in dollars; the crowd is on the rowdy side.

Pepe's Grill (tel. 2-0213), south of the main square on the waterfront drive (Avenida Rafael Melgar), is deluxe and calculating: low lights, soft music, more solicitous waiters. Tables are open to sea breezes; failing that, ceiling fans move the air. The menu is extensive with most meat and fish courses costing from $10.50 to $12.50, although a Mexican combination plate is $9. This popular place is open for dinner only, 1pm to midnight.

Though a bit humble compared to Pepe's, great food at great prices can be had at **Santiago's Grill** (tel. 2-0175), at the corner of Calle A. Rosado Salas and 15a Avenida Sur. Due to its popularity, this new eatery recently doubled in size to provide 10 tables. You can get a grouper fish filet for $7 or tasty tacos for $3. Santiago himself frequently presides over the grill; at the very least he'll be bustling about to ensure your satisfaction. Dine on the outdoor patio, next to the grill. Open for dinner from 6 to 11pm.

The **Taverna Gatto Pardo,** Avenida 10, No. 124, between Calle 1 and Rosado Salas (tel. 2-2259), gets your taste buds revved up. The minute you step inside the light aroma of garlic and oregano lets you know this is a real Italian restaurant. It's casual, with low lighting, glossy wood tables and benches, mugs and doodads hanging from the rafters, and a rock-wall waterfall back in the open patio. Select from a range of pastas, pizzas, and more substantial main courses including the combination plate that features lasagna, stromboli, and spaghetti. The powerful garlic rolls are made in-house. Although Italian food is the calling card, there's a selection of Mexican specialties too. A meal here could cost as little as $3.60 at the salad bar or $4.40 for a small pizza, or as much as $9.20 for the seafood pasta plate. Open daily from 4 to 11pm.

You'll have to be saving more than pennies to dine at Cozumel's latest in island chic, **Donatello's Ristorante** (tel. 2-0090), serving Italian fare a half a block south of the main plaza. Built to resemble an exquisite hacienda, there are three dining rooms, including a partially enclosed patio in the back built around a fountain. It's awash in apricot and blue pastels from the table linen to the walls. Attentive blacksuited waiters proffer menus that I am told cost $40 each. There's a lengthy pasta selection as well as seafood, beef, and chicken. Plan to spend $35 per person for a complete soup through dessert meal. Open daily from 5 to 11pm.

PIZZA

When Cozumel has a pizza joint, it's no dive, and so **Pizza Rolandi,** four blocks north of the main square along Avenida Rafael Melgar, is about as inviting a pizzeria as you're likely to run into anywhere. Deck chairs and red-and-white-checkered tablecloths make the interior garden very mod, and candle lamps add romance. The Four Seasons pizza, at $7, is 8 inches in diameter and serves only one person, but what a serving: It comes topped with black olives, tomatoes, asparagus, cheese, and ham. The pizza margarita costs $5, but others (seven kinds) are all priced between these two. Wine, beer, and mixed drinks are all served. Open from 11:30am to 11:30pm; closed Sunday.

LIGHT SNACKS

Another popular place is **El Portal,** across from the boat dock. This open-air restaurant boasts lots of small tables occupied by people-watchers. Try the huge, and very powerful, frosty margaritas for $2.85 and any of the Mexican snacks for $4.50 to $5.50. Fish dishes are $5 to $7. Open from 7am to 11pm Monday through Saturday and Sunday from 3 to 11pm.

Delikatessen & Deli's Cafe (tel. 2-0458), three blocks south of the plaza on 10a Avenida Sur, is a great place for picnic fixin's to go; or you can eat at one of their few small tables. Grab a large tub of yogurt and granola for $1.80. Or ask them to put together a cheese and meat sandwich for $4 (a bit more if your taste runs to imported goods). The breads are whole wheat; and the cookies are homemade oatmeal and chocolate chip (45¢). Open from 9am to 9pm Monday through Saturday; closed Sunday.

For a quick, healthful pick-me-up on a hot day, drop by the **Frutas Selectas, The Corner Store,** at the corner of Calle 1 Sur and 5a Avenida Sur, just a few steps from the Hotel El Marqués. The sweet smell of fruit greets you as you enter. Juices, liquados, "the best coffee in town," yogurt, sandwiches, and pastries are served in stark surroundings, at low prices.

---

3. What to See and Do

TOURING THE ISLAND

The question of tours brings us back to rentals, as there is no good reason to take an organized tour. You can rent a bicycle, motorbike, or car, and the motorized vehicles will take you around the southern part of the island easily in a half day, although it will take all day to cover the 42 miles on a bicycle. For car rentals, try the lobby of Meson San Miguel on the plaza, or "Rentador" in the lobby of Vista del Mar, on the waterfront, south of the plaza. *Warning:* The gas station in town is the only one on the island. However, don't believe the guy who rents you the car; you'll need only 15 liters of gas to tour the island once around, with stops and trips to the ruins included.

Head south along Avenida Melgar out of town, past the Hotel Barracuda. The Hotel La Perla is next, then the Villa Blanca. Remember that no hotel in Mexico "owns" the beach—by law, all beaches are public property, so feel free to use a "hotel" beach. On Cozumel this public ownership is more important than ever, as most of the island is surrounded by coral reefs difficult to walk across (that coral is sharp!) let alone lie on.

About 5 miles south of town you'll come to the big Sol Caribe and La Ceiba hotels, and also the car-ferry dock, for ferries to Puerto Morelos. Go snorkeling in the water by the Hotel La Ceiba and you might spot a sunken airplane. No, it's not the wreckage of a disaster; it was put there for an underwater movie.

Chancanab

A mile past the big hotels is this lagoon, which has long been famous for the color and variety of its sea life. Actually, it became

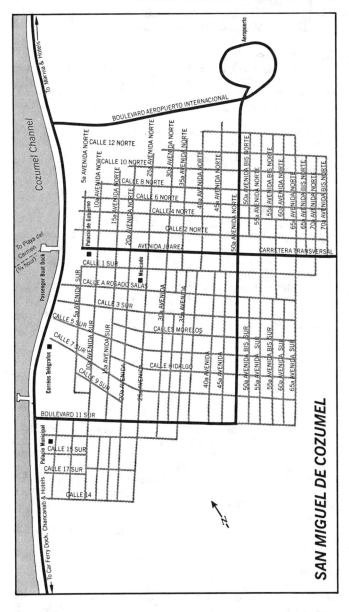

too famous. It was discovered that the intrusion of sightseers was ruining the marine habitat, and that if swimming were not controlled, snorkelers would soon have only one another to look at. So now you must swim in the open sea, not in the lagoon, which is just as well. If you don't have snorkeling gear with you, it's rentable right here. There's a $2.50 entry fee to the park.

Good Beaches

Next beach you'll come to, at 10 miles, is **Playa San Francisco,** and south of it, **Playa Palancar.** By Cancún standards they're not much, but on Cozumel they're the best, so plan most of your beach time for here. Food (usually overpriced) and equipment rentals are available.

The underwater wonders of famous Palancar Reef are offshore from Playa Palancar, and you'll need a boat to see them. Numerous vessels on the island operate daily diving and snorkeling tours to Palancar, so the best plan is to shop around and sign up for one of those.

Punta Celarain

After Playa San Francisco, the drive becomes boring as you plow through the jungle on a straight road for miles. The only distraction is the turnoff (on the left) to Cedral, a tiny market hamlet that is deserted most of the time. Otherwise, all you see is jungle until you're 17½ miles from town.

Finally, though, you emerge near the southern reaches of the island on the east coast. The lighthouse you see to the south is at **Punta Celarain,** the island's southernmost tip. The sand track is not suitable for motorbikes, but in a car you can drive to the lighthouse in about 25 minutes.

The Eastern Shore

The road along the east coast of the island is wonderful, with views of the sea and the rocky shore, surf pounding into it, and on the land side are little farms and forests. Exotic birds take flight as you approach, and monstrous (but harmless) iguanas skitter into the undergrowth. Unfortunately the desolate beauty is marred by a great deal of litter these days. Most of the east coast is unsafe for swimming because the surf can create a deadly *undertow, which will have you far out to sea in a matter of minutes.* But at a few places on this coast there are headlands and breakers that create safe swimming areas. At **Chan Río** you can swim, and also at **Punta Morena,** where there is even a small motel and restaurant. **Playa Chiqueros** is also safe, and has a little restaurant.

Halfway up the east coast, the paved road meets the transversal road back to town, 9½ miles away.

Heading On

Not ready to go back to town yet? For adventure, start out on the sand track that continues north from this junction. Follow this road for 11 very rough and rocky miles through the jungle, past little abandoned farms, along the rocky shore to **El Castillo Real,** an unimpressive but authentic Maya ruin in the middle of nowhere. The trip from the paved road to the Castillo takes 1½ hours, and then the same amount of time to return, but the time is spent watching hermit crabs scutter through the sand, watching lizards watch you, and listening to pairs of parrots squawk as they wing overhead. Don't attempt this trip in a large or a low car, or on a motorbike. Best thing to have is a VW Safari.

A scattering of other vestiges from Cozumel's Maya religious past can be found throughout the northern reaches of the island. One of the most popular trips is to **San Gervasio.** A road leads there from the airport, but you'll find it rough going. When it comes to Cozumel's Maya remains, getting there is most of the fun, and you should do it for the trip, not for the ruins. For real Maya cities, visit Tulum and Cobá, on the mainland.

Back in Town

The adventure over, spend some time strolling along the Avenida Rafael Melgar admiring the unique black coral found in Cozumel's waters, and made into all sorts of fanciful jewelry.

The new **Museo de la Isla de Cozumel,** on 5a Avenida Norte between calles 4 and 6 Norte, is a nice place to spend a rainy hour. Exhibits feature the history of the town, as well as the island's ecological systems. Open Saturday through Thursday from 10am to 1pm and 4 to 7pm; closed Friday. Admission is $2; guided tours in English are available. Upstairs is an expensive rooftop restaurant that keeps long hours.

At night, check out what's playing at the Cine Cozumel, Avenida Rafael Melgar between 2 Norte and 4 Norte. It's probably in Spanish, but when it comes to the light melodrama usually offered here, that's just as well.

WATER SPORTS

Few people come to Cozumel to spend their time on land, even if it's beach land. Like a huge boat moored permanently in the sparkling Caribbean, Cozumel has people jumping from its gunwales day and night (yes! you can go scuba diving at night!).

Snorkeling and Scuba Diving

Anyone who can swim can go snorkeling. Rental of the snorkel (breathing pipe), goggles, and flippers should only cost a few dollars for a half day. The brilliantly colored tropical fish provide a dazzling show for free.

Various establishments on the island rent scuba gear—tanks, regulator with pressure gauge, buoyancy compensator, mask, snorkel, and flippers. Many will also arrange a half-day expedition in a boat complete with lunch for a set price. Sign up the day before, if you're interested.

Sailboards are for rent at several hotels south of town, including the Divers' Inn and the Villa Blanca.

Boat Excursions

Another popular Cozumel pastime is the boat excursion, by yourself or as part of a group, with snorkeling or scuba diving or without. Various types of tours are offered, including a glass-bottom boat tour lasting 1½ hours and costing about $6 per person.

MEXICO'S CARIBBEAN COAST

The development of resort facilities at Cancún changed the entire aspect of Mexico's Caribbean coast. In times B.C. (Before Cancún), there were only a few small beachfront bungalow hotels, catering to the scuba-diving set, to be found along this coast. The ruined Maya seaport of Tulum was visited occasionally by tourists from Cozumel, but the far more impressive Maya city of Cobá, some 30 miles inland, was peopled only by ghosts and archeologists. Other Maya sites were known only to the local inhabitants, and were otherwise lost in the thick jungle. Some of the country's most heavenly beaches were virtually empty, all year round.

Then came FONATUR, the Mexican government agency charged with developing the country's tourism infrastructure, along with a host of other acronymic agencies, and the Caribbean coast began to change rapidly. Roads and electricity were provided, facilities were built on the better beaches, and one sight (Xel-ha) was declared a national park.

The coast is still undergoing great change, as you'll see by the bulldozers charging through the jungle. And though most of the lodging places are still modest, some upscale places are now available, with more under construction. Still, if it's comfort you're looking for, you'd better plan—and reserve—ahead to avoid disappointment.

A ramble down the coast from Cancún takes you past beautiful inlets crowded with brilliantly colored tropical fish, along wonderful beaches shaded by coconut palms, to the great Maya cities of Tulum and Cobá, through the farming town of Felipe Carrillo Puerto, which figured prominently in the War of the Castes, to beautiful but relatively undeveloped Lago de Bacalar, and finally to Chetumal, capital city of the state of Quintana Roo. We'll go the whole distance, north to south.

TRANSPORTATION

Without doubt, the best way to explore the coast is by private car or by tour bus. Even in your own vehicle, you must consider the distances to be covered: From Cancún to Playa del Carmen is about an hour's drive (42 miles), to Tulum and Xel-Ha about two hours' drive (81 miles), and all the way to Chetumal about five hours' drive (242 miles).

If you don't have your own car, transport along the Caribbean coast can present problems. Though there are about a dozen buses a day down the coast, you may end up waiting along the sweltering highway for an hour or more only to have a jam-packed bus roar right by you. The difficulty of transport has given rise to a lively practice of hitchhiking.

---

1. Puerto Morelos

Only a short ride (21 miles) south of Cancún along Hwy. 307 lies the village of Puerto Morelos. Its reason for being is the car ferry, which departs from a dock here on its voyage to Cozumel, several hours away. So far, Puerto Morelos has not shared measurably in the building boom that has swept this coast, so there are not many recommendable lodging places or restaurants. You need not go without a bed and a meal, however.

WHERE TO STAY AND DINE

The little **Posada Amor** (no phone) on the road to the ferry dock (right-hand side as you curve on the road toward the dock) rents 20 simple rooms with screens on the windows and mosquito netting. The rooms are quite plain but adequate. With a private bath one person pays $21, and two pay $21 to $24. With a shared bath it's $13 single and $18 double. The Posada's restaurant serves good food, and an entire meal should cost only $4 or so. No alcohol is served.

THE CAR FERRY

You won't have trouble finding the car-ferry dock (tel. 987/2-0827 or 2-0938 in Cozumel; there are no phones in Puerto Morelos), as it's the largest establishment in town. The car-ferry schedule is a complicated one, but I'll try to make it as uncomplicated as possible. On Monday there's no ferry. On Tuesday there are two ferries. For the first one, autos load around 9am if there aren't many cargo trucks. The second ferry leaves at 3pm. On the Wednesday and Thursday ferries, autos and campers load at 8am. On Thursday there's a 3pm ferry too, but it will be canceled if there's not much cargo. Friday the main cargo is gasoline trucks. No foot passengers are allowed and only cars with a driver (no other car passengers) are permitted. This ferry is never canceled. On Saturday and Sunday there's one 8am trip. *Note:* Call in advance to make sure this schedule is still valid. Cargo takes precedence over cars. Twenty-five to thirty cars can fit on each ferry, but there's space for only two to four camper vehicles. Officials suggest camper drivers stay overnight in the parking lot to be first in line for tickets. In any case, always arrive at least two hours in advance of the ferry departure to purchase a ticket and to get in line. The trip to Cozumel takes three to four hours.

The return voyage from Cozumel leaves the car-ferry dock, south of town near the Hotel Sol Caribe, at noon or so, but be there early to buy your ticket and to get in line. (Re-check this schedule as soon as you arrive in Cozumel.) You should know that in the past the schedule has been suspended for as long as a week during bouts of bad weather.

Fares are 80¢ per person, $3.50 per vehicle—obviously there's a heavy subsidy from the government! Passengers on foot are welcome on the voyage; you are not required to have a car. But since passenger boat service between Playa del Carmen and Cozumel is quite frequent now, I don't recommend that foot passengers bother with this boat.

ONWARD

Heading south on Hwy. 307 from Puerto Morelos, the village of Muchi is the next landmark. The distance from Puerto Morelos to Playa del Carmen is only 20 miles, but before you reach the latter town, you'll come to Punta Bete, 6 miles north of Playa del Carmen.

---

2. Punta Bete

There's no settlement to speak of at Punta Bete, just four hotels aimed at a scuba-diving clientele.

La Posada del Capitan Lafitte (no phone) is at the end of a 1¼-mile-long rough dirt road that heads east from the highway (you'll see a sign). The 41 white cement-block bungalows thatched with palm fronds are equipped with beds and rough-and-ready showers. You'll find a swimming pool, dining room, club house, and dive shop. Divers from North America make up virtually the entire clientele here, and pay $120 double in cash (no credit cards accepted) for a bungalow room, breakfast and lunch or dinner included. Summer rates are almost 50% less. For information, contact the Turquoise Reef Group, Box 2664, Evergreen, CO 80439 (tel. 303/674-9615, or toll free 800/538-6802 in U.S.). Don't plan on dropping in for a room; they're usually booked well in advance. A two-night deposit is required to hold a reservation.

Another Turquoise Reef Group establishment is 200 yards from the entrance to Capitan Lafitte. **Kai-Luum Camp-Tel** is a unique place that rents out large canvas tents complete with framed beds, linens, and daily maid service. Two bathroom facilities are centrally located and consist of eight showers (hot and cold water) and eight flush toilets. With two meals a day one person pays $75 a day, two people sharing the same tent pay $80, and three pay $105. Subtract 40% from these rates in summer. In summer there are usually vacancies, but Christmas and Easter week travelers should book six months in advance of arrival. The Camp-Tel has a small ecological information center with informative displays on nearby sea-turtle habitats. April through July are the best months for fishing; the Camp-Tel promotes a tag and release program. Dives to nearby coral reefs can be arranged next door at La Posada del Capitan Lafitte. For reservations, contact the Turquoise Reef Group mentioned above.

A bit further from El Marlin you'll see signs for **Shangri-La Caribe,** one mile down a semipaved road. There are 52 bungalows, 17 of which are classified as junior suites. It's very similar to Capitan Lafitte because, you guessed it, it's another Turquoise Reef Group enterprise (same address as above). Winter prices, with breakfast and dinner included, are $95 for one, $120 for two, and $165 for three. The suites are all slightly more; summer rates are 40% less.

Two and a half miles before Playa del Carmen you'll see a sign pointing left to Punta Bete. The narrow, overgrown road isn't much and you may even wonder if it's the right one. Have faith. If the new signs of the **Cabañas Xcalacoco** aren't up yet, just keep bearing right. Soon you'll reach the beach and the compound with seven cabañas facing the ocean. It's a real hideaway. The cabañas are tidy, cinder-block buildings with small porches all right on the beach. Five have king-size beds and the others have two double beds each. There are camping facilities for those wishing to hang a hammock under a thatched-roof covering. A small restaurant serves guests, but it's always a good idea to bring along packaged and canned snacks and soft drinks. Singles and doubles rent for $25 to $35 a night. For reservations or information write Apdo. Postal 176, Play del Carmen, Q. Roo 77710.

3. Playa del Carmen

This little Caribbean village came into being because of the passenger boat service to Cozumel, but recently it has developed quite a tourist trade of its own. Travelers have discovered that Playa del Carmen's beaches are far better than those on Cozumel, as much of Cozumel's coast is covered by sharp coral or is pounded by dangerous surf.

Boat and bus service is now frequent and fast to this new transportation hub of the coast. These days Playa is considered a destination resort in and of itself as people seek a less-developed alternative to Cancún and Cozumel. And enterprising businesspeople, many of them foreign, are moving in to fill the demand. Restaurants and upscale cabañas are springing up overnight, like weeds in a fertile garden. As of this writing, all establishments are north of the dock. Competition is sure to choke off many, and growth is bound to level off soon.

Vestiges of the pre-boom days are still visible; very few streets are even paved. One hotel and no restaurants have phones yet; the only phone is located on the ground floor of the Hotel Playa del Carmen. The town only recently got its own post office. As development surges northward the nudist beach is merely pushed further and further north, but beach bums and young people aren't about to abandon it just yet.

GETTING TO AND FROM PLAYA DEL CARMEN

Since Playa del Carmen is a transportation link to and from Cozumel and to the ruins of Tulum, getting there is easier than in the past, especially by ferry from Cozumel. Land transportation from Cancún and elsewhere is still not as good as it should be considering the growing demand for this village as a resort and jumping-off spot.

By Air

Aero Cozumel has four 10-minute flights a day to Cozumel at 9:20 and 11:20am and 3:20 and 5:20pm. Each plane holds 27 passengers and costs $10 per person one way. The airport is downtown a block and a half from the ferry dock and main plaza. The return from Cozumel is 20 minutes before each of the flights mentioned above.

By Bus

There are two bus stations in Playa del Carmen. Transportes de Oriente is a block from the ferry and main square. The ADO station is four blocks north of the ferry dock. At **Transportes de Oriente** there are seven buses to Cancún, the first at 5am and the last at 9pm, as well as buses to Tulum, Valladolid, Chichén Itzá, and Mérida. From Cancún there are five confirmed-seat buses, at 2, 7, and 9am, noon, and 2pm. Ten *de passo* **ADO** buses pass through Playa del Carmen on the way to Cancún. The first is at 6:30am. ADO also goes to Villahermosa and Mexico City from here.

By Ferry

Of the four ferries mentioned below, the water jet *Mexico I* is the speedier by 10 to 15 minutes. See the Cozumel section for details and prices. If the water is choppy take precautions for a seasick voyage. The ferry dock in Playa del Carmen is a block and a half from the main square and within walking distance of hotels.

Ferry Schedule
Playa del Carmen/Cozumel

Mexico I and *II*	*Xelha* and *Cozumeleño*
5:30am	5:30am
7:30	7:30
9:30	10:30
10:15	
12:15pm	Noon
2:30	2:30
4:15	5:30
5:30	7:30
6:30	9:00
7:30	

WHERE TO STAY

The town's most prominent hotels are also its most expensive. Right down by the Cozumel boat dock is the Moorish and Spanish colonial-style **Hotel Molcas** (reservations in Mérida at Turismo Aviomar; tel. 992/1-6661 or 1-6620). The very comfortable hotel cascades down the hillside, giving many rooms and the dockside restaurant fine ocean views. There's an equally nice view from the roof-deck bar and pool. The price for a single or double room is $50 in the high season and $40 all other months.

There are a number of cabañas and hotels north of the dock on the beach and on the street (officially known as 5 Avenida Norte) running parallel to the beach. If you want to stay in a bungalow and swing on a hammock right on the beach, the place to do it is three and a half blocks north of the bus station at **Cabañas Albatroz** (no phone; for reservations write Apdo. Postal 131, Playa del Carmen, Q. Roo 77710). The huts are close together, grouped around a courtyard, but no one seems to mind. There are a total of 14 cabañas for $35 to $40 in winter and $20 to $30 other times. One cabaña with a beachfront location costs $45 in season and $30 other months. The private bathrooms, all with hot water, are new, tiled, and spotless. With firm beds, this is by far the best of the cabañas. You'll get a decent break on the price if you stay a week or more. The restaurant serves all three meals.

Four and a half blocks north of the bus station on 5 Avenida Norte is the **Maya-Bric Hotel** (no phone). With two floors of rooms, a very colorful exterior, and lots of flowers you're bound to notice it. Each of the 21 rooms has two double beds, clean bathroom, stucco walls, and rents for $30 a night in season and $20 off season. There's a small, clean swimming pool, and from the rooftop you get a nice view of the ocean. This is a pleasant, conventional choice.

One of my favorite places in town is the **La Rana Cansada** (The Tired Frog). For reservations write 8048 Midcrown, Suite 146, San Antonio, TX 78218 (tel. toll free 800/365-FROG in U.S.). Five blocks north of the bus station and to the left are eight comfortable rooms with private bath, hot water, drinking water, double bed, and mosquito netting. There's a laundry service and the small kitchen serves snacks and breakfast to guests on the courtyard. The courtyard is particularly nice for relaxing. You can't find nicer hosts. In high season rooms run $20 to $25. Other times they cost $10 to $15. One room has a kitchen and rents for $25 to $35 in season and $18 to $20 other times. Add $2.50 for breakfast.

The new 13-room **Hotel Delfin,** Apdo. Postal 38, Playa del Carmen, Q. Roo 77710, at the corner of Avenida 5 and Calle 6, is another more conventional choice. It's close to the bus station, pier, and restaurants and a half block from the beach. The spacious rooms, which are simple and comfortable, come with private bath and ceiling fan. Some have sea views. On the second floor there's a terrace overlooking the street. Rates here are $15 single and $20 double in the low season and $15 to $25 single and $30 to $35 double in the high season.

WHERE TO DINE

Pleasant meals can be had in the dining room of Las Molcas Hotel. The prices are reasonable, and the food is good though not exciting. New restaurants are opening every day; ask around for recommendations and try the restaurants below for more local color than you'll find at Las Molcas.

I had another great meal at **El Capitan,** two blocks north of the bus station. This is a casual open-air, cabaña-style place with concrete floor and rickety folding chairs. Get a hearth-baked potato (50¢) and a delicious bowl of creamy mushroom soup ($1.50) for a satisfying light meal. Or see what kind of fish or beef is on the grill. The menu is limited by what the fishermen caught that day, so if they have squid or shrimp ($7), order it; it will be fresh and excellent. Open every day from 7am to 11pm.

If you're in the mood for brick-oven pizza, Italian-style (i.e., thin crust and heavy on the tomato and basil), head directly to **Restaurant Mascaras,** located on Avenida Principal in front of the plaza. It's appropriately decorated inside with a multitude of masks from Maya to Venetian. Pizza with liberal toppings is $5.75. The waiter will greet you twirling the menu like a pizza dish. I also recommend the squid (calamari) for $4. Open every day from 12:30pm to midnight; 15% service will be added to your bill.

Four blocks north of the bus station you'll find **Limones,** an attractive thatch-roofed structure understandably famous for its seafood. Although some might find the prices a bit high, it's worth dining here for the quality of the cuisine. Shrimp at $10.20 and fish filet at $5.35 are artfully prepared. Breakfasts here are also quite good and reasonably priced.

You may want to check out the beachfront restaurant of the **Cabañas Albatroz.** New owners from the United States (who also manage the popular Restaurant Limones around the corner) have enlarged the Cabañas restaurant and changed the menu. Lunchtime meals alternate with the season so you may find pizza by the slice and shrimp and fish baskets or whole fried fish and ceviche. At dinner you'll find traditional Italian specialties. It's open for breakfast too. Plan to spend $2.50 to $5 for breakfast from 7 to 11am, $3 to $5 at lunch from 12:30 to 6pm, and $7 to $14 for dinner from 6 to 8pm.

Sky Pilot, new to Playa's modest lineup of restaurants, offers something for everyone. On the second floor of a pale-blue building on Avenida 5, between Calles 4 and 11, you get the sea breezes and ocean view plus a bar and varied menu. You'll find plenty of whole wheat bread and vegetables (in sandwiches and soups) and blended fruit drinks, as well as prime beef, fish, and chicken and a variety of tacos and enchiladas. The pastries and bread are made in-house. By the time you travel, the third floor will be open for breakfast and live entertainment in the evening. You can eat here for as little as $2 or as much as $8. Open from 8am to midnight daily.

4. Xcaret

As of this writing, Xcaret is someplace magical, a touch of Maya romance. But the bulldozers have already entered the woods, so it won't last long. Get there soon.

At the turnoff there's a nice restaurant on the left. A mile in from the highway brings you to the little **Rancho Xcaret,** a turkey farm that is so authentic with its rail fences and thatched Maya *na* houses that you'll think its a Yucatecan theme park. But pay the small admission charge and walk eastward toward the sea along a path. Soon you'll pass some conserved little Maya temples and then get a glimpse of the sea.

At the end of the path is a narrow inlet, or *caleta,* bright with sun and flashing with tropical fish. The inlet has already been discovered by snorkelers, who come on foot or in boats, and by one intrepid restaurateur who has built a large palapa hut on a ledge overlooking the lagoon. The menu is still limited, but it's nice to have a beer ($1) and quesadillas ($2.65) while looking down into the tropical inlet.

Before the restaurant you'll see a sign to the cenote, only a few dozen yards away. In a great cave mouth, or grotto, its lightly salted water is as clear as glass. It's now known to tourists as well as locals, who come for a dip and a picnic. It can get crowded, so come early or late in the day if possible. Even if the air is cool the water will be warm. If you want to explore deep into the cave's recesses, bring flippers; there's a light current.

Some 10 miles south of Xcaret and a half mile east of the highway is **Pamul,** a safe cove for swimming.

When you reach the **Cabañas Pamul,** Apdo. Postal 83, Playa del Carmen, Q. Roo 77710, Km. 85 Cancún/Tulum (no telephone), you'll see only eight coral and white beachfront bungalows facing the ocean. For laid-back, peaceful lazing this is an excellent choice. The bungalows come in four pairs, each with a covered porch just steps from the beach and ocean. Each cabaña has two double beds, tile floors, rattan furniture, ceiling fans, and private baths. A small restaurant serves all three meals, but it wouldn't hurt to bring some nonperishable snacks and bottled drinks since you're miles from stores and restaurants. In-season rates are $33 single and $50 double. Rates drop about $8 per room in the off season.

In a very short time you come to Akumal, one of Mexico's newest stars in Caribbean tourism.

---

5. Akumal

Of the fledgling resorts south of Cancún, Akumal is perhaps the most developed, with moderately priced bungalows scattered among the graceful palms that line the beautiful, soft beach.

Signs point the way in from the highway, and less than a third of a mile toward the sea you will come to the Akumal gateway. The resort complex here consists of three distinct establishments that share the same wonderful, smooth, palm-lined beach protected by a breakwater.

The **Hotel-Club Akumal Caribe Villas Maya** (P.O. Box 13326, El Paso, TX 79950; tel. 915/584-3552, or toll free 800/351-1622 outside Texas and 800/343-1440 in Canada) rents bungalows easily capable of sleeping two couples or a family. Each is equipped with bath, refrigerator, and air conditioner, and costs $75 double. Rooms in the hotel are $95 double with an ocean view.

Las Casitas Akumal (in Cancún at Apdo. Postal 714, Q. Roo 77500; tel. 988/4-1945 or 4-1689) is a collection of 14 villas or bungalows rented by the day, week, or month. Each faces the sea, has two bedrooms, two baths, a living room, fan, and refrigerator, and can accommodate up to five people. A small store and restaurant nearby take care of the food problem, and a diving shop caters to the scuba set. The price for up to five people is $90 to $130 daily in season; off-season rates run $70 to $90.

Just 300 yards south of these two places is the **Hotel Akumal Cancún** (tel. in Cancún 988/4-2272), a very nice and modern 116-room, two-story hotel by the beach. Rates for its comfy rooms with bath are $69 to $77 double, $81 triple.

After Aventuras Akumal, 3 miles south along the highway, comes the beach and trailer park at **Chemuyil,** developed by the government as "the most beautiful beach in the world." Though sleepy and deserted in the summer, it's active in winter, with a snack bar, free medical clinic, and an admission fee of 25¢ per person.

About 1½ miles south of Chemuyil and a quarter mile east of the highway lies Xcacel, a gorgeous palm-shaded spot where you can pitch your tent or park your van for $1.75 per person per night, including use of changing rooms, toilets, and showers. There's a lively restaurant here as well.

After traveling less than 8 miles south of Akumal, you come to Xel-ha.

6. Xel-ha

The Caribbean coast of the Yucatán is carved by the sea into hundreds of small *caletas* (coves) that form the perfect habitat for tropical marine life, both flora and fauna. Many caletas remain undiscovered and pristine along the coast, but one caleta 72 miles south of Cancún is enjoyed daily by snorkelers and scuba divers who come to luxuriate in its warm waters, palm-lined shore, and brilliant fish. Xel-ha (that's "*shell*-hah") is a bit of paradise for swimming, with no threat of undertow or pollution. Being close to the ruins at Tulum makes Xel-ha the best place for a dip when you've finished clambering around the Maya castles. The short 8½-mile hop north from Tulum to Xel-ha is possible to do by bus. When you get off at the junction for Tulum, ask the restaurant owner when the next buses come by. Otherwise you may have to wait as much as two hours on the highway. Those who don't have a car and who don't want to chance missing Xel-ha can sign up for a tour from either Cancún or Cozumel: Most companies include a trip to Tulum and a swim at Xel-ha in the same journey.

The entrance to Xel-ha is half a mile in from the highway. You'll be asked to pay a $3 "contribution" to the upkeep and preservation of the site.

Once in the park, you can rent snorkeling equipment for $5, rent an underwater camera for $20, buy a drink or a meal, change clothes, and take showers—facilities for all these are available. When you swim, be careful to observe the "swim here" and "no swimming" signs. (*Hint:* In the swimming areas, the greatest variety of fish are to be seen right near the ropes marking off the "no swimming" areas, and near any groups of rocks.) Xel-ha is an exceptionally beautiful place!

Just south of the Xel-ha turnoff on the west side of the highway, don't miss the Maya ruins of ancient Xel-ha.

The Maya seaport of Tulum is 8 miles south of Xel-ha.

7. Tulum

At the end of the Classic period in A.D. 900 the Maya civilization began to decline and most of the large ceremonial centers were deserted. The Postclassic Period (A.D. 900 to the Spanish conquest) in the Yucatán was one of small rival states, Maya in culture but with some imported traditions from the Mexicans. Tulum is one such city-state, built in the 10th century as a fortress city overlooking the Caribbean. Aside from the spectacular setting, Tulum is not an impressive city. There are no magnificent pyramidal structures as are found in the Classic Maya ruins. The most imposing building in Tulum is the large stone structure on the cliff called the **Castillo** (castle), actually a temple-cum-fortress. At one time this was covered with stucco and painted.

The view from on top of the Castillo is quite grand. From here you get a good view of the city walls, which are constructed of lime-stone. In front of the Castillo are several palace-like buildings: unrestored stone structures partially covered with stucco. The **Temple of the Frescoes** is directly in front of the Castillo and contains some 13th-century wall paintings that are quite interesting. They are inside the temple and the lighting is bad, so if you have a flash-light it would be helpful to bring it along. Most of the frescoes are hard to see, but they are distinctly Maya in content, representing the gods Chac (rain god) and Ix Chel (the goddess of the moon and of medicine). On the cornice of this temple is a relief of the head of a god. If you get a slight distance from the building you will see the eyes, nose, mouth, and chin. Notice the remains of the red-painted stucco on this building—at one time all the buildings at Tulum were painted a bright red.

Much of what we know of Tulum at the time of the Spanish conquest comes from the writings of Diego de Landa, third bishop of Yucatán. He wrote that Tulum was a small city inhabited by about 600 people, who lived in dwellings situated on platforms along the street. The town commanded a strategic point on the Caribbean and thus supervised the trade traffic from Honduras to the Yucatán. Tulum survived about 70 years after the conquest, when it was final-ly abandoned.

The ruins are open 8am to 5pm. Admission is 35¢.

WHERE TO STAY AND DINE

It's useful to know that Tulum consists of four distinct areas. First there's the junction of Hwy. 307 and the Tulum access road, where you'll find a small hotel, two restaurants, and a Pemex gas sta-tion. Then, less than a mile down the access road, are the ruins of Tulum and a collection of small restaurants, snack shops, and souve-nir stands. Past the ruins, the road heads south along a narrow strip of sand to Boca Paila and Punta Allen. Though most of this 60-mile stretch of bad road is uninhabited, you will find several beachcomb-ers' settlements south of the ruins. The fourth area is the Mexican village of Tulum, right on Hwy. 307 about 1½ miles south of the Hwy. 307–Tulum access road junction. There's nothing much in the way of services in Tulum village. Let's look at what the first three areas have to offer, in order.

Tulum Junction

Right at the junction of Hwy. 307 and the Tulum access road is the aptly named **Motel El Crucero,** which has 16 rooms for rent plus a festive restaurant. The rooms, though basic, come with ceil-ing fans, hot and cold water, and cost $12 double. In the thatched but enclosed restaurant, meals are yours for $2.50 to $15. Beer is served, and a counter at one side of the restaurant serves as a tiny "convenience store."

Across the street from El Crucero is the **Hotel and Restaurant El Faisan y El Venado,** with similar meals, a lower noise level, and 10 nice new rooms with TV and air conditioning. Felipe and Marta Ramirez own this up-and-coming road house. She cooks. He man-ages and developes the property. Along with the new rooms comes a video bar, supermarket, and laundry service and a new swimming pool. Promotional rates when I was there were $13 single or double, but by the time you travel they may be $30. Restaurant rates are competitive with the Motel El Crucero de las Ruinas across the street.

Tulum Ruins

At the entrance to the ruins are small soft-drink stands and eateries serving up things at resort prices. Not much you can do about it, though, if you're hungry. The **Centro Chac-Mool**—it's that modern palapa on the beach north of the ruins—gives more, but charges more as well.

Boca Paila

Down the road that runs through the parking lot at the Tulum ruins are some oceanside lodgings that might appeal to the intrepid traveler. The first one is a half mile south of the ruins and the farthest one is almost 20 miles. A short distance after the ruins, the pavement leaves the mainland and becomes a potholed, narrow and sandy artery. It runs the length of a peninsula that's roughly 40 miles long and is known as the Boca Paila Peninsula named after a cut that divides it in half. At the tip end there's Punta Allen, a small lobster fishing village. A portion of the peninsula is included in the **Sian Ka'an Biosphere Reserve** and is rich in bird, plant, and animal life.

To find the **Cabañas Don Armando** (no phone), turn in at the sign for Zazil Kin. It's a casual, friendly place right on the beach. The 17 cabañas are spread out haphazardly on the sand with lots of convenient clotheslines for the use of guests. Each basic stick-walled bungalow is equipped with bed on a concrete slab, sheets, blanket, and occasional mosquito netting. Bring your own soap and towel. Your own mosquito netting might come in handy. The cabañas have candles for light. Each rents for $10 single or double. A $10 refundable deposit entitles you to bedding, key, and flashlight. Do note that unless the door is open, some of the bungalows have no windows and therefore no ventilation except through the cracks. There are four bathrooms separated for men and women. For dinner they might be serving up a big plate of chicken, beans, and rice for $2.65.

Where the paved road ends you'll see the **Cabañas Chac-Mool**, Domocilio Conocido, Tulum Pueblo, Q. Roo (fax 915/4-4564), a stucco, rock and thatched-roof bungalow establishment that's ordinary and extraordinary all at once. All bungalows have sand floors and one or two beds suspended from the ceiling and covered with mosquito netting. These rent for $50 in season. A separate building serves bathroom needs for both sexes and there's a restaurant serving all three meals. A flashlight is a must here, but there's usually electricity between 5 and 10pm.

The **Cabañas Tulum** (no phone), 4 miles south of the Tulum ruins, are little thatched bungalows facing a heavenly stretch of ocean beach (deadly surf). Each bungalow comes with cold-water shower, two double beds, screens on the windows, table, one electric light, and a veranda good for hanging a hammock. The cost is

Staying in a Nature Reserve

You're 2½ miles past the Boca Paila bridge and more than halfway down the peninsula when you reach the **Caphe Ha Guest House,** Spencer 408, P. H. Polanco 11580, Mexico, DF (tel. 5/254-0457). And you've entered the part of the peninsula south of Boca Paila (the cut where the lagoon meets the ocean) that ends at Punta Allen. By this time too you've already passed the guard station as you entered this portion of the **Sian Ka'an Biosphere Reserve.** The Reserve is a 1.3-million-acre jungle territory set aside to protect 320 bird and animal species and 1,200 plants found in Mexico and the Caribbean. The guest house is within the reserve. You are welcomed by owner Sue Brown Baker. Caphe Ha is actually two mosquito-proof, solar-powered one-bedroom cottages and a main house all with shared bath. The setting is on 5 acres in a dense coconut palm grove just steps from a plush beach that goes on for miles. There are no nearby neighbors, restaurants, telephones, or other inns. You can't beat it for seclusion. What your $90 single or $130 double per night buys is breakfast and dinner daily, and as many guided fishing, diving, and birding excursions as you have time to experience. Caphe Ha means "between waters" and for guests that means fishing in either the lagoon or the ocean. Tackle is provided. Guests have the run of the main house, and everyone usually pitches in to help with the family-style meals served there. Baker suggests guests arrive before 3pm mosquito time. For information and reservations in the United States call Jeff Frankel in New York (tel. 212/219-2198).

Directions to Caphe Ha: Turn right at the Tulum ruins parking lot and follow that road down the coast. After about 1½ miles the road becomes dirt. Follow it for about 15 miles (which takes an hour because of the pot holes). Come to a bridge; cross it and set your odometer. At exactly 3 miles you'll see two posts on the left, the entrance to Caphe Ha. By the time you reach the entrance in the rainy season, you've slogged and dodged your way through and around numerous pools of varying depths on the narrow, sandy road that at times offers glimpses of the ocean.

$16 double per night. A small restaurant serves three meals a day at fairly low prices; beer and soft drinks are on sale, but the Restaurant y Cabañas Ana y José next door serves good, reasonably priced food. The Cabañas Tulum are usually full between November 15 and March and again in July and August. Plan ahead. Electricity goes on between 6:30 and 10:30pm, so bring candles or a flashlight.

Those who enjoyed the good food at the friendly palapa restaurant run by Ana and José (mentioned above) will enjoy the **Restaurant y Cabañas Ana y José.** Eight simple but very comfortable cabañas are next to the restaurant. Eight more may be ready by the time you travel. All have baths, tile floors, and little brick patios.

The rock-walled bungalows in front are a little larger and some face the beautiful wide beach just a few yards off. Single or double rates are $30, a bargain considering the comfort plus peace and quiet. The restaurant, open 8am to 10pm, is easy on the budget. Breakfast runs $1.50 to $3.50. Fish entrees range from 80¢ to $10 with lobster $12 in season. By the way, Gordo, the confident pet parrot, trods the restaurant's sand floor right up to the table, politely accepts a finger perch to the table, then turns into the devil when prohibited from perching on your plate and helping himself.

Pez Maya Fishing and Beach Resort, P.O. Box 9, Cozumel, Q. Roo. (tel. 487/20072), or Worldwide Sportsman, Isla Morada, Fla. (tel. 305/664-4615 in Fla., or toll free 800/327-2880 in the rest of the U.S.), caters to sportsfishing enthusiasts from its location in a beautiful oceanside palm grove south of Tulum. The Pez Maya sells its comfortable cabañas through fishing packages that include transportation from Cancún, all meals, tackle, boat, and guide for seven nights and six days of fishing. A private boat and fishing guide are assigned to each of its seven stucco and rock bungalows. Packages start at three nights for $1,734 per person. Since food is planned around reservations, drop in guests can't be accommodated. If you are on the peninsula and want to look it over, follow directions under Caphe Ha. Pez Maya's hot pink cement pilar appears on your left a few yards after the Boca Paila bridge. There's also an 800-foot sand airstrip adjacent to the compound.

About a mile south of the turnoff to Tulum, on Highway 307, is the road to Cobá, another fascinating Maya city. Less than a mile past the Cobá road is Tulum village, with little to offer the tourist. If you're driving, turn right when you see the signs to Cobá, and continue on that road for 30 miles.

8. Cobá

The Yucatán is rich in breathtaking Maya cities, but in its time, fewer were grander than Cobá. Linked to important cities many miles distant by excellent, straight roads through the jungle, Cobá itself covered numerous square miles on the shores of two Yucatecan lakes.

Today the city's principal monuments are on display again, but unless you take a tour or rent a car, they're difficult to reach.

Pay the small admission fee at the little entrance shack, and stroll into the ruins. Keep your bearings as it's very easy to get lost on the maze of dirt roads in the jungle.

The Grupo Cobá boasts a large, impressive pyramid just in the entry gate to the right. Were you to go straight, you'd pass near the badly ruined *juego de pelota* (ball court).

Straight in from the entry gate, walk for 10 or 15 minutes to a fork in the road. The left fork leads to Nohoch Mul group, which contains El Castillo, the highest pyramid in the Yucatán (higher than the great El Castillo at Chichén-Itzá and the Pyramid of the Magician at Uxmal). The right fork (more or less straight on) goes to the Conjunto Las Pinturas. Here, the main attraction is the Pyramid of the Painted Lintel, a small structure with traces of the original bright colors above the door. You can climb up to get a close look.

Throughout the area, intricately carved stelae stand by pathways, or lie forlornly in the jungle underbrush.

It can be hot here deep in the jungle. You'd be well advised to visit Cobá in the morning, or after the heat of the day has passed.

WHERE TO STAY AND DINE

The very nice **Villa Arqueológica Cobá** (tel. 988/4-2574 in Cancún, or toll free 800/528-3100 in U.S.), a Club Med operation, is here, right at lakeside, a five-minute walk from the ruins. The hotel has a French polish because of the Club Med affiliation and, as you might expect, the restaurant is top-notch, with full meals for about $10.50. The 40 comfortable rooms have private bath and air conditioning, and cost $52 to $75 single or double. Besides rooms, the hotel has a library of books on Mesoamerican archeology (with books in French, English, and Spanish), and a swimming pool. You can make reservations (definitely a must) in Mexico City at Hoteles Villa Arqueológicas, Avenida Masaryk 183, Colonia Polanco, México, DF 11570 (tel. 5/203-3086).

If you arrive without a reservation and the Villa is full, try **El Bocadito** (no phone) in town, a restaurant and lodging with a handful of rooms priced at $8 single and $12 double. For this you get modern construction, washbasin, and a cold shower. There are only nine of these rooms, and they may well be full unless you arrive to claim one early in the day. Don't expect anything fancy, but the proprietors do their best. The same can be said for the restaurant.

---

9. Felipe Carrillo Puerto

From the Cobá turnoff, the main Highway 307 heads southwest through Tulum village. About 14 miles south of the village are the ruins of **Chunyaxche,** on the left-hand side. The ruins aren't very exciting, but the price is right: Admission is free after you sign the register. In exploring Chunyaxche, I was virtually eaten alive by mosquitos in the beautiful jungle. You may have better luck, though.

After Chunyaxche, the highway passes 45 miles of jungle-bordered road with few distractions. Then comes an oasis of sorts.

Felipe Carrillo Puerto (pop. 15,000) is an oasis in the jungle along the road to Ciudad Chetumal, and has this to offer: several banks (off the zócalo), gas stations, a market, a small ice plant, a bus terminal, the intersection with the road back to Mérida, and a presentable handful of modest hotels and restaurants to serve the traveler's needs. Carrillo Puerto is the turning point for those making a "short circuit" of the Yucatán peninsula, as Hwy. 184 heads west from here to Ticul, Uxmal, Campeche, and Mérida. It is quite possible you may have to spend the night here, and very probable that you will arrive in town hungry.

As you spend your hour or your overnight in Carrillo Puerto, recall its strange history: This was where the rebels in the War of the Castes took their stand, guided by the "Talking Crosses." Some remnants of that town—Chan Santa Cruz—and that time are still extant. Look for signs in town pointing the way. For the full story, refer to Chapter I, "Yucatán's Fascinating History."

WHERE TO STAY AND DINE

The highway goes right through the town, becoming Avenida Benito Juárez in town. Driving from the north, you will pass a traffic circle with a bust of the great Juárez. The town market is here.

One block south from the traffic circle on the left-hand side is **Hotel El Faisan y El Venado** (tel. 983/4-0043). The hotel is a new addition to the popular restaurant of the same name. The 13 tidy rooms, all with private bath and hot water, come with either fan or air conditioning. Realistic photographs of the rooms are on display in the restaurant. A double with a fan costs $8; with air conditioning the price is $11.

As for the restaurant, it's one of the townfolks' favorites, with a modern airy dining room equipped with ceiling fans, and even a small air-conditioned section (used mostly for private parties). Chances are that many tables will be filled at mealtimes, and people will happily be chowing down from the standard Mexican menu for about $3.50 to $5.

On the main square, diagonal to the church, is an old Caribbean-style building—look for the wooden gallery on the second story. This houses the most interesting **Hotel Esquivel**, an eclectic collection of rooms, many with added-on showers, all neat and well kept if basic. The lamp tables are sections of Maya columns from temples. Original oil paintings decorate some walls. As for prices, the Esquivel charges $18 double, for a room with a fan. Parking in the rear.

10. Lago De Bacalar

From Carrillo Puerto to Chetumal (85 miles) is a 2½-hour ride. About 64 miles past Carillo Puerto you'll see the limpid waters of Lake Bacalar, a crystal-clear body of water fed by swamps and streams. It's heavenly for swimming, very quiet, and the perfect place for a resort. If you can at all arrange it, it sure beats stopping overnight in Chetumal or Carrillo Puerto. If you're in your own car, take a detour through the village of Bacalar and along the lakeshore drive. Marvel at the houses of Quintana Roo's rich and famous that were built to take in the beautiful view.

You'll soon reach the **Hotel Laguna** (tel. 99/27-1304 in Mérida) whose rooms offer two double beds and a lovely view of the lake. Most of the water along the shore is very shallow, but from the hotel's dock you can dive to a depth of 30 feet; they also have a pool.

The 23 rooms are reasonable at $30 double, $35 triple. (As it's off the beaten path, they almost always have rooms.) The hotel's restaurant is fine, but for variety you can take a 20-minute walk around the lake (away from the town) to **Cenote Azul** and feast on a grilled fresh fish dinner for $3.50 to $7. If you've come to Bacalar by bus, the hotel is a 20-minute walk from the town square. A colectivo, heading back to Chetumal, can also drop you off about 30 feet from the hotel.

As you approach the end of the lake, Hwy. 307 intersects Hwy. 186. Turn right, and you're headed west to Escárcega, Palenque, and Villahermosa; turn left, and you'll be going toward Chetumal. The turnoff to Belize is on the road *before* you enter Chetumal, but you may need to stop in the town for a meal or a bed.

---

11. Chetumal

Quintana Roo became a state only in 1974, and Chetumal (pop. 50,000) is the capital of the new state. While Quintana Roo was still a territory, it was a free-trade zone to encourage trade and immigration, and as the free-trade regulation is still in effect, much of the town is given over to small shops selling a strange assortment of imported junk and treasures at pretty inflated prices. The old part of town, down by the river (Río Hondo), preserves a Caribbean atmosphere with its wooden buildings (and sticky heat), but the newer parts are modern (and rather raw) Mexican. There is lots of noise and heat, so your best plan would be not to stay—vacant and acceptable rooms are difficult to find—but if you must, here are some hints. The bright new Central Bus Station isn't particularly central. A taxi into town will cost 90¢.

GETTING TO AND FROM CHETUMAL

For a state capital, Chetumal is rather poorly linked by public transportation to the rest of Mexico. But with time and patience connections are possible.

By Air

Aero Cozumel (tel. 988/4-2862 in Cancún) flies between Chetumal and Cancún on Monday, Wednesday, and Friday.

By Bus

The bright new central bus station at Insurgentes and Heroes isn't particularly central. In fact, it's a hot 25-minute walk into town or a $1.50 taxi ride.

Two bus lines, **Auto Transportes del Caribe** (tel. 2-0740) and **ADO** (tel. 2-0629), serve transportation needs to the Yucatán peninsula and the rest of Mexico. At least 8 direct first-class buses a day go to Cancún via Tulum, Playa del Carmen, and Puerto Morelos; 6 go to Mérida. With changes en route, 8 first-class buses a day go to Mexico City, and 12 go to Villahermosa.

Less frequent second-class buses cover most of the same routes.

Two companies make the run from Chetumal through Corozal and Orange Walk to Belize City. **Batty's Bus Service** runs 10 buses per day and **Venus Bus Lines** has 7 daily buses. A ticket to Corozal costs 90¢; Belize City costs $4. Though it's a short distance from Chetumal to Corozal, it may take as much as an hour and a half, depending on how long it takes the bus to pass through Customs and Immigration.

By Car

From Chetumal you can cut diagonally across the peninsula to Mérida; you can retrace your steps to Cancún; and you can go on south to Belize and even Guatemala. *Note:* But if you are thinking of driving the long hot trip to Escarcega and Villahermosa, don't. It's a long, lonely, and badly maintained road. The highway is fine as long as the state of Quintana Roo is maintaining it. But as soon as you cross the state line, ahead lies more than 125 miles of the worst highway in Mexico. *Zona de deslave* signs are up permanently to warn motorists that parts of the road bed are missing entirely or are so badly dipped as to nearly put you in orbit. Experience speaks. No matter what maintenance is done, rains and heavy truck traffic undo it.

Caution: Chetumal has many "no left turn streets," with hawk-eyed traffic policemen at every one. Do be alert. Chetumal isn't the friendliest of cities, and a run-in with one of the city's not-so-finest can put a damper on the trip, especially after a hot day on the road.

WHERE TO STAY

Between the bus station and the center is the nicest place to stay, the new **Hotel Principe** (tel. 983/2-4799 or 2-5167), Avenida Héroes 326. The 29 rooms are modern, fairly well-maintained, and arranged around a central courtyard. With a television in every room they charge $30 single or double. Their dining room lists an extensive breakfast menu with dishes ranging from $1.30 to $4.

The **Hotel Continental Caribe** (tel. 983/2-1100), across from the central market at Avenida Héroes 71, is a modern establishment with central air conditioning, a series of swimming pools (not always clean) in the courtyard, and a reasonably priced restaurant that's as large as a basketball court (and cold as a cave). It rents a lot of rooms at $44 single and $48 double, because Chetumal is booming and rooms are scarce—particularly comfortable, air conditioned rooms.

Down the hill from the market on Avenida Héroes, one and a half blocks toward the center of town, is the Continental Caribe's competition. The **Hotel del Prado** (tel. 983/2-0542 or 2-0544, or Fax 2-0920) has similar central air, pool, and restaurant, and charges $57 single and $59 double.

WHERE TO DINE

As for a place to dine, the situation is grim. Stick to your hotel restaurant.

CHICHÉN-ITZÁ: THE MAYA CAPITAL

The fabled pyramids and temples of Chichén-Itzá are Yucatán's best-known ancient monuments. You can't really say you've seen Yucatán until you've gazed at towering El Castillo, sighted the sun from the Maya observatory called El Caracol, or shivered on the brink of the gaping cenote that served as the sacrificial well. Chichén-Itzá is well and frequently served by buses, as it's on the main highway (no. 180) between Mérida and Cancún. Also, being on the main highway, Chichén-Itzá has a decent selection of hotels.

1. How to See Chichén-Itzá

I strongly urge you to spend the night here. No matter what the time of year, it will be hot in the middle of the day, and instead of clambering up pyramids you should be taking a siesta after lunch, in a cool hotel room. If you come on a day-trip, you'll arrive just in time to hike the pyramids in the heat of the day. You'll have to rush through this marvelous ancient city in order to catch another bus, which will take you away just as the once-fierce sun is softening to a benevolent gold and burnishing the temples.

Here's the plan: Drive a rental car or get a bus from Mérida or Cancún in the morning, find your hotel room, then head for the ruins. After lunch, take that siesta, then return to the ruins for a few more hours. The next morning, get to the ruins early, before the intense heat. When the heat of the day approaches, head for your next destination. This may involve paying the admission fee more than once, but the fee is minimal, the experience maximal!

Note that it's possible (but not probable) that your chosen hotel at Chichén-Itzá might be booked up. If you want to make a reservation, be advised that it is difficult to reach Chichén by phone; however, most hotels have a means by which you can make reservations in Mérida. Read the hotel descriptions for details.

An alternative to staying at Chichén is to stay in the sleepy town of Valladolid (that's "Bye-ah-doh-*leet*"), 25 miles east of the ruins. You can get an early bus from Cancún, spend the day at the ruins, then trundle back to Valladolid in an hour. In recent years Valladolid has acquired some nice, simple hotels (see below), and since they're a distance from the ruins, prices are very low and crowds are not a problem.

ORIENTATION
Highway 180 used to plough right through the midst of the archeological zone, but has now been re-routed to pass completely around the zone to the north. Coming from Cancún, you must bear left at the fork where the old highway and the new bypass divide. Bearing left will take you to the Villa Arqueológica, Hotel Hacienda Chichén, and Hotel Mayaland, in that order, before coming to a dead end at one entrance to the zone.

Chichén-Itzá's little airstrip is on the bypass to the north of the zone.

The town of Pisté is on the highway about a 15-minute walk or a $3 taxi ride (one mile) west of the archeological zone. The town boasts two moderately priced hotels and one deluxe lodging; restaurants are in the town proper, or on the road between the town and the zone.

2. Where to Stay and Dine

CHICHÉN-ITZÁ
The best place to stay, in my opinion, is right next to the archeological zone. The hotels here are the most efficient and charming, and they're within walking distance to the ruins. In case your first choices are full, there are alternatives both to the west of the zone in Pisté, and to the east of the zone, out in the country and, as discussed below, in Valladolid.

Top Hotels Near the Ruins
The **Hotel Hacienda Chichén** is a short walk from the ruins, and guests stay in the bungalows built for those excavating the ruins some years ago. There's a fine pool—which, by the way, is open also to those who drop in for the $7 lunch—and all is quite plush. Rates

are $67 single or double. Each cottage is named for an early archeologist working at Chichén. You can make reservations for the Hacienda by contacting the Mayaland Resorts, in the Hotel Casa del Balam at Calle 60 no. 488, corner of Calle 57 (Apdo. Postal 407, Mérida, Yucatán 97000; tel. 92/24-8844, or toll free 800/451-8891 in U.S.).

The **Hotel Mayaland,** sister hotel to the Hacienda Chichén and very close to it, is perhaps the most genteel and sumptuous of Chichén-Itzá hotels. Built positively to reek of jungle adventure, it boasts such subtle touches as a front doorway that frames perfectly El Caracol (the observatory) as you walk from the lobby outside. It has a swimming pool and restaurant-bar, of course, and very attractive air-conditioned rooms and bungalows for $70 double, $75 triple. Make reservations as at the Hacienda Chichén.

The **Hotel Villa Arqueológica** (tel. 985/6-2830, or toll free 800/528-3100 in U.S.) is part of the Club Méditerranée operation, as you might guess by a glance at the lavishness of the layout: tennis courts, a pool, and gardenlike grounds. On my last inspection tour I was quoted rates of $64 for one or two people—a very reasonable price for what you get; December through April rates may go up 20 to 30%. Meals are more expensive here than at the nearby Hacienda Chichén or at the Hotel Misión. For reservations in Mexico City, contact the Club Méditerranée office at Avenida Masaryk 183, Colonia Polónco, Mexico, DF 11570 (tel. 5/203-3086).

In Pisté

The **Hotel Misión Chichén-Itzá** (tel. Pisté 4) is a fancy establishment. With two floors of rooms, a pretty pool, a shopping arcade, and a restaurant-bar, the Misión is the "compleat" place to stay: Double rooms cost $47. You can drop in for breakfast ($4), lunch, or dinner ($10). For reservations in Mexico City, go to Florencia 15-A in the Pink Zone, or call 533-5953 or 553-3560.

About a mile west of the ruins in Pisté is the **Stardust Inn** (no phone)—the newest addition to this hotel strip. For reservations write Calle 81-A 513, Mérida, Yucatán 97000. The 57 modern rooms are quite nice, with television and air conditioning. The two-story structure is built around a pool and shaded courtyard. A room with two double beds will cost you $40. Unfortunately there is a video bar/disco below the hotel.

In the Country

A good place to stay overnight is the **Hotel Dolores Alba,** 1½ miles past the ruins on the road going east to Cancún. (If you go to Chichén-Itzá by bus from Mérida, ask for a ticket on a bus that is going *past* the ruins—to Valladolid or Puerto Juárez—and then ask the bus driver to stop at the Dolores Alba; he will be glad to do so. Or take a taxi from the ruins to the hotel.) The 28 rooms are kept clean and neat, and several of them have been equipped with air conditioners to help the ceiling fans. Besides the motel-style rooms, which are older, you'll find two modern, air-conditioned rooms and a separate cottage that sleeps four in two bedrooms. Prices are $17 single, $21 double, $31 triple, and $31 for four (in the cottage). All rooms have a shower, of course, and there's a pretty little swimming pool besides. Good meals are available here at decent prices, but you should realize that when it comes to dining you have little choice—the nearest alternative restaurant, or tienda to buy your own supplies, is several miles away. For your trips to the ruins, the Dolores Alba provides free transportation to guests without cars. By the way, this hotel is run by the same family that runs the Dolores Alba in Mérida (tel. 992/21-3745), at Calle 63 no. 464. Either hotel will help you to make reservations at the other one.

Best Dining Bets

Choices are limited here, but you won't go hungry, and you may even have a memorable meal. If not, the conviviality of fellow adventurers at dinner makes up for uninspired fare.

The acknowledged leader in the culinary arts is the French-style dining room at the **Villa Arqueológica**. Mexican and continental specialties share the menu here, and a full dinner with wine will cost about $15 to $20.

After the Villa, the place to dine is the **Hotel Mayaland**. Food here is much simpler, but still presentable and filling. Plan to spend about $11 for lunch or dinner.

IN PISTÉ If you have to eat in Pisté, don't expect much. There are many eateries, but there is little difference among them. Because they cater to day-tripping tour buses, quality and atmosphere aren't a priority. Expect to find your silverware encased in plastic and outdated mood music pulsing in the background. For a pleasant meal try the **Hotel Misión,** which is posh and charges $10 for a fixed-price meal. The restaurant **Xaybe,** across from the Hotel Misión, is air-conditioned and nice if somewhat sterile.

VALLADOLID

Although it remained untouched by tourism for centuries, Valladolid is no newcomer to Yucatán. It was founded in 1543 near the site of a Maya religious center called Zací. The Franciscans built an impressive monastery here, called the **Convento de San Bernardino de Siena** (1552), and the town can boast of half a dozen colonial churches and two cenotes.

The main square is called the **Parque Francisco Cantón Rosado,** and when you find your way there, you'll be just a few steps from a variety of acceptable hotels and restaurants. Walking around the main square, here's what you'll find: El Parroquía de San Servasio (the parish church) on the south and the Palacio Municipal (town hall) on the west.

Where to Stay

Near El Parroquía, at the southwest corner of the square, is the **Hotel San Clemente,** Calle 42 no. 206, at Calle 41 (tel. 985/6-2208 or 6-2065), a modern, colonial-style building covered in white stucco. From the second-floor balcony, you get a bird's-eye view of the church. The 64 rooms, some with air conditioning, ceiling fan, and tidy bath, are located on two floors around a central garden quadrangle complete with swimming pool (which may or may not have water in it). Rates, compared to those at Chichén or Cancún, are low: $18 double, all included.

The north side of the square holds the **Hotel El Mesón del Marqués,** a nice old colonial building at Calle 39 no. 203 (tel. 985/6-2073). Signs in English advertise the restaurant (very tidy) and gift shop. Most of the 27 rooms are in a modern addition, however, and come with air conditioning for $21 single, $26 double, $31 triple. The addition is behind the pretty tree-shaded courtyard, and therefore away from street noise. There's a nice little swimming pool in the courtyard here.

Another option in Valladolid is not on the main square proper, but just a block off it. It's the **Hotel Don Luis,** Calle 39 no. 191, at Calle 38 (tel. 985/6-2024). From the north side of the square (which is Calle 39) go east one block, and the Hotel Don Luis is on the left-hand side: You'll spot the sign. Despite its being on a busy street, the Don Luis' rooms are quiet, big, and air-conditioned. All are doubles, many with two double beds. A thoughtful touch is that the washbasin is located *outside* the bathroom, so one can wash while another showers. The swimming pool in the courtyard is attractive and very clean, and prices are low: $18 single, $19 for a double room with fan; an extra person in a room pays $1.50.

Where to Dine

The hotel restaurants are not bad here.

At the aforementioned **Hotel El Mesón** you can dine inside, where it's cool, or outside around a pretty little courtyard with a splashing fountain. While it's an idyllic place, bear in mind that there is precious little breeze at midday; you might be better off in the ventilated dining room.

Casa de los Arcos Restaurant (tel. 6-2467) is a newer place on Calle 39, no. 200-A. It has a lovely, breezy courtyard with a black and white tiled floor. Poultry and meat dishes hover between $4 and $5.50, while fish goes for between $4.25 and $7.50. It's across from Hotel Don Luis. Open from 7am to 10pm daily.

But for a real Valladolid adventure, take a stroll through the **Bazar Municipal,** that little arcade of shops beside the Hotel El Mesón del Marqués. The little cookshops here open at mealtimes, and their family-owners set out tables and chairs in the courtyard. Local farmers and traders in town on business come to chow down. You won't find a printed menu often, let alone one in English. But a quick look around at nearby tables will tell you what's cooking, and a discreet point of a finger will order it. Ask the price as you order, for the record, so you won't be charged something exorbitant when it's too late.

3. What to See at Chichén-Itzá

This Maya city was absorbed by the Toltecs in A.D. 987, when, as legend has it, a man named Kukulcán, who was the same as Quetzalcóatl from the Toltec capital of Tula, arrived from the west "for the redemption of his people." Here he built a magnificent metropolis combining the Maya Puuc style with Toltec motifs of the feathered serpent, warriors, eagles, and jaguars.

TOURING THE RUINS

The archeological zone at Chichén is open from 8am to 5pm daily. Admission costs 80¢, free on Sunday and holidays. There are actually two parts of Chichén-Itzá: the northern zone, which is distinctly Toltec; and the southern zone, which is of an early period with mostly Puuc architecture. A day is needed to see all the ruins here, preferably from 8am to noon, and 2 to 5pm. Parking is 25¢; children under 12 are free.

There is a Light and Sound Show in English at 9pm for 85¢. The sophisticated computer system frequently breaks down, so before you leave the ruins for dinner, ask if it's working; you don't want to make the trip for nothing. If you're also going to Uxmal and only have time to see one show, I think the show at Uxmal is better.

Before marching off to El Castillo, however, it's important that you understand the basics of the Maya system for measuring time. Without such an understanding, El Castillo is merely an impressive pile of rock. With an understanding, it's a marvelous and complex celestial sundial, which has kept perfectly accurate time for centuries.

The Maya Sense of Time

The amazingly exact and intricate Maya calendar system begins with the year 3113 B.C., before Maya culture even existed. From that date, the Mayas could measure time—and their life cycle—to a point 90,000,000 years in the future! Needless to say, they haven't felt the need for the whole system yet. For now, just note that they conceived of world history as a series of cycles moving within cycles.

THE SOLAR YEAR The Maya solar year was very precisely measured, and consisted of 365.24 days. Within that solar year there were 18 "months" of 20 days each (total: 360 days) plus a special 5-day period.

THE CEREMONIAL YEAR A ceremonial calendar, completely different from the solar calendar, ran its "annual" cycle at the same time. But this was not a crude system like our Gregorian calendar, which has saints' days, some fixed feast days, and some moveable feasts. The Maya ceremonial calendar "interlaced" exactly with the solar calendar. Each date of the solar calendar had a name, and each date of the ceremonial calendar also had a name; so every single day in Maya history has two names, which were always quoted together.

The ceremonial calendar was a very complex and ingenious system with 13 "months" of 20 days, but running within that cycle of 260 days was another of 20 "weeks" of 13 days!

THE DOUBLE CYCLE After 52 solar years and 73 ceremonial "years," during which each day had its unique, unduplicated double name, these calendars ended their respective cycles simultaneously on the very same day, and a brand-new, identical double cycle began. Thus, in the longer scheme of things, a day would be identified by the name of the 52-year cycle, the name of the solar day, and the name of the ceremonial day.

MYSTIC NUMBERS As you can see, several numbers were of great significance to the system. The number 20 was perhaps most important, as calendar calculations were done with a number system with base 20. There were 20 "suns" (days) to a "month," 20 years to a *katun*, and 20 katuns (20 × 20, or 400 years) to a *baktun*.

The number 52 was of tremendous importance, for it signified, literally, the "end of time," the end of the double cycle of solar and ceremonial calendars. At the beginning of a new cycle, temples were rebuilt for the "new age," which is why so many Maya temples and pyramids hold within them the structures of earlier, smaller temples and pyramids.

The Maya, obviously, were obsessed by time. (You'd have to be, to deal with such a system!) Time for them was not "progress," but the Wheel of Fate, spinning endlessly, determining one's destiny by the combinations of attributes given to days in the solar and ceremonial calendars. The rains came on schedule, the corn was planted on schedule, and the celestial bodies moved in their great dance under the watchful eye of Maya astronomers and astrologers.

It's no wonder that Chichén's most impressive structure, El Castillo, is in fact an enormous "time machine," and that this imperial city included a huge and impressive astronomical observatory.

El Castillo

Begin with the beautiful 75-foot **El Castillo** pyramid, built with the calendar in mind: There is a total of 364 stairs plus platform, which makes 365 (days of the year), 52 panels on each side that represent the 52-year cycle of the Maya calendars, and 9 terraces on each side of the stairways, a total of 18 terraces to represent the 18-month Maya solar calendar. If this isn't proof enough of the mathematical precision of this temple, come for the spring equinox (March 21), and when the sun goes down you'll see the seven stairs of the northern stairway plus the serpent head carving at the base touched with the last rays of the fading sun; within a 34-minute period the "serpent" formed by this play of light and shadow appears to descend into the earth as the sun leaves each stair, going from the top to the bottom, ending with the serpent head. To the Maya this is a fertility symbol: The golden sun has entered the earth: time to plant the corn.

El Castillo, also called the Pyramid of Kukulcán, was built over an earlier structure of Toltec design. A narrow stairway, entered at the western edge of the north staircase, leads into the structure, where there is a sacrificial altar-throne encrusted with jade, and a chac-mool figure. The stairway is open at odd and irregular hours, is claustrophobic, usually crowded, very humid, and uncomfortable.

Plan your visit for early in the day, if possible. By the way, you can indeed reach the top of the pyramid via the interior staircase.

Main Ball Court (Juego de Pelota)

Northwest of El Castillo is Chichén's main ball court, the largest and best preserved anywhere. It is only one of nine ball courts built in this city.

The game was played with a hard rubbery ball. Players on two teams tried to knock the ball through one or the other of the two stone rings placed high on either wall, using only their elbows, knees, and hips (no hands). The losing players, so it is said, paid for defeat with their lives. Actually, a debate still rages as to whether winners or losers were sacrificed. Conventional wisdom has it that losers (being losers) were killed. The other school of thought has it that Maya gods valued the same things as humans. And since victory is the highest achievement on earth, the winners would be the only appropriate sacrifices for the gods. It would therefore be an honor and privilege for winners to be sacrificed.

The game must have been an exciting event, heightened by the marvelous acoustics of the ball court. Have someone walk to the North Temple at the far end, and speak or clap hands. You'll hear the sound quite clearly at the opposite end, about 450 feet away.

The North Temple has sculptured pillars, and more sculptures inside. For a look at the teams after a game, walk along the bas-reliefs on each wall. Two opposing teams are facing the center. At the midpoint in the wall, Death accepts the sacrifice of one team's captain, who has been decapitated by the captain of the other team, who wields an obsidian knife.

TEMPLE OF JAGUARS (TIGRES) Near the southeastern corner of the main ball court is a small temple with serpent columns and carved panels showing jaguars *(tigres)*. Up the flight of steps and inside the temple, a mural chronicling a battle between Mayas and Toltecs was found. The Toltecs, with the feathered serpents, are attacking a Maya village of thatched houses, or *na*'s.

Tzompantli (Temple of Skulls)

When a sacrificial victim's head was cut off (some unlucky ball player, for instance), it was stuck on a pole and displayed here, in a tidy row with others. Just in case the skull population dropped, the architects have provided rows of skulls carved into the platform. Also carved into the stone are pictures of eagles tearing hearts from human victims. The word *Tzompantli* is not Maya, but came from central Mexico with the Toltecs.

Platform of the Eagles

Next to the Tzompantli, this small platform has reliefs showing eagles and jaguars clutching human hearts in their talons and claws.

Platform of Venus

East of the Tzompantli and north of El Castillo, near the road to the Sacred Cenote, is the Platform of Venus. Don't look for beauty, for the planet Venus, in Maya-Toltec lore, is thought to have been represented by a feathered monster, or a feathered serpent with a human head in its mouth, not a luscious lady. A chac-mool figure was discovered "buried" within the structure, which is why it is sometimes called the Tomb of Chac-Mool.

The Sacred Cenote

Follow the dirt road that heads north from the Platform of Venus, and after five minutes you'll come to the great natural well that may have given Chichén-Itzá (Well of the Itzáes) its name. By now you must have heard the sacrificial virgin lore. It seems that the priests herded a rather different breed of person to death in the watery depths here. Anatomical research done in the earlier part of this century by Ernest A. Hooten suggests that children and adults, male and female, were used as sacrificial victims. Judging from Hooten's evidence, the victims may have been outcasts: diseased, feebleminded, or generally disliked.

Whatever the worth of the sacrificial victims, the worth of other presents to the rain god Chac was very considerable. Edward Thompson, American consul in Mérida and a Harvard professor, bought the hacienda of Chichén in the beginning of this century, explored the bottom of the cenote with dredges and divers, and brought up a fortune in gold and jade. Most of these he spirited out of the country and lodged in Harvard's Peabody Museum of Archeology and Ethnology. Later excavations, in the 1960s, brought up more treasure. It appears, from studies of the objects recovered, that offerings were brought from throughout Yucatán, and even farther away.

Temple of the Warriors

One of the most impressive structures at Chichén, the Temple of the Warriors (Templo de los Guerreros), also called the Group of the Thousand Columns, is due east of El Castillo. Climb up the steep stairs at the front to reach a figure of chac-mool, and several impressive columns carved in relief to look like enormous feathered serpents. The building gets its name from the carvings of warriors marching along its walls. Other motifs, as you may have guessed by now, include feathered serpents, jaguars, and eagles.

South of the temple was a square building called by archeologists the market (mercado). Its central court, surrounded by a colonnade, may well have been just that.

Beyond the temple and the market, in the jungle, are mounds of rubble that have yet to be uncovered, excavated, analyzed, or reconstructed.

The main Mérida-Cancún highway used to cut straight through the ruins of Chichén, and though it has now been diverted, you can still see the great swath it cut. South and west of the old highway's path are more impressive ruined buildings. On the way to these buildings is a shady little stand selling cold drinks.

Tomb of the High Priest

Past the refreshment stand, to the right of the path, is the Tomb of the High Priest (Tumba del Gran Sacerdote), which stood atop a natural limestone cave in which skeletons and offerings were found, giving the temple its name.

Next building along, on your right, is the House of Metates (Casa de los Metates), named after the concave corn-grinding stones used until recently by the Maya.

Past it is the Temple of the Stag (Templo del Venado), fairly tall though ruined. The relief of a stag that gave the temple its name is long gone.

Chichán-chob (Little Holes), the next temple, has a roof comb with little holes, three masks of rain-god Chac, three rooms, and a good view of the surrounding structures. It's one of the older buildings at Chichén, built in the Puuc style during the Late Classic Period.

El Caracol

Construction of the Observatory (El Caracol), a complex building with a circular tower, was carried out over quite a long period of time. No doubt the additions and modifications reflected the Mayas' increasing knowledge of celestial movements, and their need for ever more exact measurements. Through slits in the tower's walls, Maya astronomers could observe the cardinal directions and the approach of the all-important spring and autumn equinoxes, and the summer solstice. The temple's name, which means "snail," comes from a spiral staircase within the structure.

On the east side of El Caracol, a path leads north into the bush to the Cenote Xtoloc, another natural limestone well. The Sacred Cenote of Chichén was reserved for sacrifices; its water was not used for drinking (good thing!). The city's daily water supply came from Xtoloc.

Temple of Panels

Just to the south of El Caracol are the ruins of a steambath (Temazcalli), and the Templo de los Tableros, named for the carved panels on top. This was once covered by a much larger structure, only traces of which remain.

Edifice of the Nuns

If you've visited the Puuc sites of Kabah, Sayil, Labná, and Xlapak, the Nunnery here (Edificio de las Monjas) will remind you at once of the "palaces" at the other sites. It is enormous, and was built in the Late Classic Period. Like so many other Maya buildings, a new edifice was built right over an older one. Suspecting that this was so, an archeologist named Le Plongeon, working earlier in this century, put dynamite in between the two and blew part of the newer building to smithereens, thereby revealing part of the old. You can still see the results of Le Plongeon's delicate exploratory methods.

On the eastern side of the Nunnery is an annex (Anexo Este) in highly ornate Chenes style, with, as usual, lots of Chac masks and serpents.

The Church

Next to the annex is one of the oldest buildings at Chichén, ridiculously named The Church (La Iglesia). Masks of Chac decorate two upper stories. Look closely and you'll see among the crowd of Chacs an armadillo, a crab, a snail, and a tortoise. These represent the Maya gods called *bacab,* whose job it was to hold up the sky.

Akab Dzib

The Temple of Obscure Writing (Akab Dzib) is due east of the Edifice of the Nuns along a path into the bush. Above a door in one of the rooms are some Maya glyphs, which gave the temple its name. In other rooms, traces of red hand-prints are still visible. The earliest part of this building is very old, and may well be the oldest at Chichén. It was reconstructed and expanded over the centuries.

Old Chichén

For a look at more of Chichén's oldest buildings, constructed well before the Toltecs arrived, follow signs from the Nunnery southwest into the bush to Old Chichén (Chichén Viejo), about half a mile away. Be prepared for this trek with long trousers, insect repellent, and a local guide. The attractions here are the Temple of the First Inscriptions (Templo de los Inscripciones Iniciales), with the oldest inscriptions discovered at Chichén, and the restored Temple of the Lintels (Templo de los Dinteles), a fine Puuc building.

GRUTAS DE BALANKANCHÉ

Spelunkers take note: The Grutas (caves) de Balankanché are 3½ miles from Chichén-Itzá on the road to Cancún. Expect the taxi to cost $5. You can see the caves with a guide only. Guides begin English-language tours at 11am and 1, 3, and 4pm every day. Admission costs $1.30 per person.

Getting down into the caves takes some doing as you will probably end up taking a taxi to the caves, and having it wait for your return. The entire excursion takes about two hours. Check at the main entrance to the Chichén ruins for current tour hours at the caves, which may or may not prove to be fully accurate.

The natural caves became wartime hideaways after the Toltec invasion of Yucatán. You can still see traces of carving and incense-burning, as well as an underground stream that served as the sanctuary's water supply.

THE ROAD TO MÉRIDA

Next stop on our circuit of Yucatán is its colonial capital and commercial metropolis. The 75-mile trip from Chichén-Itzá to Mérida will take between one and a half and two hours.

Along the way, tiny Maya hamlets with thatched houses (called *na*) dot the highway. Sometimes the frames of sticks are covered in mud plaster and whitewashed. The women take pride in wearing the traditional white *huipil*, which always has embroidery around the neckline, and several inches of lacy slip showing at the hem.

This is henequen country, and just east of Mérida you'll pass a big Cordemex plant that gathers in the leaves from the surrounding fields. Tied in bundles, the leaves form huge piles by the plant, waiting to have the sisal fibers extracted and made into rope and cloth. Henequen has been the principal industry of Yucatán for centuries, and the vast henequen haciendas were owned by absentee landlords and worked by peasants who were little better than slaves. The great haciendas have been split up in recent years, but the hacienda complexes—house, smokestack, factory, chapel, workers' houses, gateway, narrow-gauge railways—still stand along the road. In every direction stretch the numberless stone-walled fields where the spiny henequen plants grow, taking years to reach maturity.

VIII

MÉRIDA: THE COLONIAL CAPITAL

1. WHERE TO STAY
2. WHERE TO DINE
3. WHAT TO SEE AND DO

Yucatán's charming capital city (pop. 300,000) has been the hub of peninsular life since the Spanish founded it in the mid-1500s on the ruins of the defeated Maya town of Tiho. Little remains of Tiho, but a great deal remains of the Spaniards' colonial town. There's lots to see and do, many fine places to dine, and many good hotels in which to stay. You'll like it here.

You're liable to hear North American accents on Mérida's streets in January and February, July and August, for that's when most foreign visitors come. If you visit in the summer months, be advised that the weather can be intensely hot and humid. Consider taking a hotel room with air conditioning. If you don't, make absolutely sure the fan in your room works well. You're going to need it.

Also be advised that brief showers wash down Mérida's streets in late May, June, and July, during the rainy season. You may have to duck under cover any day until mid-October, but the rains are most frequent in the first two or three months.

GETTING TO AND FROM MÉRIDA
Unless you have a private car, it's simple: Arrive by air or by bus.

By Air
Mérida enjoys nonstop direct and connecting flights from numerous cities.

Flying into Mérida's modern airport, you'll find yourself on the southwestern outskirts of town, where Hwy. 180 enters the city.

At the airport itself are car rental desks for Avis, Budget, Dollar, Hertz, National, and VW Rent, as well as reservations and information desks for numerous hotels. In addition, you'll find a Tourist

Information desk run by the state government of Yucatán. Next to it is a big fluorescent sign listing many hotels in town. Each hotel has its own little button. Select your desired hotel, pick up the courtesy telephone, push the hotel's button, and the hotel's number will be dialed automatically!

Taxis between the airport and downtown hotels cost about $5. The "Transporte Terrestre" minibuses charge $3.60 per person for the ride downtown, so if you're traveling in a group, take a cab as it'll work out to be cheaper.

City bus no. 79 ("Aviación") operates between the center and the airport. This is the cheapest way to go, of course, with a one-way ticket costing only 10¢, though the buses are not all that frequent. Other city buses run along the Avenida de los Itzáes, just out of the airport precincts, heading for downtown.

You can make reservations and buy air tickets from one of the many travel agencies in Mérida.

The two national carriers have offices downtown as well: **Aeroméxico** is at Avenida Paseo de Montejo no. 460 (tel. 99/27-9000). At the airport, phone them at 24-8554 or 24-8576. **Mexicana** is at Calle 58 no. 500 (tel. 99/24-6623) and Calle 56-A no. 493, at Paseo de Montejo (tel. 99/24-7421 or 23-0508). At the airport, their number is 23-8602 or 23-6986. Two regional airlines, **Aero Caribe** and **Aero Cozumel,** Paseo de Montejo 500, (tel. 99/23-0002 and 28-0099 at the airport) have flights to and from Cozumel, Chetumal, Cancún, Oaxaca, Villahermosa, and Ciudad del Carmen.

By Train

Just in case you arrive by train, you should know that the station is about eight blocks northeast of the Plaza Mayor on Calle 55 between Calles 48 and 46.

The station is open from 7am to 10pm on Monday through Saturday and from 8 to 11am and 5:30 to 8:30pm on Sunday. Tickets go on sale at 8pm for the 10pm train and one hour in advance of departure for all others. First-class *Estrella* service may be available by the time you travel. Until then make do with second-class trains without a pullman or diner. And be alert for train thieves that we've been warned prey on unsuspecting travelers. From Mérida there's a 10pm train to Mexico City (a 40-hour trip) that goes through Campeche, Palenque, Cordoba, and Orizaba; a 6am train to Tizimin (four hours); and another at 4pm to Valladolid (four hours).

By Bus

Mérida's main bus station, run by the Unión de Camioneros de Yucatán, is on Calle 69 between Calles 68 and 70, about six blocks southwest of the Plaza Mayor. The ADO line runs from here, as do Unión de Camioneros buses. The station has a travel agency with tours to the ruins, a newsstand, and various stalls selling souvenirs and snacks.

Coming from the east (Cancún, Chichén-Itzá, Valladolid), your bus may make a stop at the old bus station on Calle 50 between

65 and 67. If you're headed for the Plaza Mayor, you might as well get off here. It's six blocks to the plaza from here as well.

As for departures, buses to Uxmal depart at 6, 7, 8, and 9am, and noon, 3, 5:30, and 7pm; return trips are at 6:30, 8:30, and 11:30am, and 2:30, 5:30, and 7:30pm.

There's one bus a day from Mérida's bus station on the route Mérida-Uxmal-Kabah-Sayil-Labná-Xlapak-Mérida. It departs Mérida at 8am, and allows you about 20 minutes' time to visit each of the ruins, returning to Mérida in the afternoon. In effect, it's a low-price unguided tour bus.

A special bus for the sound and light show performance at Uxmal departs Mérida at 5:30pm, returning after the show.

Going via Mayapán, catch a bus to Oxcutzcab, which will take you through Kanasin and Acanceh, to Ruinas de Mayapán, and then through the villages of Mayapán, Mama, etc. Be sure to tell the driver you want to get off at the *ruinas*, or he'll assume you want to go to the village, a couple miles farther on.

For Chichén-Itzá there are first-class ADO buses at 8:30am and 3pm. If you're planning to go out and back in a day (something I don't recommend if you enjoy seeing impressive ruins), take the 8:30am bus and reserve a seat on the 3pm bus returning from Chichén. A one-way ticket on the two to two-and-a-half-hour trip costs $1.60; a round-trip ticket is twice as much.

To Cancún and Puerto Juárez (the dock for boats to Isla Mujeres), there are first-class ADO buses almost every hour on the hour throughout the day, from 6am to just past midnight. The trip takes about five hours and costs $5.

For buses north to Progreso, you must go to a special bus terminal at Calle 62 no. 525, between Calles 65 and 67. Buses leave every 15 minutes between 5am and 9pm. First-class buses take 45 minutes for the trip and second-class buses take an hour or more.

There are buses to Campeche from the main bus station about every 30 minutes or so throughout the day on the three- or four-hour trip (the duration depends partly on which route you pick, the short way via Hwy. 180, or the longer route past Uxmal and Kabah via Hwy. 261).

About 18 ADO buses per day head to Villahermosa ($8.50) via the Palenque junction, a trip of about 11 or 12 hours.

Six buses a day make the long grind all the way to Mexico City for a fare of $16.

ORIENTATION

As with most colonial Mexican cities, Mérida's streets were laid out in a grid. Even-numbered streets run north-south, odd-numbered streets run east-west. In the last few decades, the city has expanded well beyond the grid, and several grand boulevards have been added on the outskirts to ease traffic flow.

A word of warning about street numbers: What with unnumbered dwellings and -A, -B, and -C additions, these progress agonizingly slowly. Example: I wanted to get from 504 to 615-D on Calle 59 and did—after walking 12 blocks! Otherwise, the street grid is fairly easy to find your way in.

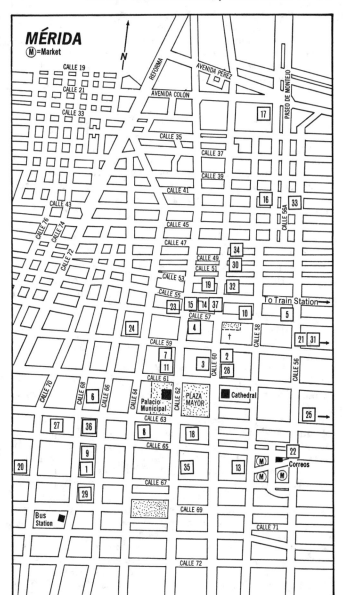

Plaza Mayor

The center of town is the very pretty Plaza Mayor, sometimes called the Plaza Principal, the main square, with its shapely, shady trees, plus benches, vendors, and a social life all its own. Around the plaza are the massive cathedral, the Palacio de Gobierno (state government headquarters), the Palacio Municipal, and the Casa de Montejo, a mansion built by the founder of Mérida and now occupied by a bank. Within a few blocks of the Plaza Mayor are several smaller plazas, each next to a church; the University of Yucatán; and the sprawling market district.

Paseo de Montejo

Mérida's most fashionable address, however, is over seven blocks northwest of the Plaza Mayor. It's the Paseo de Montejo, a wide tree-lined boulevard laid out during the 19th century and lined with houses and mansions built by politicos and henequen barons. The Paseo, which extends northward for over a dozen blocks, is home to Yucatán's anthropological museum, several upscale hotels and auto dealerships, and the U.S. Consulate.

GETTING AROUND

Most of the time, you'll walk, because many of the most attractive sites are within a handful of blocks from the Plaza Mayor.

Taxis are usually easy to find in the center of town. A short ride, perhaps between the Plaza Mayor and the bus station or the Paseo de Montejo, might cost $2.20 to $2.50.

Another way to tour the town is in a horse-drawn carriage. Look for a rank of them near the cathedral, then haggle for a good price. An hour's tour might cost $6 to $7.

City buses are the cheapest of all, charging only 10¢ for a ride. You might conceivably take one to the large, shady Parque Centenario on the western outskirts. Look for the bus of the same name ("Centenario") on Calle 64.

As for rental cars, you may well want one of these for your explorations of Mayapán, Uxmal, Kabah, etc. You don't really need one to get around Mérida, or to Chichén-Itzá or Cancún. The bad news is that rental cars are very expensive these days in Yucatán, averaging $50 or $60 per day for a VW Beetle rented in Mérida. The good news is that you can often haggle for a lower price. You should, in any case, shop around the local agencies for a good price.

Keep these tips in mind as you scour the city for a rental car deal: Kilometers and insurance are the most expensive charges; daily rental and fuel are the least. Don't be impressed by a very low daily charge, unless it includes unlimited kilometrage. In every single case, get the absolutely final figure for a rental before you decide; if you can't get kilometers included, estimate the distance you'll travel by adding up the highway mileages, then add 15% for wrong turns and detours. Keep in mind that you can often get lower rates if you rent for more than a day or two, and if you promise to pay at the end of the rental in cash dollars (you'll need a credit card at first for the paperwork, though). For more information on car rental, see "Car Rentals" in Chapter XIII.

Here are two of the local agencies that seem to be good. Please write and tell me about your car rental experiences, both good and bad:

Budget Rent-A-Car, (tel. 99/24-9791), at the airport, offers an unlimited mileage rate that works out to about $55 per day, all included except gas.

You might also try **Volkswagen Rent,** Calle 60 no. 486-F, between 57 and 55 (tel. 99/21-8128), which tends to be slightly lower than Budget.

FAST FACTS

The information below will help answer your questions concerning the location of various services in Mérida.

Banks: Banamex, in the Palacio Montejo on the Plaza Mayor, has its own casa de cambio, which usually provides a better rate of exchange than the banks. Other banks are located on and off Calle 65 between Calles 62 and 60.

Consulates: The **U.S. Consulate** is at Paseo de Montejo no. 453, corner of Avenida Colón (tel. 99/25-5011 or 25-5409), next to the Holiday Inn. It's open from 7:30am to 4pm on Monday through Friday, but follows a specific schedule for visas and travelers' problems. Visa matters are dealt with only on Monday, Wednesday, and Friday between 7:30 and 11am. Other kinds of problems are considered the same days from noon to 3:30pm and on Thursdays from noon to 4pm.

The **British Vice-Consulate** is at Calle 53 no. 489, corner of Calle 58 (tel. 99/21-6799). Open in principle from 9:30am to 1pm, you may find no one. The vice-consul fields questions about travel to Belize as well as British matters. The **Alliance Française** has a branch at Calle 56 no. 476 (tel. 99/21-6013).

Medical Care: If Moctezuma's Revenge gets serious, ask your hotel to call a doctor after you've got an estimate of his fee. The city's Hospital O'Horan (tel. 99/24-4224 or 24-4111) is on Avenida de los Itzáes at Calle 59-A, north of the Parque Centenario.

Post Office: Mérida's main post office is at the corner of Calles 65 and 56, in the midst of the market. It is open from 8am to 7pm on Monday through Friday, Saturday from 9am to 1pm; closed Sunday.

Telephones: Long-distance casetas are at the airport, the bus station, at Calles 59 and 62, and Calles 59 and 64, on Calle 60 between 55 and 53 in "El Calendario Maya," and at the intersection of Avenidas Reforma and Colón in a farmacia. Remember that international calls are expensive, but at least from a caseta you won't pay a hotel's gross "service charge."

Tourist Information: The most convenient source is the office operated by the Estado de Yucatán (tel. 24-9290 or 24-9389), in the hulking edifice known as the Teatro Peón Contreras, on Calle 60 between 57 and 59, open Monday through Friday from 9am to 9pm, Saturday from 9am to 4pm, Sunday from 9am to noon.

You can also try the Palacio Municipal, on the western side of the Plaza Mayor (opposite side from the cathedral), which has a tourism office open daily from 8am to 8pm, Sunday from 11am to 5pm.

The Secretaría de Turismo (SECTUR) building (tel. 24-9431 or 24-9542), where not much seems to be happening, is at the corner of Calles 54 and 61.

1. Where to Stay

The hotel situation in Mérida is wonderful: wide selection, many styles, and prices range from an amazing backpackers' special at $11 double, to the Holiday Inn's $87 double.

So low are the prices, and such are the attractions of this city, that it is possible some of Mérida's hotels might not be able to accommodate you in the busy months of February, July, and August unless you reserve in advance. To be certain of getting exactly the room you want, particularly in the better hotels, call in advance.

TOP HOTELS

Mérida's best places to stay are new, modern, efficient, pleasant, and moderately priced.

The **Holiday Inn Mérida,** Avenida Colón 498, Mérida, Yucatán 97000, between Calle 60 and the Paseo de Montejo (tel. 99/25-6877, or toll free 800/465-4329 in U.S.), is a lavish lowrise layout right next to the U.S. Consulate. If you check into one of the 214 rooms, each with individual climate controls, color television, AM/FM radio, servi-bar refrigerator, and purified water, have your bathing suit handy, for the hotel has a nice swimming pool complete with swim-up bar. Other assets include a pair of tennis courts, two restaurants, several bars, and a nightclub. The price for a room is $87 single or double. Though the Holiday Inn is at a prestigious address, you'll find yourself taking taxis often to reach the main plaza, the colonial monuments, and the shopping streets.

In terms of price and style, you can't do better than the **Hotel Los Aluxes,** Calle 60 no. 444, Mérida, Yucatán 97000, at Calle 49 (tel. 99/24-2199). Pronounced "ah-*loo*-shes," the name refers to the magical elves who acted as guardian angels to the ancient Mayas. This modern 109-room hotel is one of Mérida's newest; and offers you a patio café with thatch-shaded tables, a coffeeshop, an elegant restaurant, a swimming pool and sundeck on the mezzanine level, and a staff ready to please. Air-conditioned rooms are priced at $63 single or double, $17 triple, all included. The hotel has its own parking lot.

MODERATELY PRICED HOTELS

Very moderately priced, the following hotels offer modern accommodations, swimming pools, air conditioning, and all the other comforts and pleasures of mid-range hotels.

Near the Plaza Mayor

One of Mérida's most popular and centrally located hotels, **Casa del Balam,** Calle 60 no. 48, Mérida, Yucatán 97000 (tel. 99/24-8844 or toll free 800/451-8891 in U.S.), is near the corner of

Calle 57. The three- and six-story hotel is built around a lush interior courtyard. Each of the 52 colonial-style rooms is accented with Mexican textiles, folk art, dark furniture, iron headboards, and tile floors with area rugs. It's hard to top for location and comfort. Singles and doubles both run $65.

Across the street the **Hotel Mérida Misión,** Calle 60 no. 491, Mérida, Yucatán 97000, corner of Calle 57 (tel. 99/23-9500), is actually a large modern addition grafted onto a gracious older hotel. The location, right across the street from the university and the Teatro Peón Contreras, and only two short blocks from the Plaza Mayor, is excellent. Enter the hotel's cool lobby from the noisy street, and you enter an oasis complete with bubbling fountain, high ceilings, and a nice little swimming pool. Though the public rooms are colonial in style, the 150 air-conditioned guest rooms are modern, and priced at $44 single, $46 double, $48 triple.

The **Hotel Maria del Carmen,** Apdo. Postal 411, Mérida, Yucatán, 97000, Calle 63 no. 550, betwen Calles 68 and 70 (tel. 99/23-9133), is an older but modern-style four-story hostelry complete with pretty swimming pool and enormous rubber tree. The public rooms are paved in marble and supported by mirrored pillars; the guest rooms have tidy tiled private bath, color TV, FM music, telephone, and in many cases two double beds. The hotel has its own restaurant and bar, and rents its guest rooms for $41 single, $48 double. It's a popular lodging for groups both North American and European.

The **Hotel Castellano,** Calle 57 no. 513, two blocks northwest of the Plaza Mayor, Mérida, Yucatán 97000 (tel. 99/23-0100), has been patronized by North American visitors for decades. You enter by way of a small semicircular drive to the porte-cochère, then through wrought-iron gates along a sea of gleaming marble to a lobby done in a modern interpretation of colonial style. The hotel is fairly large for Mérida, with 170 guest rooms on 12 floors, the rooms outfitted with private bath, black and white or color television, air conditioning, and radio. Hotel guests enjoy the use of a swimming pool, solarium, restaurant, lounge, and coffeeshop, as well as souvenir shops and a travel agency. The location is pretty convenient to the square. The rate for a room, single or double, is $50. This is a good, dependable choice for comfortable accommodations in Mérida.

Small but sleek, the **Hotel del Gobernador,** Calle 59 no. 535, Mérida, Yucatán 97000, at the corner of Calle 66 (tel. 99/23-7133), qualifies as being among Mérida's most modern mid-range hotels. Each of the 43 rooms and 16 junior suites has air conditioning, telephone, and radio, with prices of $37 single, $42 double, $5 for each extra person. If you have more than two people in your party, you're liable to want a junior suite for only a few dollars more; these have two double beds each. You'll enjoy use of a small swimming pool here, a cafeteria, bar, and parking lot.

Another good choice is the **Hotel Calinda Mérida Panamericana,** Calle 59 no. 455, Mérida, Yucatán 97000, between 52 and 54 (tel. 99/23-9111 or 23-9444, or toll free 800/228-5151 in U.S.). The Panamericana has a secret: you enter an ornate

19th-century doorway to register at the front desk. Then you pass through a classic Spanish atrium with its fancy stone and woodwork, and head for a modern annex that holds the up-to-date guest rooms, the restaurant, and the swimming pool. The old building is quite charming; the new one is quite efficient. For one of the 110 rooms with bath, air conditioning, television (with satellite programming), and perhaps a five-city view, you pay $52 to $61 single or double; 12 junior suites cost about $6 more per room, 6 suites yet another $4.

Along Paseo de Montejo

The thoroughly modern **Hotel El Conquistador,** Calle 56-A no. 458, Mérida, Yucatán 97000 (tel. 99/26-2155 or Fax 26-8829), is on the Paseo de Montejo (that's Calle 56-A) at Calle 35. Rising nine stories over the boulevard, it holds 64 modern guest rooms, 20 junior suites and 5 full suites, each with two double beds, balcony, private marble bathrooms with tub and shower, telephone and television; standard rooms are priced at $52 single or double. Two shiny elevators, and a small interior swimming pool on the second floor, are available for your enjoyment, along with a solarium, restaurant, cafeteria, and lobby bar with live entertainment. Though the hotel itself is modern, it stands amid a bevy of dowager colonial mansions from Mérida's gilded age.

Two other choices on the Paseo de Montejo are under identical management. The first is the veteran 90-room **Hotel Montejo Palace,** Paseo de Montejo 483-C, at Calle 41, on the west side of the boulevard, Mérida, Yucatán 97000 (tel. 99/24-7644 or 24-7678). The decor is colonial, more or less, but the nice front porch and sidewalk coffeeshop and restaurant add a touch of modern comfort and ambience. Guest rooms here have white stucco walls and dark wood in the colonial manner, color television, two double beds, little balconies, and air conditioning for modern comforts. Two elevators trundle you among the floors. For a guest room here, single or double, it's overpriced at $50 single or double.

The Montejo Palace's sister establishment, cater-corner across the boulevard on the east side, is the **Hotel Paseo de Montejo,** Paseo de Montejo 482, at Calle 41, Mérida, Yucatán 97000 (tel. 99/23-9033 or 23-9550). The Paseo de Montejo appears a bit older and more used, but is still a comfy place with an elevator and a little swimming pool. Your quarters here will have tidy tiled private bath, color TV, plastic laminate furniture, and a clean if well-used air. Rooms cost $35 single or double. It's a popular place with tour groups.

BUDGET HOTELS

Mérida's lineup of hotels is a budget traveler's dream-come-true. From the very expensive to the very low-priced, from the modern to the romantically old-fashioned, everyone can find a place that suits. Most hotels offer at least a few air conditioned rooms (and current weather reports will tell you whether or not you'll need this), and a few of the places in the budget lineup even have swimming pools!

Modern, with Colonial Touches

As in many Mexican towns, the hotel lineup in Mérida includes numerous establishments that are basically modern in amenities and construction, but colonial in inspiration and decor. Mérida has quite a few of these, in a nice range of prices. Expect a serviceable and comfortable if not particularly charming room, and a fairly central location, in any of these places.

At the corner of Calles 59 and 60, a mere half-block northeast of the Plaza Mayor, is the 43-room **Hotel Caribe** (tel. 99/21-9232), popular for its location, with three floors arranged around a quiet central courtyard. The restaurant's tables are set out in a portico surrounding the court; on the top floor is a small but quite serviceable swimming pool, a sundeck, and a vantage point for views of the cathedral and the town. Most of the rooms here have an air conditioner, television, phone, ceiling fan, and a tile bathroom, usually with a walk-in shower. Attached to the hotel is a sidewalk café, El Mesón, with wrought-iron tables set in the shady Parque Cepeda Peraza. Prices for a room with ceiling fan are $20 single and $25 double; with air conditioning, you pay $25 single, $30 double. Suites cost about $5 more per room.

The **Hotel Janeiro,** Calle 57 no. 435, Mérida, Yucatán 97000, between Calles 48 and 50, about seven blocks from the Plaza Mayor (tel. 99/23-3602), is owned by the same family as the Dolores Alba (see below). Since buying the Janeiro, they've spruced up the 22 rooms and added a nice little swimming pool and patio tables for breakfast or snacks. Rooms come with ceiling fan for $17 single or double; with air conditioning and TV for $21. They have parking places for a few cars.

Only a block and a half north of the Plaza Mayor is the small **Hotel del Parque,** Calle 60 no. 497, Mérida, Yucatán 97000, at Calle 59 (tel. 99/24-7844). The hotel entrance and restaurant are quite colonial, but the 21 rooms are actually in the modern structure next door. Although the rooms are quite small, they're bright with floral wallpaper, tiled baths, and ceiling fans. The hotel has its own large enclosed parking lot. Figure to pay $18 single, $20 double here.

Colonial Inns

A few of Mérida's lodging places have an authentic colonial ambience, somewhat faded, it's true, but still charming.

The **Hotel Dolores Alba,** Calle 63 no. 464 Mérido, Yucatán 97000, between Calles 52 and 54 (tel. 99/21-3745), is an old Mérida house converted to receive guests. Thirty rooms here come with air conditioning, ceiling fans and showers, plus decorations of local crafts. A big open court and another court with a nice clean swimming pool give a sense of space. The colonial-style dining room is open for breakfast and dinner. You'll pay $16 single, $18 double, $23 triple for a room with a fan. The Dolores Alba is run by the Sanchez family, who also have the Hotel Janeiro, and the Hotel Dolores Alba at Chichén-Itzá. Make reservations at one hotel for space at the other hotel, if you like.

Once a Private Mansion

The hotel **Posada Toledo,** Calle 58 no. 487 at the corner of Calle 57 (tel. 99/23-2256), was once a private mansion but is now run as an inn with 19 rooms and a rooftop deck, good for sitting and viewing the city in the cool of the evening. The place seems to be a cross between a garden and a museum with antique furnishings, antique facilities, and lots of verdure. Rates are $26 single and $27 double with ceiling fan or with air conditioning.

A 19th-Century Grand Hotel

Perhaps the finest example of old-time hotel architecture in the city is the **Gran Hotel,** facing the Parque Cepeda Peraza at Calle 60 no. 496, Mérida, Yucatán 97000, between Calles 59 and 61, a half block north of the Plaza Mayor (tel. 99/24-7622 or 24-7730). The ambience is 19th century rather than colonial, and all the more enjoyable for that. Thirty high-ceilinged rooms on three levels surround a central plant-filled court. Corinthian columns and fancy ironwork vie for your attention with lofty portals and heavily worked wood trim. It is a worthy place. A century ago, the Gran Hotel was undoubtedly one of Mérida's best places to stay, and the management has undertaken extensive renovations in recent years to reclaim some of its past glory. Rates for the rooms with bath here are $26 single, $30 double. The hotel has a good restaurant, El Patio Español, in a rear courtyard.

Low-Budget Hotels

The **Hotel Peninsular,** Calle 58 no. 519, Mérida, Yucatán 97000, between Calles 65 and 67 (tel. 99/23-6996 or 23-6902), is right in the heart of the market district less than three blocks southeast of the Plaza Mayor. In such a busy district, you'll be surprised to find this warren of tidy, quiet little rooms at the end of the long entrance corridor. There's even a small restaurant. Prices are $13 single, $15 double with ceiling fan; $16 single, $19 double with air conditioning.

Four blocks northeast of the Plaza Mayor is the **Hotel Mucuy,** Calle 56 no. 481, Mérida, Yucatán 97000, between Calles 56 and 58 (tel. 99/21-1037). The hotel is named for a small dove said to bring good luck to places where it alights, and you should have good luck, as many alight here. The two floors of rooms, 26 in all, with window screens, tile shower, and ceiling fan, are lined up on one side of a garden with fine grass and bougainvillea. The owners are Sr. Alfredo and Sra. Ofelia Comin, who live on the premises. Señora Comin speaks English. Rates are $15 single, $17 double, $19 for three persons. A laundry sink and clothesline are available for guests' use. The roses and bougainvillea seem to be in bloom all summer here.

With its inviting modern appearance, the lobby outperforms

the rooms at the **Hotel Monjas,** Calle 66 at 63, Mérida, Yucatán 97000 (tel. 99/21-9862). But the 20 basically furnished rooms are clean, and come with ceiling fan, private bath, and either one double bed or two or a double and a twin. The location is excellent and so are the prices at $11 single or double and $15 for a room for three.

---

2. Where to Dine

Although Mérida cannot approach such cosmopolitan centers as Mexico City and Guadalajara in terms of diversity of restaurants, it has a comfortable number of good places to dine. Continental cuisine, Mexican specialties, American favorites, even Middle Eastern and French dishes are available.

You should make a point of trying some of the special dishes of Yucatán during your stay in Mérida. I'll give you a few suggestions, but first you must know how things are seasoned and prepared.

SEASONINGS, SAUCES, AND SURPRISES

The hot pepper of Yucatán, called *chile habanero,* is among the hottest in all Mexico, and if you tangle with one, you won't soon forget it. But you needn't worry, as dishes are not heavily doused in habanero, although it is used. Often it lurks in a fiery sauce served on the side.

A popular sauce is *achiote,* made of sour orange juice, salt, onion relish, habanero peppers, and cilantro (fresh coriander leaf). There's also *pipián,* a sauce made with pumpkin or sunflower seeds; and escabeche, a thick, mildly piquant concoction reminiscent of a stew, though the word means "pickle."

Yucatecan Specialties

Huevos Motuleños: Said to have originated in the Yucatecan town of Motul, these breakfast eggs come atop a tortilla, garnished with beans, peas, ham, sausage, and grated cheese.

Sopa de Lima: This lime soup is tangy and flavorful, made with chicken stock.

Cochinita Pibil: Try suckling pig wrapped in banana leaves and baked in a barbecue pit (if it's authentic), flavored with achiote. Look also for the similar pollo pibil, made with chicken.

Papadzules: Tortillas are stuffed with hard-boiled eggs and seeds (cucumber or sunflower) in a tomato sauce.

Pavo Relleno Negro: Pavo means turkey, and Yucatán was the original home (along with New England) of this marvelous bird. Stuffed turkey, Yucatán-style, is filled with chopped pork and beef and cooked in a rich, dark sauce.

Poc-chuc: This translates into slices of pork with onion in a tangy sauce of sour oranges or limes.

Venado: Venison (deer), a popular dish, is served numerous ways, perhaps as pipián de venado, steamed in banana leaves and served with a sauce of ground squash seeds.

Queso Relleno: Called "stuffed cheese," this dish is made with a mild yellow cheese stuffed with minced meat and spices.

Beer: As for drinks, Yucatecan beers such as Carta Clara and Montejo (lager) and León Negro (dark) are delicious, but harder and harder to find as the gigantic brewing companies from central Mexico move in and crowd the market.

Liquor: *Xtabentún* (shtah-ben-*toon*) is the local high-octane firewater, traditionally made by fermenting honey, then flavoring the brew with anise. Today the xtabentún you buy in the market may have a lot of grain neutral spirits in it instead of fermented honey. Think of the drink as Yucatecan ouzo or pastis. It comes *seco* (dry), or *crema* (sweet).

THE BEST PLACES

Here are my favorite dining places in Mérida.

Mexican

A place to try if you're feeling romantic is the **Restaurante Portico del Peregrino,** Calle 57 no. 501 (tel. 21-6844), right next door to the ever-popular Pop and across the street from the university. The restaurant aims to recapture the 19th century in Mexico, and does this rather well. You enter through a little garden court, then through a cross-topped gateway into another little courtyard set with tables and shaded by vines and trees. If the weather is too warm for outdoor dining, escape to the air-conditioned bliss of the two enclosed dining rooms, which are well stocked with antique beveled mirrors and elegant sideboards. There's also a modern street-side salon. Table settings are done with white cloths and decent glassware. For less than $10 you can have soup, fish filet, a brochette of beef, or pollo pibil, plus rum-raisin ice cream for dessert. The Peregrino is open for lunch and dinner, noon to 3pm and 6 to 11pm, every day of the week.

La Casona, Calle 60 no. 434, between Calles 47 and 49 (tel. 23-8348), is only a block north of the Hotel Los Aluxes. Here, a gracious old Mérida house has been converted to a charming restaurant. The white stucco portico leads to a lush garden; gleaming red floor tiles and tidy tablecloths show that this is a proper place for a good meal, and romantic enough for a special night. The cuisine is Yucatecan and continental, especially Italian, so you can choose among such dishes as pollo pibil, filet mignon with brandy and cream, linguini with mushrooms, or "lasaña multicolor" for your main course. The price of a dinner depends heavily on what you select, but it should be in the range of $12 per person. Come any night of the week for dinner. It's a good idea to drop by earlier in the day (or the evening before) to secure a reservation and to see what's cooking. Open from 1pm to midnight daily.

The pollo pibil at the **Restaurant Santa Lucía,** on Calle 60 near Calle 55 (tel. 21-5670), may be the best in town, and the camarones en brochette are another standout. Santa Lucía has the unusual distinction of offering Lebanese specialties and traditional Yucatecan dishes on the same menu, and doing both equally well. It's small, atmospheric, friendly, and you get a free glass of xtabentún (anise and honey liqueur) after dinner. On Thursday nights you can see the parade to the Santa Lucía Park, and hear the mariachi band. Come any day for lunch or dinner to its location near Santa Lucía Park, and expect to pay about $7 to $10 per person for dinner.

French
Those in the mood for French cuisine will want to try the **Yannig Restaurante,** Ave. Perez-Ponce 105, between calles 21 and 21A (tel. 27-0339). Chef Yannig Oliviéro was trained in France, and serves up the old favorites and some of his own creations: onion or garlic soup, Roquefort salads and crêpes, pâté maison, beef with unripe pepper sauce, fish amandine, coq au vin, pêche Melba. The bright, cheery, cozy little restaurant is a pleasant change from the normal fluorescent lighting. Plan to spend $4 to $6 for a light meal, $9 to $12 for a feast with wine. Only dinner is served, Monday, Tuesday, and Friday from 5 to 11:30pm and Thursday, Saturday, and Sunday from 1 to 10:30pm; closed Wednesday.

Yucatecan
As Yucatecan cuisine spreads throughout Mexico, the fame of poc-chuc pork goes with it. The dish, a delectable concoction of grilled pork, tomatoes, onions, cilantro (fresh coriander leaves), and salt, was created in Mérida at **Los Almendros,** Calle 50-A no. 493, between Calles 57 and 59, facing the Plaza de Mejorada (tel. 21-2851). Actually, the first Los Almendros is deep in the Maya hinterland, at Ticul, but the branch in Mérida has become the favorite spot to sample local delicacies. Start with venison broth (sopa Mestiza), then have poc-chuc, pollo pibil, or pavo relleno negro (baked turkey with a black stuffing of ground pork, roasted peppers, and Yucatecan spices). You'll find lots of similarly exotic and delicious entrees, all for about $3 to $5 with descriptions in English! The daily special plate, always a good bargain, costs about $5 and constitutes a full meal. Over the years, I've been alternately delighted and mildly disappointed at Los Almendros. You must try it, though.

Lebanese
In Yucatán? A Middle Eastern restaurant? Why? Because 19th-century Mexico, and particularly Yucatán, had a significant population of Ottoman traders, mostly from the sultan's province of Lebanon. The **Restaurant Cedro del Libano,** Calle 59 no. 529, between Calles 64 and 66 (tel. 23-7531), is a simple but tidy place with experienced waiters and a menu that lists berenjena con tijini (eggplant with tahini), labne (yogurt), labin (like buttermilk), tabouli, kibi, and alambre de kafta (ground meat grilled on skewers). I had the fatta Cedro del Libano, which turned out to be chicken topped with chick peas, yogurt, and sliced almonds. Meat dishes cost about $3 to $4, and a full meal can be had for $10 or so. Hours are 11:30am to 11:30pm every day.

Vegetarian

Any Mexican town of considerable size has a vegetarian restaurant, and Mérida is no exception. Here it's the **Restaurante
Vegetariano La Guaya,** Calle 60 no. 472, between 55 and 53,
just a few steps north of the Parque Santa Lucia (tel. 23-2144). Enter to find a little patio café in a courtyard, combined with a
bookstore featuring health-related titles. Lots of different salads
are offered here, as well as a Hindu dish of oats, wheat, and fish,
named Kama Sutra! Full meals tend to cost about $4 to $6, and are
served Monday through Saturday evenings from 5 to 11pm.

Fajita Fix

Fajitas, that northern Mexico invention that's slipped over the
U.S. border, has also made its way to Mérida at **El Patio de las
Fajitas,** Calle 60 no. 467 at 53 (tel. 28-3782). The mansion-turned-
restaurant is festooned in colorful tablecloths and plants centered
around a central courtyard. You won't see piles of mesquite wood
though. These folks say they do fajitas *the* authentic way, which is to
marinate the pork, shrimp, chicken, or beef, then grill it on a siz-
zling iron platter with a dash of garlic oil, lime juice, and at the last
minute, warm beer for a flaming effect. Each order comes with guacamole salad, flour tortillas, and Mexican salsa. Although fajitas
reign supreme, they serve hamburgers, quesadillas, beans ranchero
style, and other Mexican specialties. You can snack for as little as
$3.20 or spend as much as $8.40 for the fajita supreme, a combination of three meats that easily feeds two. Open from 1 to 10pm;
closed Monday.

FULL SERVICE, BUDGET PRICES

Probably the most popular meeting place in town is the **Café-
Restaurant Express,** facing the Parque Cepeda Peraza at Calles 59
and 60 (tel. 28-1691). Here, hordes of townspeople—mainly men
—sit and idle the hours away, totally devoid of atmosphere, with all
attention focused on the sidewalk or at least a newspaper. The menu
is vast—lengua à la Mexicana (Mexican-style tongue), pollo pibil
(the chef wraps and marinates the chicken in banana leaves before
cooking), huachinango milanesa (red snapper). Top off whatever
you choose with pasta de guayaba con queso (guava paste with
cheese). Or simply while away some time here with coffee, good and
strong. Plan to spend $2 for breakfast, about $5 for the set-price
lunch, and $5 or $6 for dinner. Open 7am to 11pm every day.

Soon after your arrival in Mérida you'll discover **El Mesón** (tel.
24-9022), the tiny place just to the left of the Hotel Caribe's entrance. Wrought-iron tables are set in the shady Parque Cepeda
Peraza (alias Parque Hidalgo), and they're often full. The food is
usually pretty good; I especially enjoy the sopa de verduras (vegetable soup), and prices are great: The set-price meal, usually served

right into the evening hours, is $5.00. El Mesón is open for three meals a day, every day.

For a light lunch, try **Pop,** on Calle 57 between Calles 60 and 62, next to the university (tel. 21-6844). The little place is air-conditioned, clean, bright, and modern, and seems to be where the gilded youth of Mérida have their afternoon snack. Apple pie, Bavarian fudge cake, the best hamburgers in town, and the air conditioning are the attractions. Prices are okay: $1.25 or less for a hamburger, $2.50 for a huge fruit salad with ice cream. "Pop," by the way, is the first month of the 18-month Maya calendar.

A Plaza Café

For after-dinner ice cream or Mexican pastries and cakes, the **Dulcería y Sorbetería Colón** sets out bent-wire café tables and chairs in the portico on the Plaza Mayor (Calle 61 side). Besides serving dessert at budget prices—50¢ for ice cream or cake—it provides the best vantage point for people-watching in the late afternoon or evening. Try some of their exotic tropical fruit ice creams such as coconut or papaya. Open 8am to midnight daily. Try to pick a time of day when auto traffic (with its noise and smelly fumes) is not so heavy in the square.

For Breakfast

A good breakfast choice, particularly if the day is already hot, is the aforementioned **Pop,** which is air-conditioned and has set breakfasts priced at $1 for a continental breakfast, $2 with two eggs, and $2.50 with two eggs plus bacon or ham.

To make your own breakfast, feast your eyes (and later your appetite) on pastries and sweet rolls from the **Panificadora Montejo,** at the corner of Calles 62 and 63, which is the southwest corner of the main plaza. It's hard not to overeat with your eyes as you choose from a dozen or more delectable breakfast treats. With a hot drink a suitable light breakfast can be thrown together for about $1.50.

For those (like me) who simply cannot start a day without fresh orange juice, here's good news. Juice bars with the name of **Jugos California** or **Jugos Florida** have sprouted up all over Mérida. Three of these thirst-quenching establishments are on or just off the main plaza: one on Calle 62 near Calle 61, one on the Calle 63 side of the plaza, and another just across the corner from it on Calle 62! Demand is brisk, and prices are not high for what you get: a tall ice-cream-soda glass of juice squeezed right before your eyes for 80¢.

---

3. What to See and Do

Mérida is pretty, congenial, friendly, and in summer it's also very, very hot. Just before the coming of the muggy, rainy months

(June through September), Mérida can get up to 108°F (42°C). You'd do well to arise early, snatch a quick breakfast, and do your walking well before the noonday sun does its worst. Then have lunch, and a siesta, and issue forth in the evening, refreshed and ready for the next round.

If you're lucky enough to be visiting in January or February, you'll be able to spend most of the day outdoors without discomfort.

Start your explorations of old Mérida at the city's focal point, the Plaza Mayor.

PLAZA MAYOR

This beautiful town square, now shaded by topiary laurel trees, began its history as the Plaza de Armas, a training field for Montejo's troops. Later called the Plaza Mayor, it was renamed the Plaza de la Constitución in 1812, then the Plaza de la Independencia in 1812. Other common names for it include Plaza Grande, Plaza Principal, and even (sometimes) zócalo.

The city was laid out by the conquering Montejos on the classic Spanish colonial plan. Surrounding the plaza were the cathedral, the archbishop's palace, the governor's palace, and the mansions of notables. Let's examine each in turn.

The Cathedral

On the east side of the plaza, the cathedral was under construction from 1561 to 1598. It looks like a fortress, as do many other early churches in Yucatán. That was actually their function in part for several centuries, as the Mayas did not take kindly to European domination. Much of the stone in the cathedral's walls came from the ruined buildings of Maya Tiho.

Inside, decoration is sparse and simple, the most notable feature being a picture over a side door of Ah Kukum Tutul Xiú visiting the Montejo camp. To the left of the main altar is a smaller shrine with a curious burnt cross, recovered from the church in the town of Ichmul, which burned down. The figure was carved by a local artist in the 1500s from a miraculous tree that burned but did not char. The figure burned, though, along with the church, and broke out in blisters as it did. The local people named it Cristo de las Ampollas (Christ of the Blisters).

Also take a look in the side chapel (open from 8 to 11am and 4:30 to 7pm), which has a life-size diorama of the Last Supper. The Mexican Jesus is covered with prayer crosses brought by supplicants asking for intercession.

The archbishop's palace and a seminary once stood to the right (south) of the cathedral. The palace was torn down during the Mexican Revolution (1915); part of the seminary remains, but is now used for shops.

Palacio de Gobierno

On the north side of the plaza, this site was first occupied by a mansion built for the colonial administrators; the present building dates from 1892.

Between 8am and 8pm (Sundays from 9 to 5pm) you can visit the palace and view the large murals painted mostly between 1971 and 1973. Scenes from Maya and Mexican history abound, the painting over the stairway combining the Maya spirit with ears of sacred corn, the "sunbeams of the gods." Nearby is a painting of the mustached benevolent dictator Lázaro Cárdenas, who in 1938 expropriated 17 foreign oil companies and was hailed as a new Mexican liberator.

Palacio Municipal

Facing the cathedral across the plaza from the west side is the Palacio Municipal, or City Hall, with its familiar clock tower. It started out as the cabildo, the colonial town hall and lock-up, in 1542. It had to be rebuilt in the 1730s, and rebuilt again in the 1850s, when it took on its present romantic aspect.

Palacio Montejo

Also called the Casa de Montejo, it was begun in 1549 by Francisco Montejo "El Mozo," and was occupied by Montejo descendants until the 1970s. It now houses a bank branch (Banamex), which means you can get a look at parts of the palace just by wandering in during banking hours (9am to 1:30pm, Monday through Friday). Note the arms of the Spanish kings and of the Montejo family on the Plateresque façade, along with figures of the Conquistadores standing on the heads of "barbarians" overcome by their exploits. Look closely and you'll find the bust of Francisco Montejo the Elder, his wife, and his daughter.

THE MARKET DISTRICT

Mérida's bustling market district is just a few blocks southeast of the Plaza Mayor, roughly the area bounded by Calles 63 to 69, and 62 to 54. The market proper is right next to the post office, at the corner of Calles 56 and 65. Wade into the clamor and activity, browsing for leather goods, hammocks, Panama hats, Maya embroidered dresses, men's formal guayabera shirts, and handcraft items of all kinds. A few tips and pointers might be helpful.

Hammocks

The supremely comfortable Yucatecan fine-mesh hammocks (hamacas) are made of string from several materials. Silk is wonderful, but extremely expensive, and only for truly serious hammocksleepers. Nylon is long-lasting. Cotton is attractive, fairly strong and inexpensive, but it wears out sooner than nylon. There are several grades of cotton string used in hammocks.

What will probably serve your needs best is a cotton hammock of good-quality string. Here's how to find it: First, look at the string itself. Is it fine and tightly spun? Are the end loops well made and tight? Grasp the hammock at the point where the body and the end strings meet, and hold your hand level with the top of your head. The body should touch the floor; if not, the hammock is too short for you. Next, open the hammock and look at the weave. Are the strings soiled? Are there many mistakes in the pattern of the weave?

Then, decide on size. Keep in mind that any of these hammocks is going to look big when you stretch it open, but many will seem small when you actually lie in them, so you want a hammock as big as you can afford.

Hammocks are sold as *sencillo* (single, 50 pairs of end strings, about $5), *doble* (double, 100 pairs of end strings, about $8 to $10), *matrimonial* (larger than double, 150 pairs of end strings, about $12 to $15). The biggest hammock of all is called *una hamaca de quatro cajas,* or sometimes *matrimonial especial,* and it is simply enormous, with 175 pairs of end strings; if you can find one, it'll cost you about $18 to $20. Buy the biggest hammock you think you can afford. You'll be glad you did. The bigger ones take up no more room, and are so much more comfortable, even for just one person.

Where should you buy your hammock? Street vendors will approach you at every turn. "Hamacas, Señor, Señorita?" Their prices will be low, but so may be their quality. Buy from these guys if you're willing to take the time and go through all the steps listed above. Otherwise, booths in the market will have a larger selection to choose from, at only slightly higher prices.

For years I've been recommending the store called **La Poblana, S.A.,** Calle 65 no. 492, between Calles 60 and 62 (tel. 21-6503), with no complaints. Sr. William Razu C., the owner, is usually on the job and ready to whip out dozens of hammocks for your inspection. Prices are marked, and bargaining is not encouraged. If you've spent some time in the market for hammocks, and you seem to know what you're talking about, Sr. Razu may usher you upstairs to a room wall-to-wall with hammocks, where you can give your prospective purchase a test-run. La Poblana sells ropes and mosquito nets for hammocks as well, and also Maya women's dresses and men's guayaberas.

Panama Hats

Another very popular item is this soft, pliable hat made from fibers of the *jipijapa* plant in several towns along Highway 180 in the neighboring state of Campeche. If you travel through the town of Becal, for instance, you'll see a sculpture in the main square composed of several enormous concrete hats tipped against one another. It's a fitting monument to a townfolk who have made their wealth (such as it is) weaving the pliant fibers into handsome headgear while sitting in humid limestone grottoes and caves. The caves provide just the right atmosphere for shaping the fibers. Stop and ask for a demonstration, and any citizen will be glad to oblige.

There's no need to journey all the way to Becal, however, as Mérida has the hats in abundance. Just the thing to shade you from the fierce Yucatecan sun, the hats can be rolled up and carried in a suitcase for the trip home. They retain their shape quite well.

Jipi hats come in three grades, judged by the quality (pliability and fineness) of the fibers and closeness of the weave. The coarser, more open weave of fairly large fibers will be sold for a few dollars (or by street vendors in Cancún and Cozumel for up to $10!). The middle grade, a fairly fine, close weave of good fibers, should cost about $10 in a responsible shop. The finest weave, truly a beautiful hat, can cost twice this much. For most people, the middle grade is fine.

A tried and true *sombrería* is **La Casa de los Jipis,** Calle 56 no. 526, near Calle 65 (no phone), where a phlegmatic señora will show you the three grades of hats, grumping the while. Find your size, more or less, and the señora will tie a ribbon around the hat for final adjustment. If you'd like to see how the hats are blocked, wander into the shady depths of the rear of the store.

Crafts Museums and Shops

For a look at the best of Yucatán's crafts and handwork, drop by the **Museo Regional de Artesanías,** Calle 59 between Calles 50 and 48, open for free from Tuesday through Saturday, 8am to 8pm, Sunday until 2pm, closed Monday. Another place to examine crafts is at **La Casa de las Artesanías,** Calle 63 no. 513, between Calles 64 and 66, a beautiful restored monastery with exhibits of crafts, and a shop where you can buy them. There are also two galleries here with changing exhibits, plus a bookstore, a bulletin board listing cultural events, and an inexpensive cafeteria. The Casa is open from 10am to 8pm on Monday through Friday and Saturday until 6pm.

EXPLORING CALLE 60

Many of Mérida's old churches and little parks are located along Calle 60 north of the Plaza Mayor. Plan a stroll along this street, perhaps continuing to the Paseo de Montejo and its Museo Regional de Antropología.

Parque Cepeda Peraza

As you leave the Plaza Mayor, you'll pass the site of the Seminario de San Ildefonso, an early hospital, on your right. You then come to the little Parque Cepeda Peraza (also called the Parque Hidalgo), named for the 19th-century General Manuel Cepeda Peraza. Part of Montejo's original plan for the city, the parque borders the church called **La Iglesia de Jesus,** or El Tercer Orden (the Third Order), built by the Jesuit order in 1618. The entire city block in which the church stands was part of the Jesuit establishment, and the early schools started by these worthies ended up being the Universidad de Yucatán. The Biblioteca (library) Cepeda Peraza, founded by the general in 1867, is beside the church.

Down Calle 59 a few steps past the park and the church is the former **Convento de la Mejorada,** a late-1600s work of the Franciscans.

Parque de la Madre

This park is sometimes called the Parque Morelos. By its statue shall you know it, this little park with its modern madonna and child. The statue is a copy of the work by Lenoir that stands in the Luxembourg Gardens in Paris.

Teatro Peón Contreras

Designed by Italian architect Enrico Deserti in the beginning of the present century, the enormous yellow building holds the state Tourist Information Office (facing the park). The main entrance, with its Carrara marble staircase and frescoed dome, is closed most of the time, unfortunately.

Universidad de Yucatán

On the west side of Calle 60, at the corner of Calle 57, is the university, founded in the 19th century by Felipe Carrillo Puerto with the help of the aforementioned General Cepeda Peraza. Wander in, ask directions to the **fresco** (1961) by Manuel Lizama, and the painting will tell you the whole story of the founding.

Heading north on Calle 60, the Hotel Mérida Misión is on your left, the Hotel Casa del Balam on your right. Soon you'll come to the Parque Santa Lucía.

Parque Santa Lucía

Facing the park is the ancient **Iglesia de Santa Lucía** (1575). The plaza itself, surrounded by an arcade on the north and west sides, used to be the place at which visitors first alighted in Mérida from their stagecoaches. The plaza is floodlit at night, and on Thursday there are concerts of local music at 9pm. On Sunday, the plaza fills up with vendors and browsers during the weekly Antiques and Crafts Bazaar.

To reach the Paseo de Montejo, walk up Calle 60 to Calle 47, turn right, and the Paseo is two blocks away.

PASEO DE MONTEJO

Most guidebooks compare the Paseo to Paris' Champs-Elysées, but you'll see at once that they're pretty different. Even so, it is a broad, tree-lined thoroughfare lined with imposing banks, hotels, and a number of the 19th-century mansions put up by henequen barons, generals, and other Yucatecan potentates.

Museo Regional de Antropología

Most impressive mansion of all is that occupied by the local anthropology museum on the Paseo Montejo, at the corner of Calle 43 (tel. 23-0557). The **Palacio Cantón** (1909–1911) was designed by Enrico Deserti, the architect who designed the Teatro Peón Contreras, and built during the last years of the Porfiriato as the home of General Francisco Cantón Rosado (1833–1917). The general got to enjoy his palace for only six years, until his death. After this short occupancy the imposing edifice began a new career as a school, then as the official residence of Yucatán's governor, before becoming first the archeological museum, and now the Regional Museum of Anthropology.

Don't neglect to admire the building itself as you walk around. It's the only Paseo mansion that you'll get to visit. Note especially a great luxury of the time: the little art deco elevator.

The museum is open from 8am to 8pm on Tuesday through Saturday, to 2pm on Sunday, closed Monday. Entry costs less than half a dollar.

On the right as you enter is a room for changing shows. After that are the permanent exhibits, with captions in Spanish only.

Starting with fossil mastodon teeth, the exhibits take you down through the ages of Yucatán's history, giving special attention to the daily life of its inhabitants. You'll see how the Maya tied boards to babys' skulls in order to reshape the heads, giving them the slanting forehead that was then a mark of great beauty, and how they filed teeth to sharpen them, or drilled teeth to implant jewels. Enlarged photos show the archeological sites. The one of Mayapán, for instance, clearly shows the city's ancient walls. Even if you know little Spanish, the museum provides a good background for your Maya explorations.

Monumento a la Patria

Continue your stroll along the Paseo, and you'll walk by the **Parque de las Americas,** planted with trees and shrubs from throughout the New World, to the grandiose Monumento a la Patria (Monument to the Fatherland), done by Rómulo Rozo in the 1950s in neo-Maya style.

PARQUE CENTENARIO

Due west of the Plaza Mayor, along Calle 61 or 65, lies the large Parque Centenario, bordered by the Avenida de los Itzáes, which leads to the airport and Campeche. The parque is a fine place for an afternoon stroll, especially with children. There's a small zoo with Yucatecan animals.

A DAY-TRIP TO PROGRESO

Want to zoom out to Progreso for a day? There's a good beach, not touristy but very Mexican, a fantastically long *muelle* ("mu-*wey*-yeh," or pier) that shoots out into the bay to reach water deep enough for ocean-going ships, and a few seafood restaurants (nothing great, though).

To get there, go to the special Progreso bus station on Calle 62 at no. 524, between Calles 65 and 67. Buses leave every 15 minutes during the day, starting at 5am. The trip takes 45 minutes.

Once in Progreso, Calle 19 runs along the beach. The bus station is about four blocks south of this street. The beach seems endless, and is crowded with coconut palms (and on weekends, with Mexican families). The **Restaurant Carabela,** Calle 69 no. 146, on the seashore Avenida Malecon, will serve you a fish platter for $6 or so, shrimp for just a bit more.

A Stop at Dzibilchaltún

Along the road north to Progreso lie the Maya ruins of Dzibilchaltún, worth a stop if you're interested in ruins and have the time. Before you go, pick up the detailed official guide to the site written by archeologist E. Wyllys Andrews V, and published by the Instituto Nacional de Antropología e Historia. Besides providing full descriptions of the site and its buildings, it has a handy plan of the central portion of the ruins.

Five buses per day (7:10 and 10:50am, and 1:20, 5:20, and 7:30pm) depart the Progreso bus station in Mérida (see above) for Chablekal, which is near the entrance to the Dzibilchaltún ruins.

Only the first three are really of interest, and of these I recommend the very earliest so as to beat the heat.

The site is 9 miles north of Mérida along the Progreso road, then 4½ miles east off the highway, on the grounds of the former Hacienda Dzibilchaltún. There's a small museum at the site with exhibits of stelae, figurines, and pottery. A group of seven strange clay dolls show a variety of diseases and birth defects.

Though it was founded about 500 B.C. and flourished around 750 A.D., Dzibilchaltún was in decline long before the coming of the Conquistadores. It was not rediscovered until 1941. Excavations were carried out from 1956 to 1965. Today the most interesting points are grouped around the Cenote Xlacáh, the sacred well. They are the complex of buildings around Structure 38, the Central Group of temples, the raised causeways (or *saches),* and the Seven Dolls Group, centered on the Temple of the Seven Dolls. It was beneath the floor of the temple that those seven weird little dolls (now in the museum) were discovered.

Dzibilchaltún is unusual in that it is out here on flat land normally covered in low scrub rather than thick jungle. It's not well known, so you will have the pleasure of exploring the site without crowds of other people around.

Flamingo Sanctuary

Celestun, an hour and a half from Mérida on the Gulf Coast, is a flamingo sanctuary as well as an offbeat, sand-street fishing village that's an excellent inexpensive getaway. If you're driving, follow highway 281 toward the Gulf Coast on a single-lane road past numerous old henequen haciendas. Or take one of the frequent buses from Mérida. The town proper is on a narrow strip of land separated from the mainland by a lagoon. As you cross over the lagoon bridge going into town you'll notice small boats moored on both sides. They are waiting to take visitors to see the flamingos. For an hour-and-a-half flamingo-sighting trip the cost is around $20 or twice that if you stay a half day. Besides flamingos, you'll see cranes, sandpipers, and other waterfowl feeding on shallow sandbars. *Note:* The best time to see the flamingos is around 7am and the worst is mid-afternoon when sudden storms come up. Be sure not to allow the boat operators to frighten the birds; they've been known to do it for photographers, but it's caused a lot of problems in the habitat.

To find overnight lodging, follow the bridge road straight ahead to the end. The last street is Calle 12, which parallels the ocean front. Here you'll find less than a half dozen hotels all charging around the same $11 single or double. A couple of them are on the beach. Two or three restaurants serve excellent seafood. I highly recommend the **Restaurant Celestun** owned by Elda Cauich and Wenseslao Ojeda. It's on the corner of the bridge road and Calle 12. The house specialty is a super delicious shrimp, crab, and squid omelet locally called a *torta.*

EVENING ENTERTAINMENT

There are band concerts every Sunday at 9pm in the Plaza Mayor. Every Thursday in **Santa Lucía Park,** on the corner of Calles 60 and 55, you can hear some festive music and serenades by different mariachis. They begin at 9pm and stop when their enthusiasm turns to thirst.

Take a stroll past the **Jardín de los Compositores** (Garden of Composers), behind the Palacio Municipal, to see what's happening. This is the venue for many concerts, movies, and general happenings. Another good place to check is the **Teatro Peón Contreras** at Calles 60 and 57. Ask at the Tourist Information Office right in the building about current shows. They often have Yucatán's own ballet folklórico in performance, but usually on Sunday mornings at 11 rather than at night.

Hotel bars, lounges and discos depend largely on the crowd of customers presently staying at each hotel. Most of Mérida's downtown hotels are filled with tour groups whose members, after an exhausting day, seek to rest rather than rock.

For a cross-cultural experience, you might want to try the club named **Tulipanes,** Calle 42 no. 462-A (tel. 27-2009 or 27-0967), which has a restaurant, bar, and disco. Every evening from 8:30 to 10 they put on a floor show inspired, however remotely, by Maya customs, ancient and modern. Cover charge is about $7; the restaurant menu tends toward Yucatecan specialties such as pollo pibil, venison steaks, and chuleta Yucateca (pork chops with achiote).

Another possibility is the evening Maya folklore spectacular at the Hotel Calinda Mérida Panamericana, a show entitled "Mukuykak."

IX

UXMAL AND THE
PUUC CITIES

1. MAYAPÁN
2. TICUL
3. UXMAL
4. KABAH
5. SAYIL
6. XLAPAK
7. LABNÁ
8. LOLTÚN

Though it is not quite as famous as Chichén-Itzá, Uxmal is equally impressive, and perhaps even more dramatic. And when you consider that Uxmal, 50 miles south of Mérida, is only one of a half-dozen impressive archeological sites in the Puuc (hill country) region, you've got an attraction of major proportions.

You can and should spend more than a day in touring the region. Secure a reservation at one of the excellent hotels right at Uxmal to use as your base. Though it's possible to visit Uxmal itself in a day, try to spend at least two days (one night), or even three (two nights) before heading back to Mérida, or onward to Campeche, or across the peninsula to the Caribbean coast.

Want the full rundown? First there's Mayapán, the ancient Maya capital city, badly ruined now but in a lush setting. It's thrilling to consider yourself walking among the ruins of the great Maya capital. Then there's Uxmal, with several of the most beautiful and awe-inspiring buildings ever constructed by humans. Then 17 miles southeast of Uxmal is Kabah, with a unique palace, several other grand buildings, and a decorative style very different from that at Uxmal. From Kabah it's only a few miles to Sayil, with its immense palace reminiscent of Minoan structures. Xlapak ("Shla-*pahk*") is almost walking distance (through the jungle) from Sayil, and Labná just a bit farther east. A short drive east from Labná brings you to the caves of Loltún. Backtrack to the main road (Hwy. 261) and you can head southwest to spend the night in Campeche.

Those with only a little time will have to limit themselves to seeing Uxmal on a day-trip by bus (see Chapter VIII, "Getting To and From Mérida," for details). The ideal way to tour the ruined cities south of Mérida is to rent a car, plan to stay the night in a hotel at Uxmal, and allow two full days for sightseeing before hitting Campeche or returning to Mérida, or driving on toward Tulum and Cancún. How interested are you in Maya archeology? If you enjoy it as much as I do, rent a car in Mérida, take your time, and enjoy yourself.

Another way to do it is to ignore Mayapán, get an early start in your rental car, and head south on Hwy. 261 directly to Uxmal. Spend the morning there, and the afternoon at Kabah, Sayil, Xlapak, and Labná, and then head on to a place to sleep in Campeche, or return to Mérida. This tour would be about 275 miles round trip.

Here, then, is a stone-by-stone description of the ruined Maya cities south of Mérida, starting with Mayapán and the old pottery-making town of Ticul.

---

1. Mayapán

Founded by an offshoot of the wandering Itzá tribe, some time between 1263 and 1283, for over 250 years Mayapán was the center of power in the Yucatán. By the time of its rise, the once powerful cities of Uxmal and Chichén-Itzá were dwindling city-states that paid tribute to Mayapán. By 1461 Mayapán too was conquered and lay in ruins.

You can take a village bus to the Ruinas de Mayapán (not to be confused with the village of Mayapán (see Chapter VIII, "Getting To and From Mérida," for details). But the easiest way is to drive. Ask directions frequently—it's very easy to take wrong turns or to get onto unmarked roads by mistake.

Head out of Mérida toward Kanasin and Acanceh ("Ah-kahn-*keh*"), about 12 miles.

This is not as easy as it sounds, as signs are few and sometimes wrong. Here are some hints: Get to Calle 67 in the Mérida *colonia* (suburb) named Miraflores, on the eastern edge of the city. Head east on 67, bear right at its end, then take an easy left at a big intersection. Follow the wide, divided highway complete with speed bumps, cross Mérida's *circunvalación* (ring road)—you'll see signs to Cancún (left) and Campeche (right)—and continue straight on. Soon you'll enter Kanasin. Watch for signs that say *desviación* (detour) as you approach the town. As in many Yucatán towns, you're being redirected to follow a one-way street through the urban area. Go through the market, pass the church and the main square on your left, and continue straight out of town.

The next village you come to, at Km 10, is San Antonio Tehuitz, an old henequen hacienda. At Km 13 is Tepich, another hacienda village, with those funny little henequen-cart tracks crisscrossing the main road. After Tepich comes Petectunich, and finally Acanceh.

In **Acanceh** there's a partially restored pyramid to the left of the church, overlooking the main square. Another large one, the "stucco palace," is a couple of blocks from the market. To unlock the gate to the pyramid, you'll have to find the custodian, Anatolio Narvaez. His house is on the street to the right of the market about halfway down. Ask—everyone knows where he lives. There's little stucco left on the palace, but to find it, follow the street to the right of the market, turn right at the first corner, left at the next one, and right again. The grass-covered pyramid is about halfway down the block. A few animal figures in stucco relief are preserved under a makeshift cover on top.

Even if you just see the pyramid from the street, without tracking down the Sr. Narvaez for the key, it's a good excuse to detour through the village with its whitewashed rock walls and tidy oval-shaped thatched huts.

Should you need sustenance, Acanceh's market, complete with little loncherías, is just to the right of the church. Just before you reach the main square, drop in at the tortilla factory on the left-hand side of the road.

Turn right in the main square (around that statue of a smiling deer) and head for Tecoh with its huge, crumbling church (5½ miles) and Telchaquillo (6¾ miles). This route takes you past several old Yucatecan haciendas, each complete with its big house, chapel, factory with smokestack, and workers' houses. Shortly after the village of Telchaquillo, a sign on the right-hand side of the road will point to the entrance of the ruins, on the right.

A hundred yards in from the road, after passing the guards' hut, are the remains of **Mayapán**. The main pyramid is ruined but still lofty and impressive. Next to it is a large cenote (natural limestone cavern, used as a well), now full of trees, bushes, and banana plants. A small temple with columns and a fine high-relief mask of Tlaloc, the hook-nosed rain god, are beside the cenote. Other small temples, including El Caracol, with its circular tower, are in the nearby jungle, reached by paths.

These piles of stones, though impressive, give one no idea of what the walled city of Mayapán must have been like in its heyday. Supplied with water from 20 cenotes, it had over 3,000 buildings in its enclosed boundaries of several square miles. Today, all is covered in dense, limitless jungle.

The guard will sell you the requisite admission ticket for 50¢ and help you with any bits of information you may need.

Heading onward, continue along the main road to Tekit (5 miles), turn right and go to Mama (4⅓ miles) on a road as thrilling as a roller coaster ride, turn right again for Chapab (8 miles), and finally you'll reach Ticul (6¼ miles), the largest town in the region.

2. Ticul

You can have lunch here, or get a soft drink, or change some money, or pick up snacks in the market, or even stay the night in modest comfort, if necessary.

This sprawling town actually has only 20,000 inhabitants, many of whom make their living embroidering huipiles (the Maya women's costume), weaving straw hats, shoemaking, and shaping pottery. Workshops and stores throughout the town, and especially in the market area, feature these items.

The main street is Calle 23, also sometimes called the Calle Principal. It's where you'll find the market, a hotel, and Los Almendros, Ticul's best-known restaurant.

WHERE TO STAY AND DINE

The nicest hotel in town is actually a motel on the outskirts. The **Hotel-Motel Cerro Inn** is just at the edge of town on Calle 23, 1¼ miles from the market, on the highway to Muna and Mérida (no phone). Its nine basic rooms, dark but cool, with showers and fans, face a shady grove and a nice palapa restaurant. Prices are $11 for one bed, $13 for two. There's an atmospheric thatched-roof restaurant with entrees from $3 to $5. This place doesn't look so great as you enter, but it's not bad at all.

The restaurant called **Los Almendros** is on Calle 23 not far from the market (tel. 2-0021). Set in the courtyard of a big old Andalusian-style house, this is the original of the chain with branches now in Mérida and Cancún. The specialties are Mayan, such as papadzules (the stuffed tortillas) and poc-chuc. Ask for the illustrated menu in English that explains the dishes in detail, so you're not in for a mystery meal. Stop in any day for lunch or dinner, and your bill will come to about $4.50 to $6 per person.

At no. 218 on Calle 23, past the mercado, is **Restaurant Los Delfines** (no phone). It's a wonderful place run by Miguel Angel Cachon and his wife Aida. Most main courses cost between $3 and $6 liquor is available with meals. Open every day from 8am to 6pm.

Right near the market there's a cantina called "Bar 'Tu Hermana'" (Your Sister). I can't recommend it, but as a veiled insult or the punch-line to a ribald joke, it's unbeatable!

WHAT TO SEE AND DO

Ticul's annual festival, complete with bullfights, dancing, and carnival games, is held during the first few days of April. All during the year it's entertaining to watch the men pedal three-wheeled carts to taxi locals around town.

Spelunker's Challenge

Just outside the village of Yotolín (which is between Ticul and Oxkutcab) are some impressive caves called Yaxnic ("Yash-neek"), on the grounds of the old, private Hacienda Yotolín. Virtually undeveloped, and full of colored stalactites and stalagmites, the caves are visited by means of a perilous descent in a basket let down on a rope.

Arranging this spelunking challenge takes time, but since the thrill may be worth it, here's the procedure. Several days (or even weeks or months) before your intended cave descent, go to Yotolín and ask for the house of the *commisario*. He will make the proper introductions to the hacienda owners who in turn will tell you how and when to prepare for the experience.

ONWARD

It's 14 miles from Ticul to Muna. At Muna, turn left and head south on Hwy. 261 to Uxmal, 10 miles away, or take the shortcut at Santa Elena. Buses depart Ticul for Muna almost hourly during the day. At Muna, change to a bus heading south to Uxmal.

---

3. Uxmal

Prepare yourself for one of the highlights of your Yucatán vacation, for the ruins of Uxmal are truly breathtaking. *Note:* There's no gasoline at Uxmal, so top off the tank in Mérida or Ticul before continuing.

If you've decided to come directly from Mérida on highways 180 and 261, you get a bonus: the chance to tour a real Yucatecan hacienda, **Yaxcopoil.** This unpronounceable Maya name designates a fascinating old hacienda on the road between Mérida and Uxmal. It's difficult to reach by bus, but if you're driving, look for it on the right side of the road 21 miles south of Mérida, 10 miles south of Uman, on Highway 261. Take a half hour to tour the house, factory, outbuildings, and museum. You'll see that such haciendas were the administrative, commercial, and social centers of vast private domains, almost little principalities, carved out of the Yucatecan jungle. Yaxcopoil is open 8am to dusk on Monday through Saturday, and on Sunday between 9am and 1pm.

When you leave Yaxcopoil, you still have 28 miles to drive to reach Uxmal. Although the ruins of Uxmal are visible from the highway, the impressiveness of this site will not strike you until you enter the archeological zone and walk around. Coming from the north along Hwy. 261, you'll pass four hotels before you reach the ruins proper, three of them moderately priced and one quite inexpensive. Here's what to expect.

WHERE TO STAY AND DINE

Unlike Chichén-Itzá, which has several classes of hotels from which to choose, Uxmal has mostly one class: comfortable and moderately priced. Unfortunately, dining options are limited in Uxmal; the only places to dine are in the hotels. The food isn't bad, but it's pretty standardized. A nice exception is the French cuisine at the Villa Arqueológica. In all three of the nicer hotels, the atmosphere will more than make up for the unexceptional fare.

My favorite of the hotels here is the oldest one, the **Hotel Hacienda Uxmal,** Uxmal, Yucatán 97840 (tel. 4-7142; for reservations, contact Mayaland Resorts in the Hotel Casa del Balam in Mérida, Calle 60 no. 488, Mérida, Yucatán 97000; tel. 99/24-8844). Right on the highway across from the ruins, the Hacienda Uxmal was built as the headquarters for the archeological staff years ago. The 71 rooms are large and airy, with equally large bathrooms, screens on the windows, ceiling fans, and blocky, substantial furniture. The rambling building groups many rooms around a central garden courtyard complete with fine swimming pool and bar. A dining room and gift shop fill out the spare rooms. Singles and doubles cost $67; huge triple rooms cost $74. A mariachi band usually plays at pool-side in the evenings. It's a five-minute walk to the ruins from the hotel. Check-out time is 1pm, so you can spend the morning at the ruins and take a cooling dip (you'll need it!) before you check out and get on the road again.

Even closer to the ruins is the **Villa Arqueológica** (tel. toll free 800/528-3100 in U.S.)—the hotel driveway starts at the ruins parking lot. A Club Med operation, the Villa Arqueológica has a swimming pool, tennis court, library, audio-visual show on the ruins in English, French, and Spanish, and 46 air-conditioned rooms that are fully modern. Room prices here are $52 single or double; $58 triple; meals are à la carte only.

Farther out, north of the ruins 1¼ miles on the highway, is the **Hotel Misión Uxmal** (tel. 24-7308), a new and modern 49-room hotel that you can't help but notice as you drive. Same services here: restaurant, bar, pool, etc. The comfortable, air-conditioned rooms go for $70 double.

Should you arrive at Uxmal without reservations and find that the nicer places are full, you do have one more option, but only if you have strong legs and a sun hat, or a car. The **Rancho Uxmal** (no phone), on Hwy. 261 north of the ruins 2¼ miles, is a modest little place with a thatched-roof restaurant, a few primitive camping spots, and 10 modest rooms with showers and fans. They go for $20 double. In the restaurant, most main-course plates cost around $5. It should take you about 30 minutes to walk to the ruins from here, but remember—that sun gets awfully hot.

Unidad Uxmal

There is a service center at the ruins, called the Unidad Uxmal. Within the modern complex are toilets, a first-aid station, a small museum, and shops (for publications, photo supplies, and craftwork). This is the place for a cold drink and excellent ice cream.

Otherwise, for an imformal, quick meal the Hacienda Uxmal has a little lunchroom and bar called the **Posada Uxmal, Café-Bar Nicte-Ha,** in a building right across the highway from the turnoff to the ruins. A ham and cheese sandwich costs about $4.50, a fruit salad $3.25. The café-bar is open from 1 to 8:30pm.

SEEING THE RUINS

The ruins of Uxmal are open from 8am to 5pm every day. Admission is $1.25; free on Sunday and holidays. (Inquire here about tour times if you'll be going to the caves of Loltún).

It can give you quite a thrill to ponder what Uxmal must have been like in its heyday: great lords and ladies clad in white embroidered robes and feathered headdresses moving here and there; market day, when the common people would come from their thatched huts and gather nearby in a tumultuous scene of barter and brouhaha. Uxmal flourished in the Late Classical Period, about A.D. 600 to 900, and then became subject to the Xiú princes (who may have come from the Valley of Mexico) after the year 1000. Four and a half centuries later, the Xiú conquered Mayapán (1440s). The conquistadores moved in shortly after, ending forever the glories of Maya cultural independence.

A 45-minute sound and light show is staged each evening, in Spanish for 80¢ at 7pm, and in English for $1.75 at 9pm. The special sound and light bus from Mérida only stays for the Spanish show. If you came on this bus for the show, you've got to find your own ride back to Mérida. After the impressive show, the chant "Chaaac, Chaaac" will echo in your mind for weeks.

The Pyramid of the Magician

As you enter the ruins, note first of all the *chultún* (cistern) just inside the fence to the right, the ticket booth being to your left. Besides the natural underground cisterns (such as cenotes) formed in the porous limestone, these chultúnes were the principal source of water for Maya civilization. You'll see more of them at Sayil and at sites near it.

After buying your ticket and walking a few steps farther, you'll be confronted with Uxmal's dominant building, the Pyramid of the Magician. Legend has it that a mystical dwarf who had hatched from an egg built this pyramid in one night, which is where it gets its name. Actually, there are several temples underneath the one you see. It was common practice for the Maya to build new structures atop old ones, even before the old structures were ruined.

The pyramid is unique because of its oval shape, its height and steepness (wait till you see the steps on the other side!), and its odd doorway. The doorway is on the opposite (west) side near the top, and is actually a remnant of the fourth temple built on this site (what you see today is the fifth). In contrast to the clean, simple style of the rest of the pyramid, the doorway is in Chenes style, with elaborate decoration featuring stylized masks of the rain god Chac. In fact, the doorway is a huge Chac mask, with the door as mouth.

The View from the Top

It's a tiring and even dangerous climb, but what a view! You're now in an ideal position to survey the rest of Uxmal. Next to the Pyramid of the Magician, to the west, is the Nunnery Quadrangle, so called (by the 16th-century Spanish historian Fray Diego Lopez de Cogullado) because it resembles a monastery or convent. To the left (south) of the Nunnery is the ruined ball court, and south of that are several large complexes. The biggest building, with a 320-foot-long façade, is called the Governor's Palace. Near it is the small House of the Turtles. Behind the Governor's Palace is the Great Pyramid, only partly restored, and beyond that the Dovecote, a palace with a lacy roofcomb that looks as though it'd be a perfect apartment complex for pigeons.

These are the main structures you'll notice from atop the Pyramid of the Magician, but there are others. For instance, the small ruined pyramid directly south is called the Pyramid of the Old Woman, which may be the oldest building at Uxmal. Due west of the pyramid is the Cemetery Complex, a temple with roofcomb that's pretty ruined. There's also a Northern Group, mostly covered with jungle and in ruins.

Uxmal is special among Maya sites because of the broad terraces or platforms constructed to support the building complexes—look closely and you'll see that the Governor's Palace is not on a hill or rise, but on a huge square terrace, as is the Nunnery Quadrangle.

Now that you've got your breath, prepare for the climb down. If you came up the east side, try going down the west.

The Nunnery

No nuns lived here. It's more likely this was a military academy or a training school for princes, who may have lived in the 70-odd rooms. The buildings were constructed at different times: The northern one was first, then the southern one, then east, then west. The western building has the most richly decorated façade, with interesting motifs of intertwined snakes. Masks of the rain god Chac, with his hooked nose, are everywhere. The richness of the geometric patterns on the façades is one of the outstanding features of Uxmal.

As you head toward the archway out of the quadrangle to the south, notice that above each doorway in the south building is a motif showing a Maya cottage, or *na,* looking just like you see them today. All of this wonderful decoration has been restored, of course —it didn't look this good when the archeologists discovered it.

The Ball Court

The ball court is ruined, and not so impressive. Keep it in mind, and compare it to the magnificent restored court at Chichén-Itzá.

The Turtle House

Up on the terrace south of the ball court is a little temple decorated with colonnade motif on the façade, and a border of turtles. It's small, but simple and harmonious—one of the gems of Uxmal.

The Governor's Palace

This is Uxmal's masterwork, an imposing edifice with a huge mural façade richly decorated in mosaic designs of the Puuc style. "Puuc" means "hilly country" and Uxmal has many examples of this rich decoration. The Puuc hills, which you passed over coming from Mérida, are the Maya "Alps," a staggering 350 feet high! Maya towns near the hills favored this style of geometric patterns and masks of Chac, giving the style its name.

The Governor's Palace may have been just that: the administrative center of the Xiú principality, which included the region around Uxmal. The Xiú rulers later conquered the emperors at Mayapán, and became supreme in the region. The fall of Mayapán allowed Yucatán to split into smaller principalities. It was just great for the conquistadores, who arrived less than a century after the fall of Mayapán and mopped up the principalities one by one. The great breaking up the hegemony of Mayapán.

Before you leave the Governor's Palace, note the elaborate stylized headdress patterned in stone over the central doorway.

The Great Pyramid

A massive structure partially restored, it has interesting motifs of birds, probably macaws, on its façade, as well as a huge mask—the Uxmalians went in for masks in a big way. The view from the top is wonderful.

The Dovecote

It wasn't built to house doves, but it could well do the job in its lacy roofcomb. The building is remarkable in that roofcombs weren't a common feature of temples in the Puuc hills, although you will see one (of a very different style) on El Mirador at Sayil if you visit that site.

LEAVING UXMAL

South and west of Uxmal are several other Maya cities well worth your exploration. Though the scale of these smaller cities is not as grand as that of Uxmal or Chichén-Itzá, each has its gems of Maya architecture. You will not be spending your time looking at the same old pyramids and temples. Rather, the great façade of masks on the Codz Poop at Kabah, the enormous palace at Sayil, and the fantastic caverns of Loltún may be among the highpoints of your trip.

Transportation to these sights is not easy. Though buses do run occasionally along the road south from Uxmal to Kabah, it is difficult to reach the other sites without a private car.

If you're off to Kabah, head southwest on Hwy. 261 to Santa Elena (8⅔ miles) then south to Kabah (8 miles).

---

4. Kabah

The ancient city of Kabah sits astride the highway, but you turn left into the parking lot. Buy your ticket from 8am to 5pm daily for 25¢.

The most outstanding building at Kabah is the one you notice first: that huge palace on a terrace. It's called the Palace of Masks, or **Codz Poop** ("rolled-up mat") from a motif in its decoration. Its outstanding feature is the façade, completely covered in masks of the hook-nosed rain god Chac. All those eyes, hooked noses, and grimacing mouths, used as a repeated pattern on a huge façade, have an incredible effect. There's nothing like this façade in all of Maya architecture.

Once you've seen the Palace of Masks, you've seen the best of Kabah. But you should take a quick look at the other buildings, and follow the paths into the jungle, for a look at the **Tercera Casa** (Third House), or "Las Columnas." This temple has fine colonnaded façades on both front and, even better, back.

Across the highway, you'll pass a conical mound (on your right) that was once the **Great Temple,** or Teocalli. Past it is a great arch. This triumphal arch was much wider at one time, and may have been a monumental gate into the city. For all their architectural achievements, the Maya never discovered the principle of the true arch made of many small fitted stones and a keystone. Instead, they used this corbelled arch, which is simply two flat stones leaned at an angle against one another. Compare this ruined arch to the one at Labná (below), which is in much better shape.

5. Sayil

About 3 miles south of Kabah is the turnoff (left, east) to Sayil, Xlapak, Labná, Loltún, and Oxkutzcab. Drive along 2½ miles and find the ruins of Sayil, just off the side of the road. The ruins are open from 8am to 5pm, and there's a small admission.

Sayil is famous for **El Palacio,** the tremendous 100-room palace that is a masterpiece of Maya architecture. The rows and rows of columns and colonettes give the building a Minoan appearance. There are some nice decorative details, but for the most part El Palacio impresses one by its grandeur and simplicity.

Off in the jungle past El Palacio is **El Mirador,** a small temple with a slotted roofcomb, an odd structure. Beyond El Mirador, a crude stele has a phallic idol carved on it, with greatly exaggerated proportions. The Maya didn't normally go in for this sort of thing, and this crude sculpture may well be unique.

Climb to the top of El Palacio if the heat is not too intense. The breeze up here is cooling, and the view of the Puuc hills delightful. Sometimes it's difficult to tell which are hills and which are unrestored pyramids, as little temples and galleries peep out at unlikely places from the jungle foliage. That large circular basin on the ground below the palace is a catch basin for a chultún (cistern). This region has no natural cenotes (wells) to catch rainwater, so the people had to make their own.

6. Xlapak

Back on the road, it's just under 3½ miles to Xlapak ("Shla-*pahk*"), a small site with one building. The Palace at Xlapak bears the inevitable rain god masks. If you do this tour of the ruins in the summer rainy season, it may be at this point that Chac responds to your earnest pleas for a break from the heat. When I was there, Chac let loose a downpour. It soaked through. Cool, though. Admission is free.

7. Labná

Labná is only about 1¾ miles past Xlapak, open 8am to 5pm. Admission is 25¢. The first thing you should look at here is the monumental arch. Good old Chac takes his place on the corners of one façade, and stylized Maya huts are fashioned in stone above the doorways. El Mirador, or **El Castillo** as it is also called, stands near the arch, with its roofcomb towering above it.

The **Palacio at Labná** is much like the one at Sayil: huge, restrained, monumental. It's not in quite as good shape as that at Sayil, but still impressive. In the decoration, find the enormous mask of Chac over a doorway, and also the highly stylized serpent's mouth, out of which pops a human head. *Note:* The afternoon light is best for photographs.

8. Loltún

About 18½ miles past Labná on the way to Oxkutzcab (that's "Ohsh-kootz-*kahb*") are the caverns of Loltún, on the left-hand side of the road. The entrance fee is $1.10 per person, and tours are given at 9:30am, 11am, and 12:30pm every day. Before driving out, you should confirm these times at the information desk at Uxmal.

No sign marks the entrance to the caves, so look for a tidy fence with a small park behind it, entered by a gravel drive. Wander in, and someone will fetch a guide. If they tell you that you've missed the last tour of the day, offer to pay a substantial tip (a few dollars) and you will get your tour.

You will also have to tip the guide at the end of the hour-long tour; I'd suggest a dollar or two if the tour has been a good one.

The caves are fascinating. Not only were they the home of ancient Maya but they were used as a refuge and fortress during the War of the Castes (1847–1901). You can examine statuary, wall carvings and paintings, chultúnes (cisterns), and other signs of Maya habitation. Besides the Maya artifacts, you'll be impressed by the sheer grandeur and beauty of the caverns themselves.

HEADING NORTH, SOUTH, EAST, WEST

From Loltún, you can drive the few miles to Oxkutzcab, and from there north on Hwy. 184 to Ticul, Muna, and Mérida (62 miles). Or you can head back past Sayil, then south on Hwy. 261 to Campeche. Those intrepid souls out to do a circuit of the northern peninsula can strike out southeast toward Tekax, Tzucacab, and Polguc on Hwy. 184. After about 124 miles you'll arrive in the town of Felipe Carrillo Puerto, where there are restaurants, hotels, banks, and gas stations. Carrillo Puerto thus serves as your jumping-off point for the tour north to Tulum, Xel-ha, Cozumel, and Cancún. See Chapter VI for more information.

THE ROAD TO CAMPECHE

Highway 261 heads south for several miles, then passes beneath a lofty arch that marks the boundary between the states of Yucatán and Campeche. You then pass through Bolonchén de Rejón (*bolonchén* means "nine wells").

Grutas de Xtacumbilxuna

Just under 2 miles south of Bolonchén you'll notice a sign on the side of the road pointing west to the Grutas de Xtacumbilxuna (though the sign spells it "Xtacumbinxunan"). The parking area is a half mile west of the highway—only a 10-minute walk.

Legend has it that a Maya girl, to escape an unhappy love affair, hid herself in these vast limestone caverns. It wouldn't be hard to do, as you'll see if you sign the guest register and follow the guide down for the 30- or 45-minute tour in Spanish (tip the guide at the end).

But if she did hide down here, the girl left no trace. Unlike the fascinating caves at Loltún, filled with traces of Maya occupation, these have only the standard bestiary of limestone shapes: a dog, eagle, penguin, madonna and child, snake, and so on, the fruit of the guide's imagination. The caves are open whenever the guide is around, which is most of the time.

Chenes Ruins

At Hopelchén there's a turnoff for Dzibalchén, near which you can see several unspoiled, unexcavated, all but undiscovered ruined cities in the Chenes style. You've got to be an explorer for these **Chenes ruins.** It's good if you have some food and water. Head for Dzibalchén, 25½ miles from Hopelchén, then begin asking for the way to Hochob, San Pedro, Dzehkabtun, El Tabasqueño, and Dzibilnocac.

From Hopelchén, Hwy. 261 heads west, and after 26 miles you'll find yourself at the turnoff for the ruined city of Edzná, 12½ miles farther along to the south.

Edzná

At one time, a network of Maya canals crisscrossed this entire area, making intensive cultivation possible, and no doubt contributing to Edzná's wealth as a ceremonial center. But today what you'll see at this "House of Wry Faces" (that's what *edzná* means) is a unique pyramid of five levels with a fine temple, complete with roofcomb, on top.

The buildings at Edzná were mostly in the Chenes, or "well country" style, so named because of the many wells found in the region. *Note:* The afternoon light is better for photographing the temple.

Back on Hwy. 261, it's about 8¾ miles to the intersection with Hwy. 180, and then another 19¼ miles to the very center of Campeche.

X

CAMPECHE: PIRATES' PRIZE

1. WHERE TO STAY
2. WHERE TO DINE
3. WHAT TO SEE AND DO

Capital of the state of the same name, Campeche (pop. 162,000) started life in 1517 as a military camp for the invading Spaniards under Francisco de Córdoba, but the town really came to life as a municipality after its founding by Francisco de Montejo as Salamanca de Campeche in 1531.

Being right on the shore, having no bay with headlands, or outlying islands, to protect it, Campeche was prey to constant attack by Caribbean pirates. The townspeople, fed up with these depredations by the late 1600s, poured money into construction of fortifications so massive that it was not worth the pirates' while to assault them. The city's system of *baluartes* (bulwarks, or ramparts) is still visible. Many of its strong points now serve as museums, libraries, and other public buildings. So the citizens of Campeche are still getting a return on their investment after almost three centuries!

Before the creation of Cancún, when most traffic into Yucatán came by road from Villahermosa and Ciudad del Carmen, Campeche benefited by being the last rest-stop on the drive to Mérida. But since the opening of the airport at Cancún, and the finishing of Hwy. 261 (which bypasses Campeche), tourist trade to Campeche has declined considerably. The city's economy now depends on its traditional source of wealth—harvesting fish, shrimp, and other crustaceans from the teeming waters of the gulf—and on its new bonanza, oil.

Though it is slightly out of the way, Campeche is a very pleasant coastal town with a smooth, leisurely pace, and many well-preserved colonial paving-stone streets and buildings. You won't regret a night spent here.

GETTING TO AND FROM CAMPECHE

By Air
Aeroméxico (tel. 981/6-6656 or 6-5628) flies once daily to both Mexico City and Cancún. If you happen to arrive by air, you'll have to take a taxi into town ($5).

By Train
Campeche's train station is about 1¼ miles northeast of the downtown waterfront, on Avenida Héroes de Nacozari, which intersects Avenida de los Gobernadores. A taxi should cost about $3.10 to the center, but there may not be any if you arrive in the wee hours of the morning. From Campeche there's a 2am train that continues to Palenque, arriving around noon there. Another train leaves for Mérida at 5pm and arrives there around 10pm. Readers have warned us of thievery on the Campeche to Palenque train, so be careful.

By Bus
First- and second-class buses arrive and depart from the terminal on Avenida Gobernadores, corner of Calle de Chile, about four blocks northeast of the **Baluarte de San Pedro (9).** You can walk to the center of town from here if your bags are not too heavy (turn left as you leave the station). Otherwise, a taxi to the hotels will cost a little over a dollar. (By the way, buses to Mérida run nine times a day.)

ORIENTATION
Virtually all of your time in Campeche will be spent within the confines of the old city walls. You'll certainly pass one of the old baluartes as you come toward the center of town, which is the modernistic Plaza Moch-Couoh on the waterfront, next to which rises the modern office tower called the Edificio Poderes or Palacio de Gobierno, headquarters for the State of Campeche. Next to this is the futuristic Cámara de Diputados, or Casa de Congreso, or state legislature's chamber, which looks somewhat like an enormous square clam.

Just behind it, the **Parque Principal** (central park) will more likely be your focal point for touring.

The city's two best hotels are within sight of the Palacio de Gobierno on the waterfront.

Finding an Address
Unlike most towns in Mexico, Campeche boasts a systematic street-naming plan whereby streets that run roughly north to south have even numbers, and those running east to west have odd num-

bers. Thus along Calle 14 you will cross in succession Calles 51, 53, 55, 57, etc., and if you turn right off Calle 14 onto Calle 51 you will cross Calles 12, 10, 8, etc., in your course down 51. Not to confuse you further, but the streets are numbered so that numbers ascend toward the south and west. After you get downtown and walk around for five minutes you'll have the system down pat. Bus, train, and airport terminals are all a good distance from downtown, and as Campeche is hardly a good town to negotiate by bus, I would recommend a taxi to get you from the various depots to the center.

FAST FACTS

Post Office: Look for the **Correos** (post office) in the **Edificio Federal (3)** (tel. 981/6-2134), at the corner of Avenida 16 de Septiembre and Calle 53, near the Baluarte de Santiago. The **telegraph office** is here as well.

Tourist Office (1): The state of Campeche operates a convenient and helpful tourist office (tel. 981/6-6068 or 6-6767) on the waterfront near the Palacio de Gobierno. Look for the modernistic bulwark with a slender vertical sign ("Turismo") on top. When you get to the structure, don't walk up the ramp toward the sign, but rather walk around to the right to reach the entrance, which faces the sea. Hours are 8am to 2:30pm and 4 to 8:30pm; closed Sunday and holidays. They speak some English and are very helpful. At the **ADO bus station** there's also a tourist information booth staffed daily except Sunday.

---

1. Where to Stay

Though Campeche's tourist trade has largely dried up, there are still some good places to stay.

TOP HOTELS

Right at the center of town, on the waterfront, are the city's two best but fairly ordinary hotels.

The **Ramada Inn (4)**, P.O. Box 251, Campeche 24000 (tel. 981/6-2233 or 6-4611), is officially at 51 Avenida Ruiz Cortines. Most of the 120 rooms and suites have views of the sea, and all have air conditioning, color television, servibar, and a terrace for sunset watching. Other extras include a swimming pool, fenced parking lot, plus a nice restaurant, bar, coffeeshop, and discothèque. Prices are quite reasonable for all this: $53 double; junior suites cost $2 to $6 more per room.

Just south of the Ramada Inn is Campeche's old standby, the 100-room **Hotel Baluartes (5)**, 61 Avenida Ruiz Cortines, Campeche 24000 (tel. 981/6-3911). This was the city's original luxury digs, but it's been extensively modernized, and now has all of the

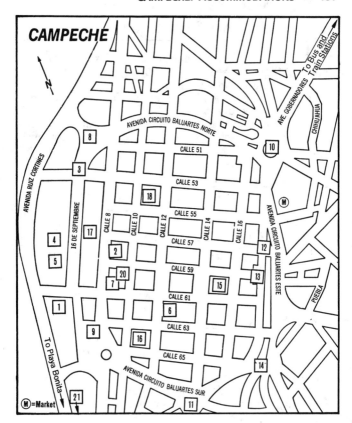

services of its neighbor, including air conditioning, swimming pool, and many rooms with sea views. Prices are $42 single and $46 double.

A guidebook such as this one contains literally hundreds of different facts and details. The data in this book have been carefully researched. But nothing stops the relentless march of time, and facts change daily. You can help us keep this guide current, and thus help future travelers to Mexico, by writing to us and describing your travel experiences south of the border. Our address is: Prentice Hall Travel, 15 Columbus Circle, New York, NY 10023. And thanks!

2. Where to Dine

The best all-around restaurant choice in Campeche is the **Restaurant Miramar (7)**, calles 8 and 61, very near the town hall building. The decor is pleasant, with lots of light-colored stone, arches, and some dark wood and ironwork. The menu offers typical Campeche seafood dishes: lightly fried, breaded shrimp (ask for "camarones empanizadas") for $7, arroz con mariscos (shellfish and rice) for $3.50, and for dessert, queso napolitana, a sort of very rich, thick flan for $1.25.

3. What to See and Do

"Campeche" is derived from the Maya name Ah Kim Pech. Founded in 1531, later abandoned, and refounded by Montejo the Younger in 1540, it became the springboard for the Montejo's conquest of Yucatán.

Campeche's dearth of tourists is a blessing, in a way, because it allows you to see this charming old city without the crowds.

CITY WALLS AND BULWARKS

As the busiest port in the region during the 1600s and 1700s, Campeche was a choice prize to pirates, who attacked it repeatedly starting as early as 1546. The Campechanos, eventually tired of the depredations, began construction of the city's impressive defenses in 1668. By 1704, all of the walls, gates, and bulwarks were in place.

Today, seven of the bulwarks remain, and four are worthy of a visit.

Baluarte de San Carlos

Southernmost of the seaside bulwarks, the **Baluarte de San Carlos/Museo de la Ciudad (9)** is near the modern Palacio de Gobierno at the intersection of the Circuito Baluartes and the Avenida Justo Sierra, near where Calles 63 and 8 meet. It's a good place to begin your tour, as it is now set up as the Sala de las Fortificaciones (Chamber of Fortifications). A permanent exhibition of photographs and city plans show the city in history. There's a model of the city too showing how the city looked in its glory days. Take a look here from Tuesday through Saturday from 8am to 8pm and Sunday until 1pm. There's a small admission.

Baluarte de la Soledad

Walk north along Calle 8, and you'll pass the Puerta de Mar, or Sea Gate, the ancient entry to the city enclosure from the port area. Just beyond the Puerta de Mar is the **Baluarte de la Soledad (17)**, or Bulwark of Solitude, just off the zócalo where Calles 57 and 8 meet. This bastion now houses the Sala de Estelas, or Chamber of Steles. The Maya votive stones were brought from various sites in this ruin-rich state. Many are badly worn, but the excellent line drawings beside the stones allow you to admire their former glory. Admission is free, and hours are the same as for the Baluarte de San Carlos.

The Plaza

While you're in the area, take a stroll through Campeche's pretty little zócalo, or Plaza de la Independencia, complete with cathedral. Construction of the church was begun in 1540, though it was frequently interrupted, and not completed for over a century and a half.

Baluarte de Santiago

Walk north along Calle 8 and at Calle 51 you'll come to the **Baluarte de Santiago (8),** northernmost of the seaside bulwarks, now fixed up as Campeche's Jardín Botánico (Botanical Gardens). This is the perfect place to take a breather in your walking tour, among the plants both common and exotic, on a bench in the cool shade. Want to learn about what you're seeing? The garden offers tours in English at noon and at 4pm, Tuesday through Saturday; in Spanish almost every hour in the morning and evening.

Admission to the Jardín Botánico is free. It's open on Tuesday through Saturday from 9am to 6pm, on Sunday from 9am to 1pm; closed Monday.

Baluarte de San Pedro

Head inland (east) on Calle 51, and at Calle 18 you'll see the **Baluarte de San Pedro (10),** where there's a crafts showroom called the Exposición Permanente de Artesanías. Besides the bastion itself, you can look over the products of Campechano craftspeople. Hours are as at the Baluarte de San Carlos.

Other Baluartes

If you're not tired yet, make the complete circuit of the bulwarks. Follow Calle 18 south, passing the **Baluarte de San Francisco (12)** at Calle 57, then the **Puerta de Tierra (13)** (Land Gate) at Calle 59, where there's a light and sound show on Friday at 9pm. Admission is around $2. The **Baluarte de San Juan (14),** at Calle 65, is where you turn west toward the sea. The **Baluarte de Santa Rosa (18),** at Calles 14 and 67 (Circuito Baluartes), is now a library.

Three blocks' walking brings you back to the Baluarte de San Carlos.

MUSEO REGIONAL DE CAMPECHE

Over the years, Campeche has moved its museum collections around quite a bit. The best of the lot have now come to rest in the

Museo Regional de Campeche (15), in the former mansion of the Teniente de Rey (Royal Governor) at Calle 59 no. 36, between calles 14 and 16.

The museum's displays are similar to those in the Palacio Cantón in Mérida. Pictures, drawings, and models are combined with original artifacts, bringing to life the ancient Maya culture. The curious skull-flattening deformation of babies is shown in the most direct way: with an exhibit of the actual deformed skulls. Another highlight is the Late Classic (A.D. 600–900) Maya stele carved in a metamorphic rock that does not exist in Yucatán, but was brought hundreds of miles from its quarry.

A model of the archeological site at Becán shows Maya society in daily life. Other displays demonstrate Maya architecture, techniques of water conservation, aspects of their religion, commerce, art, and their considerable scientific knowledge.

Hours for the museum are 8am to 2pm and 2:30 to 8pm on Tuesday through Saturday, 9am to 1pm on Sunday; closed Monday. Admission is free.

Museo de Campeche

Actually the restored **Templo de San José (16)** (St. Joseph Church), at the corner of calles 10 and 63, this is the venue for many traveling art exhibits that come to Campeche. Drop by to see what's up. Admission is free, and hours are the same as at the Museo Regional. Visit here Monday through Friday from 8am to 2pm and 5 to 8pm. It's free.

Museo Fuerte San Miguel

For the best panoramic views of the city head south on Calle 8 to the **Museo Fuerte San Miguel,** the most important of the city's defenses that was started in 1771. Turn at the sign "Ruta Escenica." Santa Anna used it when he attacked the city in 1842, but today it houses a small exposition of Mesoamerican culture and pre-Hispanic pottery from the area and a room of model ships. See it on Monday through Saturday from 8am to 8pm and on Sunday until 1pm.

STROLLING THROUGH CAMPECHE

One of this pleasant city's most enjoyable pastimes is simply to stroll along its colonial streets, particularly calles 55, 57, and 59. Many of the buildings are in classic Mexican colonial style. Glance through a grand doorway to find a fine courtyard, or a Moorish colonnade, or a few high-ceilinged rooms. Remember that Campeche was a wealthy port. Its merchants could afford to build themselves the best, and to live in style.

You'll probably hear about **Playa Bonita,** about 4 miles west of town, but unless you're really in need of some cooler air, I recommend saving your swimming for the Caribbean. The last time I was there the beach was pretty dirty and the water was not so appealing.

XI

PALENQUE: FABULOUS JUNGLE CITY

1. WHERE TO STAY
2. WHERE TO DINE
3. WHAT TO SEE AND DO

Lying west of the mighty Río Usumacinta in the wild and mountainous jungle province of Chiapas, Palenque was a unique and eccentric outpost of Maya culture. Strictly speaking, it is not part of the Yucatán peninsula. But as a masterwork of Maya art and architecture, it has no equal. With its great Temple of the Inscriptions built above a king's fabulous tomb, Palenque has intrigued archeologists, mythologists, and visitors for decades.

It's a long way from Cancún or Mérida to Palenque, but if you have the time, and a healthy interest in Maya culture, you'll want to make the pilgrimage.

GETTING TO AND FROM PALENQUE

The fastest way is by air, but you can also go by bus or car. You may end up going via Villahermosa, which is covered in the following chapter.

By Air

Aviacsa has direct daily flights between Tuxtla Gutiérrez and Palenque and on Monday, Wednesday, and Friday between Comitan near San Cristóbal and Ocosingo near Palenque. Contact the airline either through a travel agency or at their central office, Hangar de Govierno 2, Aeropuerto Francisco Sarabia, Tuxtla Gutiérrez, Chiapas 29000 (tel. 961/3-6751, or Fax 961/2-7405). **ATC Tours and Travel** (mentioned below under "Excursions") operates day trips by charter plane to or from San Cristóbal de las Casas. For the latter trip, there's a four-person minimum for a cost of $55 per person. It's possible that San Cristóbal's airport may function again in 1991 and flights would leave directly from that city.

By Train

Plans were shaping up to add a first-class *Estrella* train in 1991 between Mexico City and Mérida that would pass through Palenque. For current information when you travel, use the train contacts mentioned in Chapter XIII, "Fast Facts for Yucatán." At this writing, Train 49 passes through on its way to Campeche and Mérida from Mexico City. Many thefts have been reported on it, so use it with caution.

By Bus

From Villahermosa's second-class station there are two buses to Palenque, at 8 and 11am. From San Cristóbal there's one bus that leaves at 10am.

In Palenque three bus stations will serve most of your needs for getting in and out of the village. **Auto Transportes Tuxtla** (tel. 934/5-0369) is on Juárez on your right about a block from the Pemex station as you enter town. From here there are four buses daily to Tuxtla Gutiérrez and to San Cristóbal beginning at 7:30am. San Cristóbal de las Casas is a six-hour (minimum) trip. Two doors down is the **Terminal de Transportes** (no phone). It's known locally as the **Mérida station,** although only one bus daily goes to Mérida at 5pm. That's an eight-hour trip. The bus originates in Palenque, so chances of getting a seat are good if you buy a ticket a day in advance. Two buses a day go to Villahermosa, San Cristóbal de las Casas, and Tuxtla Gutiérrez and one goes to Ocosingo.

By Car

Highway 186 from Villahermosa is in good condition and the trip to Palenque should take about an hour and a half. From San Cristóbal the paved road is potholed in places and in some spots the road is washed out, causing traffic to slow to one lane. This is especially true in the rainy season between May and October.

To and from the Ruins

For 25¢, minivan service to and from the ruins runs every 10 minutes until 6pm from the **Chan Balu Collectivo Service** at Hidalgo and Allende.

ORIENTATION

From a Pemex station on Hwy. 186, a road turns right and heads for Palenque, 17 miles off the main road. First you'll come to Palenque Junction (the railroad station), then a few miles later to a fork in the road—there's an incredibly dramatic statue of a Maya here, so you can't miss it. Left at the fork takes you a mile or so into Palenque village (also known as Santo Domingo) with its two banks, restaurants, hotels, stores, and ice house. A right at the fork takes you past several motels to Palenque ruins; the ruins are 3½ miles from the fork. A taxi between the village and the ruins costs only about $4 and is worth it.

1. Where to Stay

There is one new fancy hotel on the outskirts of Palenque village and a few other places that provide quite acceptable accommodations. No longer are you forced to stay in Villahermosa if you want to sleep in comfort.

A TOP HOTEL

The nicest place to stay is the new **Hotel Misión Palenque** (mailing address: Domicilio Conocido, Rancho San Martín de Porres, Palenque, Chiapas 29960; tel. 934/5-0241 or 5-0110). It's located at the far end of town, a twenty-minute walk or a short taxi ride from the first-class bus station. The views of the lush, surrounding countryside are beautiful from here. There are 160 air-conditioned rooms with telephones, priced at $63 single, $67 double, or $71 triple, as well as a swimming pool and a restaurant/bar. Mexican dishes run $3 to $6, and chicken dishes cost $4.60 to $6.40. The hotel shuttles guests to and from the ruins four times a day.

MODERATELY PRICED HOTELS

The **Motel Nututum Viva,** Palenque, Chiapas 29960 (tel. 934/5-0100), is about 2 miles from the Maya statue along the road to the ruins, and then left on the road through the jungle to Ocosingo, Agua Azul, and San Cristóbal. The setting is beautiful, right on the Río Tulija, which provides excellent swimming in the cool river waters. The 40 air-conditioned rooms are huge, each with two double beds. The tiled rooms have large closets, bathtub, and shower. Prices are in the moderate category, and swimming in the river after a hot day at the ruins is a bonus. Singles cost $32, doubles, $40, and triples, $45. The hotel restaurant is inexpensive: Most meals cost $4.50 to $7; breakfasts cost $2.50.

A short distance back toward Villahermosa—only a half mile from the Maya-statue fork in the road, really—is the **Hotel Tulija,** Apdo. Postal 57, Palenque, Chiapas 29960 (tel. 934/5-0165), one of Palenque's more modern hotels with air-conditioned rooms going for $34 single, $37 double, $45 triple. The hotel restaurant offers a six-course comida at midday for $3.65, but the large-screen television may be more than one can endure. The hotel has a very nice swimming pool, and they take credit cards.

NEAR THE RUINS

Chan-Kah, Palenque, Chiapas 29960 (no phone), 2½ miles past the Maya statue on the road to the ruins, is a collection of 18 rooms in little stone and wood bungalows, rustic in design but modern in comfort. They are scattered throughout jungle-like landscaping, complete with a pool designed to look like a lake. Sliding glass doors open onto private patios. Each bungalow has a ceiling fan (no air conditioning), and is priced at $40 single, $45 double. Chan-Kah has its own thatched-roof dining room.

The **Hotel El Paraiso,** Carretera Las Ruinas, Km. 2.5, Palenque, Chiapas 29960 (tel. 934/5-0263), is a half mile from the monument and on the road to the ruins. You'll notice it first for the thatched-roof, rock-walled restaurant in front, which is large enough to be a dance hall. With colorful banners hanging from overhead beams, it appears ready for a continual party. Guest quarters, which are simple and clean with tile floors, are behind the restaurant. All eight of them rent for $30 single or double. Restaurant prices are moderate to high with fried chicken in the $3 range, soups from $1.20 to $2.70, and beef entrees between $3.60 and $6.

IN PALENQUE VILLAGE

Besides the Hotel Misión on the outskirts, the only place to stay in Palenque village is a bright, fairly new mini-hotel called the **Hotel Casa de Pakal** (no phone), on the main street (Avenida Juárez) near the central park. Each of the 14 rather small rooms here comes with that blessed air conditioning, for $15 single, $20 double. The hotel has a fancy restaurant called **El Castellano**.

The **Hotel Canada,** at the far end of Calle Merle Green (no phone), Palenque, Chiapas 29960 (tel. 934/5-0102, or Fax 5-0392), is a group of tidy cottages surrounded by dense woods and thus is pretty secluded. Rooms can be a bit musty but are quite comfortable. The price for these rooms is $22 single and $27 double. Rooms 7, 8, 9, and 10 across the street from the office are particularly good values. Each is equipped with air conditioning and a huge ceramic bathtub.

2. Where to Dine

Hardly a culinary mecca, Palenque has mostly very basic, no-frills eateries. In addition to dining at the Misión, Avenida Juárez is lined with many small restaurants, but quality and prices are inconsistent. To be safe, I'd stick to the ones mentioned below.

A five-minute walk from the statue toward the ruins is **La Selva** (tel. 5-0363), the best restaurant in Palenque. Though the restaurant has a thatched roof, inside you'll find a large, refined, and accommodating place to dine. Main-course dishes such as *pollo Palenque* (chicken with potatoes in a tomato and onion sauce) and *lomo de cerdo* (pork chops) cost $3.75 to $4.25. Figure that a full meal will cost twice that amount. Surprise of surprises, La Selva has a very respectable (for Palenque) assortment of Mexican wines. And for dessert, the flan ($1.25) is especially smooth and creamy. You'll enjoy your meal here. Frequently live music is provided for diners' enjoyment.

If you stand staring head-on in rapture (or horror) at the Maya statue at the fork in the road, just off to your left will be a wooded area, a partially paved road (Calle Merle Green), and at the end of that road is restaurant **La Cañada** (tel. 5-0102). You can get a tasty supper of chicken tacos or quesadillas and a cold bottle of beer for a mere $4; meat dishes cost twice that amount. Near the quaint dirt-floored restaurant a two-story "club" throbs to disco music. It never seems to be crowded, although it's the ideal setting for a *Night of the Iguana* romance.

Even if you do not stay or dine along Calle Merle Green, a stroll along this shady street is enjoyable. Several interesting shops are busy making and selling quality reproductions of Maya art.

In the village proper, look for the **Restaurant Maya** (no phone), facing the central park near the Correos (post office). It's breezy, open, family-run, and the most popular place in town among the tourists. Don't expect anything approaching prompt service. Fixed-price breakfasts cost between $2 to $3.50; the hearty vegetable soup is a mere $1.50; standard dishes cost $2.50 to $6; beer is 90¢. Come any time between 7am and 11pm daily.

---

3. What to See and Do

Palenque, now protected in the Parque Nacional Palenque, is one of the most spectacular of the Maya ruins with its roof-combed temples ensconced in lush vegetation high above the savannahs. It was a ceremonial center for the high priests during the Classical Period (A.D. 300–900), with the peak of its civilization being somewhere around A.D. 600–700. Pottery found during the excavations shows that there was a very early, pre-Classic people living here as early as 300 B.C. Alberto Ruíz Lhuillier, the archeologist who directed some of the explorations, states that because of "the style of its structures, its hieroglyphic inscriptions, its sculptures, its works in stucco and its pottery, Palenque undoubtedly fell within the great Maya culture. Yet its artistic expressions have a character all their own which is evident in the absolute mastery of craftsmanship, turning the art of Palenque into the most refined of Indian America."

See above, under "Orientation," for transportation details.

HOURS

The Palenque ruins are open from 8am to 5pm, although the crypt (see below) closes at 4pm. The entrance fee is small, and on Sunday it's free. By the way, a quarter mile back toward town from the parking lot, on the right-hand side (as you approach from town), is a path leading into the Cascada Motiepa, a cool, beautiful waterfall good for cooling the feet and resting the soul. Watch the mosquitos, though.

The small museum (open 8am to 5pm) has a chronological chart of Maya history, and a modest collection of votive figurines, pieces of statuary, and stones with calendar glyphs. Entrance is free once you have paid for access to the park. Be sure you save your ticket.

Plan to spend a whole day in these wonderful surroundings. When you're tired of looking at ruins, grab your bathing suit and head for the gorgeous stream and falls near the tiny museum at the end of the dirt track that goes past the "Grupo del Norte" complex of structures. A sign by the stream informs you (in Spanish) that there is no bathing allowed, but downstream a ways is a large pool out of view.

GUIDES

The official price for a two- or three-hour tour of the ancient city is $20. Some of the guides are quite knowledgeable.

TEMPLE OF THE INSCRIPTIONS

As you enter the ruins, the building to the right is the Temple of the Inscriptions, named for the great stone hieroglyphic panels found inside (most of them are now in the Archeological Museum in Mexico City) and famous for the tomb that was discovered in its depths in 1949. It took four seasons of digging to clear out the rubble that was put there by the Maya to conceal the crypt. The crypt itself is some 80 feet below the floor of the temple and was covered by a monolithic sepulchral slab 10 feet long and 7 feet wide. You can visit the tomb, and as long as you're not a claustrophobe, you shouldn't miss it. The way down is lighted, but the steps can be slippery due to condensed humidity—watch it! This is the only such temple-pyramid (resembling the Egyptian pyramids) in the Americas!

OTHER BUILDINGS

Besides the Temple of the Inscriptions, there is the Palace with its unique watchtower, the northern group (Temple of the Count and Ball Court), and the group of temples beyond the Palace (Temple of the Sun, Temple of the Foliated Cross). The official guidebook has a detailed description of this site and is well worth the money. (For a summary of pre-Columbian history, see Chapter I of this book.)

EXCURSIONS FROM PALENQUE

Popular side trips from Palenque include the day trip to Agua Azul Falls and overnight excursions to the Maya ruins of Bonampak and Yaxchilán.

Agua Azul

About 38½ miles from Palenque is the well-marked turnoff, on the right, to Agua Azul. From the road it's another 2¾ miles on a painfully broken road down the hill into the valley to reach the swimming area. The park at Agua Azul is owned and operated by an *ejido* (cooperative of owners). Pass through a gateway and pay the person on duty a small admission. Past the gateway is a parking lot, a shaded snack and soft drink place, and a camping area that charges a small fee.

Behind this are the falls, a long, broad series of cascades with sunny spots and shady spots perfect for swimming. The water is delightfully cool and is the most striking shade of pale blue (azul) I have ever seen in fresh water. The water turns a slightly milky color during the rainy season but remains oh, so cool. *Note:* Wander up and down the river, but heed the signs about where to swim—some places are dangerous.

Other than driving yourself, the most convenient way to reach Agua Azul is by collectivo van. For $5, minivans from the **Chan Balu Colectivo Service** (mentioned above) make the round trip to Agua Azul and the Cascada de Misol Ha every day (in theory) at 10am, returning to Palenque by 3pm. This allows for 30 minutes at Misol Ha and two hours at Agua Azul. They may wait until six or eight persons want to go, so check with them a day or two in advance of your proposed trip.

Bonampak and Yaxchilán

Marco Morales Fimbres, owner of **Viajes Shivalva,** will take you by four-wheel-drive vehicle to within 4½ miles of Bonampak. You must walk the rest of the way to the ruins, famous for their frescos. After camping overnight, you continue by river to the extensive ruins of the great Maya city, Yaxchilán. The trip costs $90 per person, with a five-person minimum. Morales also runs tours to Guatemala. His office is at Calle Merle Green 1, Apdo. Postal 237, Palenque, Chiapas 29960 (tel. 934/5-0411, or Fax 5-0392). Another agency, **ATC Tours and Travel,** also operates a similar trip to both ruins. Drop in or write them at Allende corner of Juárez, Palenque, Chiapas 29960 (tel. 934/5-0201, or Fax 5-0356). Their headquarters are in San Cristóbal at the El Fogon Restaurant. The **Chan Balu Colectivo Service** at Hidalgo and Allende in Palenque also advertises the trip, but there may be delays waiting for a group to accumulate and the quality of the trip may be rough. At least five people are needed to make the trip. The cost of the two-day trip is $70 per person and includes transportation and supposedly food and overnight lodging. One reader reported that the colectivo didn't provide food and they slept on wood planks in a partially walled building.

XII

VILLAHERMOSA: OIL BOOM TOWN

1. WHERE TO STAY
2. WHERE TO DINE
3. WHAT TO SEE AND DO

Villahermosa (pop. 250,000) always had some regional importance as the capital of the state of Tabasco. But since the discovery of extremely rich oil fields in the state, Villahermosa has been a veritable boom town. Huge amounts of money have cascaded in from petroleum investors and buyers of petroleum products. In a matter of a decade, Villahermosa has moved from being a sleepy state capital to a medium-sized city with growing pains.

First results of the boom were raw and undisciplined: Frantic building of highways, offices, oil field infrastructure, and hotels kept the city in chaos. Now, however, things have calmed down a bit, and the city's leaders have had some time to smooth the rough edges and to add the nice touches that may well make this town a "beautiful city," as its name announces. The Regional Museum of Anthropology, the archeological museum-in-a-park called La Venta, the new park-like office and leisure developments, the pedestrian streets in the heart of town—all have added considerably to the enjoyment of life in this city. And all are the direct result of the wealth brought in by oil.

For the visitor to Yucatán, Villahermosa is a transit point. Whether you fly to Yucatán via Mexico City and plan a stop in Palenque, or whether you fly from Mérida or Cancún expressly to visit that fascinating city, you will spend little more than a night or two in Villahermosa.

You can spend a full day here seeing the sights and getting a sense of place, and you will enjoy it—except for the heat. I know of few other places in Mexico where the heat seems so persistent, moisture-laden, and intense. Remember this when you look for a hotel room, and get one with air conditioning. Also remember it when you plan your sightseeing excursions. Hike through the Parque La Venta in the freshness of morning, and then take a siesta, or visit the air-conditioned regional museum, during the heat of the day. Save the evening for a stroll along the pedestrian streets and along the Río Grijalva, which cuts right through the center of town.

GETTING TO AND FROM VILLAHERMOSA

Travelers to Villahermosa come by road, air, bus, and perhaps soon by train.

By Air

Coming in from Villahermosa's airport, which is 6½ miles east of town, you'll cross a bridge over the Río Grijalva and turn left to reach downtown. The airport minibuses charge $3 whereas taxis want $6 at least.

The **Mexicana** ticket office is inconveniently located at the huge Tabasco 2000 complex next to the Palacio Municipal (tel. 931/3-5044, 3-5487, or 2-1164 at the airport). **Aeroméxico** has an office at the Plaza Cicom Centro between the Teatro Esperanza Iris and the Museo Carlos Pelicer (tel. 931/2-6991, 2-528, or 2-0904 at the airport). Viajes Tabasco, a travel agency, Madero 718, represents **Aviacion de Chiapas (Aviacsa)** (tel. 931/40978 or 4-2780), which flies direct to Tuxtla Gutiérrez with connections to Oaxaca and the Bays of Huatulco on the Oaxaca coast. **Aero Caribe** is at Mina 1202 near corner of Paseo Tabasco (tel. 931/4-3017 or 4-3202), but they are closed between 2 and 4:30pm. It's the new regional carrier flying between Villahermosa, Ciudad del Carmen, and Mérida with connections to Cancún, Cozumel, Chetumal, and Chichén-Itzá. **AeroLittoral,** another regional airline (tel. 931/4-3614 at the airport), flies to Tampico, Minatitlán, Ciudad Carmen, and Monterrey.

By Train

By the time you travel there may be a train to Mérida from Mexico City that makes a stop in Villahermosa. See Chapter XIII, "Fast Facts for Yucatán" for how to get current train information.

By Bus

There are two bus stations in Villahermosa three blocks or so apart. The first-class **ADO** station (tel. 2-1226 or 2-8900) is at Mina and Merino, three blocks off Hwy. 180. Pick any place in Mexico and you'll find a bus going there from Villahermosa. **Omnibus Cristóbal Colón** (tel. 931/2-2937) sells tickets to Tuxtla Gutiérrez, San Cristóbal de las Casas, Tapachula, Oaxaca, and Mexico City from a small corner office in the ADO station. (For Palenque use the second-class station mentioned below.) A helpful **tourist assistance desk** is staffed there weekdays from 7am to 9pm and until 1pm on Saturday.

The **Central Camionera de Segunda Clase** (second-class bus station) is on Hwy. 180/186 near the traffic circle bearing a statue of a fisherman. Buses marked "Mercado—C. Camionera" leave frequently from the bus station for the center of town. A taxi from either station will cost around $2.

It's one of the sleeziest stations in Mexico, but you can get buses to Palenque from here at 8 and 11am on **Sureste del Caribe.** That line also goes to Tuxtla and Campeche at 6 and 11am, 3 and 7pm, and to Mérida four times daily. **Servicio Somellera** goes to Comalcalco every 30 minutes. **Autobuses Unidos de Tabasco (AU)** travel to Veracruz.

By Car

The paved Hwy. 195 connects the Tabascan capital of Villahermosa with Tuxtla Gutiérrez, the capital of the state of Chiapas. Daily Cristóbal Colón buses ply the route from the tropical savannahs into the rugged Chiapan mountains, and the trip will take around 12 hours. Between Villahermosa and San Cristóbal de las Casas the road, although paved, may be heavily potholed in places. Sometimes a portion of the roadway caves in and traffic slows to one lane to avoid it. These conditions occur more frequently during the rainy season between May and October. The trip to San Cristóbal takes a minimum of 10 hours from Villahermosa. The paved, mountainous (and very curvy) road between San Cristóbal to Tuxtla is in good condition and the trip takes about 90 minutes. (Road repairs were in progress just outside Tuxtla, but they should be finished when you are there.)

ORIENTATION

The hotels and restaurants I recommend are located on Hwy. 180 or off the three main streets running north and south: Madero, Pino Suárez, and the Malecón. Highway 180 skirts the city, so a turn onto Madero or Pino Suárez will take you into the center of town.

Your point of focus in town can be the **Plaza Juárez,** or main square, bounded by the streets named Zaragoza, Madero, Sánchez, and Carranza. The plaza is the center of the downtown district, with the Río Grijalva to its west and Hwy. 186 to its north. If Villahermosa can be said to have a main downtown thoroughfare, then it is **Avenida Madero,** running south from Hwy. 186 past the Plaza de Armas to the river, where it intersects with the riverside avenue, the **Malecón.**

FAST FACTS

The main **Tourist Office** in the Tabasco 2000 complex, Paseo Tabasco 1504, SEFICOT building, Centro Administartivo del Gobierno (tel. 931/5-0693), is as inconvenient to reach as the name is long. It's opposite the Liverpool department store and is open from 9am to 3pm and 6 to 8pm on Monday through Friday and on Saturday between 9am and 1pm. There are three other branches: at the **airport,** staffed between 7am and 9pm on Monday through Saturday; at the **ADO bus station,** the same hours; and at **La Venta Park** from 8am to 3pm on Monday through Saturday. They can supply rates and telephone numbers for all the city's hotels as well as useful telephone numbers for bus companies, airlines, etc.

1. Where to Stay

Prices for hotel rooms in Villahermosa were once fairly high, when oil personnel had lots of money to spend. Now that oil prices have dropped, so have other prices in this town. You may be surprised at what is charged for a luxury hotel room.

TOP HOTELS

You'd expect to find Hyatt hotels in New York City, Cancún, Los Angeles, Acapulco . . . and Villahermosa? Yes, indeed. The **Hyatt Villahermosa,** Avenida Juárez 106, Villahermosa, Tabasco 86000 (tel. 931/3-4444, or toll free 800/228-9000 in U.S.), has 261 luxurious rooms with all of the Hyatt comforts, priced at what can only be described as unluxurious prices: $81 double. The dining room is lovely.

Competing with the Hyatt for the upscale trade is the 256-room **Hotel Villahermosa Viva,** Avenida Adolfo R. Cortinos 1201, Villahermosa, Tabasco 86000 (tel. 931/5-0000), out on Hwy. 180/186. Here, a luxury double with color TV and air conditioning costs $50. There's a pool of course and it's within walking distance of La Venta Park.

The **Hotel Maya Tabasco,** Avenida Grijalva s/n, Villahermosa, Tabasco 86000 (tel. 931/2-1111), down by the river in the midst of town, has 100 air-conditioned rooms within walking distance of the center for $40 single or double; there's a pool here, too.

MODERATELY PRICED HOTELS

The area around the intersections of Avenidas Juárez and Lerdo is now one of the best places to stay, for these two streets have been closed to cars and made into pedestrian malls. The best value in town, within walking distance of this area and the plaza, is **Choco's Hotel,** Avenida Constitución at Lino Merino (tel. 931/2-9444 or 2-9649). A single room costs $26 and a double runs $28. For that you get a clean room with carpeting, television, and air conditioning.

The two-story **Hotel Madan,** Avenida Piño Suarez 105, Villahermosa, Tabasco 86000 (tel. 931/21650), is another convenient downtown lodging choice. It's between Reforma and Lerdo and attached to the popular Restaurant Galerias Madan, which faces Madero. The 20 pleasant rooms all with bath are clean, carpeted, air-conditioned, and have color TV. There's a comfortable sitting room and cold water dispenser on the second floor. Rates are $21 single and $23 double.

Near the Bus Stations

Just off Hwy. 186, not far from the first- and second-class bus stations, is the **Hotel Ritz,** Avenida Madero 1009, Villahermosa, Tabasco 86000 (tel. 931/2-1611), one block in from the highway. Its three modern stories hold 72 good rooms at $30 single, $32 double, all with window air conditioners, color TV, and telephone.

While it's a block off the highway, the Ritz is not subject to any more noise than other Villahermosa hotels. Note, however, that this is not a choice particularly for those arriving late at night by bus—like other hotels in this city, it's almost sure to be full by early evening, at the latest.

2. Where to Dine

Situated in a lobby of shops, the delightfully air-conditioned **Galerias Madan,** Madero 408 (tel. 21650), serves a worthwhile comida of soup rice, pollo, mole, vegetables, coffee, and dessert for only $3.75. Antojitos, hamburgers, and set-price breakfasts are under $3. Open daily for all three meals.

Another good air-conditioned choice is **Cheje,** 732 Madero (no phone). This pleasant bamboo-paneled restaurant serves tipico meals for $2 to $5, as well as barbecued meat and fish specialties for $4.25 to $8.50. Stop in between 8am and 11pm any day.

Another choice for pleasant, economical dining is **Chilango's Snack** at 5 de Febrero and Guerrero (tel. 2-3014), on the tree-shaded Plaza Corregidora a half a block from the Museo de la Historia. Eat outside or in the open-air restaurant. The set-price lunch for $2.40 comes with soup and the plate special of meat, rice, and a vegetable. Breakfast runs $1 to $2, antojitos 75¢, and beer 50¢ to 75¢. Open from 7:30am to 9pm daily.

For **pastries,** drop in at **La Baguette,** Juárez 301 (no phone), across the pedestrian-only street from the Museo de la Historia. As the name implies, French bread is the specialty and on a back wall you'll see fresh loaves of it lined up like 2-foot long sentries. It's bagged and sold as fast as it hits the shelves for 35¢ each. Other cases hold French and Mexican pastries. Go any time Monday through Saturday between 9am and 9pm.

3. What to See and Do

Two museums, one outdoors, one indoors, are cultural highpoints of any visit to this city. There is also an interesting minor museum.

PARQUE MUSEO LA VENTA

This is a lovely outdoor museum park located outside Villahermosa on Hwy. 180 (take Paseo Tabasco northeast to Hwy. 180, turn right, and it's less than a mile on your right, next to the Exposition Park). As you walk through on a self-guided tour you'll see Olmec relics, sculptures, mosaics, a mockup of the original La Venta, and of course the colossal Olmec heads. These heads were carved around 1000 B.C., are 6½ feet high, and weigh around 40 tons. The faces seem to be half-adult, half-infantile with that fleshy "jaguar mouth" that is characteristic of Olmecan art. Even stranger is the fact that the basalt, for carving, had to be transported from the nearest source, which was over 70 miles from La Venta! A total of 13 heads have been found: 5 at La Venta, 6 at San Lorenzo, 1 at Tres Zapotes, and 1 at Santiago Tuxtla—all cities of the Olmecs. On your tour through the park, notice the fine stone sculptures and artistic achievements of the Olmecs, who set forth the first art style in Mesoamerica. Their exquisite figurines in jade and serpentine, which can be seen in the Regional Museum of Anthropology, far excelled any other craft of this period.

La Venta, by the way, was one of three major Olmec cities during the Preclassic Period (2000 B.C. to A.D. 300). The ruins were discovered in 1938, and there in the tall grasses were the mammoth heads. Today all that remains of the once-impressive city are some grass-covered mounds—once pyramids—some 84 miles west of Villahermosa. All of the gigantic heads have been moved from the site. You'll see three heads in Parque La Venta.

Parque Museo La Venta is open from 8am to 4:30pm every day: admission is around $1 to nonresidents.

REGIONAL MUSEUM OF ANTHROPOLOGY

Tabasco's Museo Regional de Antropología Carlos Pellicer Cámara was opened in February 1980 to replace the older Tabasco Museum. The new museum is architecturally bold and attractive, and very well organized inside. There is more space and therefore the number of pre-Columbian artifacts on display has greatly increased to include not only the Tabascan finds (Totonac, Zapotec, and Olmec) but the rest of the Mexican and Central American cultures as well.

The museum is beautiful, with parquet floors, wood dividers, and numerous plants. There is a very open and airy feeling about this place. Take the elevator to the top of the museum and walk down past large maps showing the Olmec and Mayan lands. Photographs and diagrams make it all easier to comprehend, but the explanatory signs are all in Spanish. Look especially for figurines that were found in this area and for the colorful *Codex* (an early book of pictographs).

The Regional Museum is a mile south of the center of town, right along the river's west bank, open every day from 9am to 8pm; admission is free.

The **Museo de Historia de Tabasco** (also referred to as the Casa de los Azulejos), at the corner of 27 de Febrero and Juárez, is another nice place to spend a half hour or so. Every room is decorated with tiles in the Spanish Italian baroque style. The museum presents the history of Tabasco from pre-Columbian times to the present through documents, artifacts, and pictures. Only a few explanations are in English. Open daily from 9am to 8pm; free admission.

The small **Museo de Cultura Popular,** Calle Zaragoza 810 at Hidalgo, is another museum worth a visit. It's a short three-block walk from the Museo de la Historia and near the post office. As you enter, on the right there's a small gift shop with baskets, carved gourds, needlepoint regional clothing, and chocolate from Tabasco. Displays in the next room show the state's regional clothing and dance costumes. In the back is a Chontal hut, complete with typical furnishings and a recorded conversation of two female villagers talking in Chontal about the high cost of living. Student guides are often on hand for a free explanation. One of them explained that he grew up in a hut like the one on display, but today there are only two huts remaining like it in his village of Tecoluta. Another room shows ceremonial pottery and household utensils. Museum hours are 9am to 8pm daily and it's free.

EXCURSIONS FROM VILLAHERMOSA

The two most popular sidetrips from Villahermosa are to the ruins of Palenque and the ruins of Comalcalco.

Palenque

To the ruins of Palenque, in the neighboring state of Chiapas southeast of Villahermosa, is a pleasant two-hour drive from Villahermosa over good roads. Travel agencies in Villahermosa will arrange the trip or you can catch one of the two morning buses from the second-class station mentioned under "By Bus" above.

Comalcalco

Comalcalco, near the Gulf of Mexico northwest of Villahermosa, is the only pyramid site in Mexico made of kilned stone. From the second-class station buses leave for the site every 30 minutes. Travel agencies in Villahermosa offer a Comalcalco day trip for $45. Generally the bus leaves at 8am and returns around 5pm. The price includes transportation, guide, and entry to the ruins, but not lunch.

XIII

FAST FACTS FOR YUCATÁN

Though Mexico is close to the United States and Canada in many ways, it is also vastly different. Lots of the simple daily chores you do at home without even thinking can become major obstacles to happiness when you attempt to do them in a foreign country. Pay telephones work differently; banks don't have those handy money machines; buses operate on very different rules; and the Mexican post office won't accept your postcards if they don't bear Mexican postage stamps.

The solutions to these and many other daily travel problems are found below, in alphabetical order.

ABBREVIATIONS: **Apdo.** = post office box; **Av.** = Avenida; **"C"** on faucets stands for *caliente* (hot) and **"F"** stands for *fría* (cold); **C.P.** = Codigo Postal (postal or "zip" code); **P.B.** in elevators is for Planta Baja, ground floor.

AIRLINES: Although airlines in Mexico say it is not necessary to reconfirm a flight, I always do. On several occasions over the years, I have arrived at check-in with a valid ticket only to discover my reservation had been canceled. Now I leave nothing to chance. In addition, because of the airline industry's general overbooking policy, I check in for an international flight the required 90 minutes in advance of travel. That puts me near the head of the line and I've never been bumped due to overbooking.

AUTO MECHANICS: Your best guide is the **Yellow Pages.** For specific makes and shops that repair them, look under *Automoviles y Camiones: Talleres de Reparación y Servicio;* auto-parts stores are listed under *Refacciones y Accesorios para Automoviles.*

I've found the Ford and Volkswagen dealerships in Mexico to give prompt, courteous attention to my car problems, and prices for repairs are, in general, much lower than in the United States or Canada. I suspect that other big-name dealerships—General Motors, Chrysler—give similar, very satisfactory service. Oftentimes they will take your car right away and service it in a few hours—a thing almost unheard of at home.

Mexico imports lots of U.S. cars of all makes, and the

country manufactures a tremendous number of Volkswagens (using the old 1600 engine).

BANKS (SEE ALSO "MONEY"):

In Mexico, banks tend to be open from 9am to 1:30pm, Monday through Friday. Although they open earlier, you'll save time at the bank or currency-exchange booths by arriving no earlier than 10am. Generally they don't receive the official rate for that day until shortly before then, and they won't exchange your money until they have the current information.

Large airports have currency-exchange counters that supposedly stay open as long as flights are arriving or departing. Otherwise, ask at airport shops.

Many banks south of the border have an employee who speaks English.

For the fastest and least complicated service, traveler's checks or cash are the best things to carry. You can usually get a cash advance on your credit card in 20 minutes or less. Personal checks may delay you for weeks—the bank will wait for it to clear before giving you your money. For money by wire, see "Money."

BRIBES:

Called *propina* (tip), *mordida* (bite), or worse, the custom is probably almost as old as humankind. Bribes exist in every country—as one sees upon picking up a daily newspaper—but in Third World countries the amounts tend to be smaller and collected more often.

BUSES:

Bus travel is the most popular form of transportation in Mexico. More and more foreign tourists are choosing to travel this way, and so here's a glossary of bus terms you'll find useful:

Bus	**Autobus**
Bus or Truck	**Camión**
Nonstop	**Directo**
Baggage (claim area)	**Equipajes**
Intercity	**Foraneo**
Gates	**Llegadas**
Bus that originates at this station	**Local**
Bus originating elsewhere; stops if seats are available	**Paso, de paso**
First (class)	**Primera**
Baggage claim area	**Recibo de Equípajes**
Waiting Room	**Sala de Espera**
Toilets	**Sanitarios**
Second (class)	**Segunda**
Nonstop	**Sin Escala**
Ticket window	**Taquilla**

Unfortunately, unlike elsewhere in Mexico, bus travel in the

Yucatán can be quite inconvenient. The new bus stations and sleek new buses that are revolutionizing bus travel in the rest of Mexico haven't arrived in the Yucatán. Thus it's disappointing to discover that several of the peninsula's most important stations (Cancún and Villahermosa, for example) are swarthy and overcrowded transportation hubs. If you use buses in the Yucatán, be sure to allow plenty of travel time. And it's best to buy your ticket (and thus reserve your seat) a day in advance, or even more than a day in the case of very long-distance and international buses, and those running on holidays.

CAMERAS AND FILM: Both are more expensive than in the States; take full advantage of your 12-roll film allowance, and bring extra batteries. A few places in resort areas advertise developing for color film, but it might be cheaper to wait until you get home.

If you're really into the sport, bring an assortment of films at various ASA/DIN speeds as you will be photographing against glaring sand, in gloomy Maya temples, in dusky jungles, through hazy humidity. The proper filters are a help, as well. *Note:* Without a permit, tripods are not permitted at archeological sites anywhere in Mexico; there's no rule about monopods though. Travelers attempting to use a video camera at the ruins may also discover there's a charge, which is usually payable at the entrance.

CAMPING: It's easy and relatively cheap south of the border if you have a recreational vehicle or trailer, a bit less easy if you're tenting. Some agencies selling Mexican car insurance in the United States will give you a free list of campsites if you ask. The AAA has lists of sites. The *RV Park & Campground Directory* (Prentice Hall Press) covers Mexico.

Campgrounds here tend to be slightly below the standards of northern ones (with many attractive exceptions to this rule, though). Remember that campgrounds fill up just like hotels during the winter rush-to-the-sun and at holiday times. Get there early.

CAR RENTALS: The car-rental business in Mexico is as far flung and well developed as in Europe and the United States, with the usual problems and procedures. As elsewhere, it's good to reserve your car in advance in Mexico, an easy task when you fly into the country, as most airlines will gladly make the reservation for you.

With a credit card (American Express, VISA, MasterCard, and so forth) rentals are simple if you're over 25, in possession of a valid driver's license, and have your passport with you. Without a credit card you must leave a cash deposit, usually a big one.

You can save yourself some money by reserving a car seven days in advance before you leave the States and by renting only as much car as you *need:* Make sure that the company you select offers the VW Beetle or Datsun—usually the cheapest car—if that will do, and make sure they will have one on hand to rent you. (Sometimes they'll say they do over the phone, but when you arrive at the office the cheapest cars will be "all booked up" for two weeks, etc.) So ask if you are guaranteed the quoted rate even if that size isn't available when you arrive (that guarantee is common when reserving in the States). Take the name of the person you spoke with and ask for your confirmation number and keep it handy. It also pays to shop price before renting, as there are great variations. And pay attention to insurance deductibles. Lets hope you don't have an accident, but if you did, one company may charge you the first $250 of the cost of repair whereas another may charge $1,000. Weekly advance rentals often have unlimited mileage, which can result in considerable savings. Be sure to double-check all math on the rental form; if you were quoted rates in the States, be sure they are the same after the peso conversion appears on the form. Return the car with the same level of gas; rental companies can sock it to you with the price of their gas.

Don't underestimate the cost of renting a car. The total amount you'll be out-of-pocket for a short one-day trip to, say, Tulum and Xel-ha (59 miles, south of Cancún), might be in the range of $60 or $75. Take your time when you look over the company's rates, estimate the total distance and time, and allow a generous margin for side trips, wrong turns, etc.—those kilometers are expensive!—and then add up all of the charges you'll have to pay before the clerk starts filling out a rental contract.

Your completed estimate should look something like this, based on a total of 225 kilometers (95 down, 95 back, 35 for wrong turns), for the very cheapest car offered (these figures have been rounded off):

Basic daily charge	$26.00
Kilometers, 225 @ 15¢	32.75
Full collision insurance	2.00
Subtotal	61.00
IVA tax @ 15%	9.15
Gas @ 80¢ per gallon	5.00
Grand Total	$75.15

You can save quite a bit of money on this daily average if you rent by the week with unlimited mileage. But however you cut it, rental costs in Mexico are much, much higher than at home.

Once you've made up your mind to rent a car, finding a rental office is a snap. Rental desks are set up in the airports, in all major hotels, and in many travel agencies. The large firms like Avis, Hertz, National, and Budget have rental offices on main streets as well.

CLOTHES FOR TRAVEL: Mexico tends to be a bit more conservative in dress (except for the capital) so shorts and halter tops are not generally acceptable except at seaside resorts. Cool clothes (the lightest weight cottons you can find) are needed at all times for Yucatán. Raingear is a must for the rainy season (May through mid-October). I prefer a fold-up plastic poncho, which is easy to pack and carry around. For more hints on clothing, see the Introduction to this book.

CLOTHING SIZE EQUIVALENTS: You'll want to try on any clothing you intend to buy, but here are some equivalents in case you're buying gifts for friends. Note that women's blouse sizes are the same in the United States and Mexico.

Women's

Dress		Shoes	
U.S.	Mex.	U.S.	Mex.
6	36	5	35
8	38	5.5	35.5
10	40	6	36
12	42	6.5	36.5
14	44	7	37
16	46	7.5	37.5
18	48	8	38
20	50	8.5	38.5
22	52	9	39

Men's

Collar		Jacket		Shoes	
U.S.	Mex.	U.S.	Mex.	U.S.	Mex.
14	36	38	48	8	41
14.5	37	40	50	8.5	41.5
15	38	42	52	9	42
15.5	39	44	54	9.5	42.5
16	40	46	56	10	43
16.5	41	48	58	10.5	43.5
17	42	50	60	11	44
17.5	43	52	62	11.5	44.5
18	44	54	64	12	45

CRIME: It's getting to be more of a problem in Mexico—which is to say that there was not much of a crime problem before. Although you will feel physically safer in most Mexican cities than in comparable big cities at home, you must take some basic, sensible precautions.

First, remember that you're a tourist, and a tourist is a mark. Beware of pickpockets on crowded buses and in markets. Guard your possessions very carefully at all times; don't let packs or bags out of sight even for a second (the big first-class bus lines will store your bag in the luggage compartment under the bus, and that's generally all right, but keep your things with you on the less responsible village and some second-class buses on country routes).

Next, if you have a car, park it in an enclosed or guarded lot at night. Vans and camping vehicles are a special mark. Don't depend on "major downtown streets" to protect your car—park it in a private lot with a guard, or at least a fence. Whatever you do, don't leave anything valuable within view inside the car.

Women must be careful in cities when walking alone, night or day. Busy streets are no problem, but empty streets (even if empty just for afternoon siesta) are lonely places.

As to the police, in the past they have been part of the problem, not part of the solution. Although Mexico no doubt has dedicated and responsible officers, the general impression is that police have little training and fewer scruples.

Scams

As money gets tighter in Mexico, the number and ingenuity of scams increase. In Mexico City there's the longstanding **shoeshine scam** in which crafty shine vendors overcharge tourists. At Yelapa Beach near Puerto Vallarta the **iguana scam** costs tourists a dollar a picture. Below are a couple of scams that could happen anywhere in the country.

Because hotel desk clerks are usually so helpful, I hesitate to mention the **lost objects scam** for fear of tainting them all. But here's how it works. You "lose" your wallet after cashing money at the desk, or you leave something valuable such as a purse or camera in the lobby. You report it. The clerk has it, but instead of telling you that he does, he says he will see what he can do; meanwhile, you should offer a high reward. This one has all kinds of variations. In one incident a desk clerk was in cahoots with a bystander in the lobby. The bystander lifted her wallet in the elevator. Another might be called the **infraction scam.** A recent one involved men acting as police who demanded money for some supposed infraction. Never get into a car with them. I avoided this one in Chetumal when my traveling companion feigned illness and began writhing, moaning, and pretending to have the dry heaves. It was more than the policeman could handle. While I'm on the subject, if you are stopped by the police, avoid handing over your driver's license. Hold it so that it can be read, but don't give it up.

Throughout the country there are legal and necessary car searches by military personnel looking for drugs. But every now and then there are police-controlled **illegal roadblocks** where motorists are allowed to continue after paying. Recently there was one operated by striking farmers on the isolated road between Chetumal and Escarcega.

Reporting a Loss

But just suppose the worst happens—you discover you've lost your wallet, your passport, your airline ticket, and your tourist permit. Whether the loss is from your negligence or by theft, you'll want to report it. Here's what to do. First always keep a photocopy of these documents in your luggage—it makes replacing them easier. If you've lost your passport, you must contact your Embassy or nearest Consular Agent (listed here). You'll have to establish a record of your citizenship, and fill out a form that will allow you to get another Mexican Tourist Card. Without the Mexican Tourist Card you can't leave the country; and without an affidavit regarding your passport and citizenship, you may have hassles at Customs when you get home. And you'll need them to get a new passport later. To be reimbursed for insured items once you return, you'll need to report the loss to the Mexican police and get a written report. If you don't speak Spanish, take along someone who does. The report involves much typewriter clacking and question answering.

Naturally each situation has circumstances of its own, and this information is offered as a tip-off to potentially tense situations. But I must reiterate that I log thousands of miles and many months in Mexico each year without serious incident and I feel safer there than at home.

CUSTOMS AND DUTY-FREE GOODS

Coming to Mexico, Customs officials are very tolerant as long as you have no drugs (that is, marijuana, cocaine, etc.) or firearms. You're allowed to bring two cartons of cigarettes, or 100 non-Cuban cigars, plus a kilogram (2.2 pounds) of smoking tobacco; the liquor allowance is 1 liter of anything, wine or hard liquor.

Reentering the **United States,** you're allowed by **federal law** to bring in a carton (200) of cigarettes, *or* 50 cigars, *or* 2 kilograms (total, 4.4 pounds) of smoking tobacco, or proportional amounts of these items, plus one liter of alcoholic beverage (wine, beer, or spirits). If you bring larger amounts of these things, you will have to pay federal duty and internal revenue tax. *But wait!* Your quotas will also be subject to **state laws** (that is, of the state in which you reenter the U.S.). The state law may not allow you to bring back *any* liquor, which means *you will have to pour it out.* It's not simply a matter of paying duty, it's a matter of absolute quotas—or no quotas at all—for some states. This liquor quota is most strictly applied at the border posts, less strictly at airports not near the border.

Here are the limits for liquor in the states that border Mexico, from information supplied by the Distilled Spirits Council, Washington, D.C.:

Arizona: You may not import more than the federal duty-free limit; any amounts over the limit will be destroyed.

California: You may bring in a "reasonable amount" of liquor for each adult, for personal use only (not for resale or as gifts).

New Mexico: You may bring in a reasonable amount duty-free.

Texas: All liquor brought into Texas is subject to state tax; for amounts of hard liquor over one quart, you must have a permit from the state liquor authorities.

Canadian returning-resident regulations are similar to the U.S. ones: a carton of cigarettes, 50 cigars, 2 pounds (not kilos) of smoking tobacco, 1.1 liters (40 ounces) of wine or liquor, *or* a case of beer (8.2 liters). All provinces except Prince Edward Island and the Northwest Territories allow you to bring in more liquor and beer— up to 2 gallons (9 liters) more—but the taxes are quite high.

DOCTORS AND DENTISTS

Every embassy and consulate is prepared to recommend local doctors and dentists with good training and up-to-date equipment;

some of the doctors and dentists even speak English. See the list of embassies and consulates under "Embassies" (below), and remember that at the larger ones a duty officer is on call at all times.

DRUGSTORES

The word is *farmacia,* and they will sell you just about anything you want, with prescription or without. Most are open every day but Sunday, from 8am to 8pm.

If you need to buy medicines outside of normal hours, you'll have to search for the *farmacia de turno*—pharmacies take turns staying open during the off hours. Find any drugstore, and in its window should be a card showing a schedule of which farmacia will be open at what time.

ELECTRICITY

Current in Mexico is 110 volts, 60 cycles, as in the United States and Canada, with the same flat-prong plugs and sockets. Light bulbs may have bayonet bases, though.

EMBASSIES

They provide valuable lists of doctors, lawyers, regulations concerning marriages in Mexico, etc. Contrary to popular belief, your embassy cannot get you out of a Mexican jail, provide postal or banking services, or fly you home when you run out of money. Consular officers can provide you with advice on most matters and problems, however. Here's a list of embassies, all of which are in the capital, Mexico City. Consulates in Cancún and Mérida are covered in the chapters on those cities.

Canada

The Canadian Embassy in **Mexico City** is at Schiller 529, in Polanco (tel. 5/254-3288). Hours are Monday through Friday from 9am to 1pm and 2 to 5pm; at other times the name of a duty officer is posted on the embassy door.

United Kingdom

The British Embassy in **Mexico City** is at Río Lerma 71, at Río Sena (tel. 5/511-4880 or 514-3327).

United States

The American Embassy in **Mexico City** is right next to the Hotel María Isabel Sheraton at Paseo de la Reforma 305, corner of Río Danubio (tel. 5/211-0042).

HOLIDAYS, PUBLIC

Banks, stores, and businesses are closed on national holidays, hotels fill up quickly, and transportation is crowded. Here are the holidays celebrated in Mexico:

January 1	New Year's Day
February 5	Constitution Day
March 21	Birthday of Benito Juárez
March-April (moveable)	Holy Week (closures usually Good Friday through Easter Sunday)
May 1	Labor Day
May 5	Battle of Pueblo, 1862 (Cinco de Mayo)
September 1	President's Message to Congress
September 16	Independence Day
October 12	Columbus Day (Mexico: Day of the Race)
November 20	Mexican Revolution Anniversary
December 24–25	Christmas Eve (evening); Christmas Day

INFORMATION

Before you leave home, you can get tourist information from any of the Mexican government tourist offices listed in Chapter I of this book. Once you're in Mexico, drop in to the tourism information offices mentioned in the text for each city or area.

LAUNDRY

All hotels can make some arrangements to have your laundry taken care of. Small laundries can be found in all but the tiniest villages. Coin laundries exist in all cities of any size—just ask at your hotel or a tourism information office.

MAIL

Mail service south of the border tends to be slow (sometimes glacial in its movements) and erratic. If you're on a two-week vacation, it's not a bad idea to buy and mail your postcards in the Arrivals lounge at the airport to give them maximum time to get home before you do. Be sure to use Mexican postage stamps!

General Delivery (Poste Restante)

If you don't use American Express, have your mail sent to you care of *Lista de Correos,* (City), (State), (Country). In Mexican post offices there may actually be a "lista" posted near the Lista de Correos window bearing the names of all those for whom mail has been received. If there's no list, ask, and show them your passport so they can riffle through and look for your letters.

You'll have to go to the central post office—not a branch—to get your mail, if the city has more than one office.

Glossary

Words you'll need to know include these:

Customs	**Aduana**
Mailbox	**Buzón**
Airmail	**Correo Aereo**
Postal Service	**Correos**

Special Delivery, Express	**Entrega Immediata**
Stamps	**Estampillas**
Money Orders	**Giros Postales**
General Delivery, Poste Restante	**Lista de Correos**
Post Office	**Oficina de Correos**
Parcels	**Paquetes**
Airmail	**Por avion**
Registered Mail	**Registrado**
Insurance(insured mail)	**Seguros**
Stamps (sometimes rubber stamps)	**Sellos**
Stamps	**Timbres**

MONEY (SEE ALSO "BANKS"): The dollar sign ($) is used to indicate pesos in Mexico. As many establishments dealing with tourists also quote prices in dollars, confusion is cleared up by the use of the abbreviations "Dlls." for dollars, and "m.n." (*moneda nacional*—national currency) for pesos, so "$1,000.00 m.n." means 1,000 pesos. Banks often charge a fee for changing traveler's checks, or give a rate of exchange below the official daily rate. Hotels usually exchange below the official daily rate as well.

Note: At this writing Mexican banks pay more for traveler's checks than for dollars in cash. Casas de Cambio often pay more for cash than traveler's checks. Some banks, but not all, charge a service fee to cash either dollars or traveler's checks. The highest I've seen was 5%. Sometimes banks post the service charge amount so you can see it, but they may not. So it pays to ask first and shop around for a bank without a fee.

Canadian dollars seem to be most easily exchanged for pesos at branches of Banamex and Bancomer.

Credit Cards

You'll be glad to know that Mexico is well into the age of living on the little plastic card, and that you will be able to charge some hotel and restaurant bills, almost all airline tickets, and many store purchases. You can get cash advances of several hundred dollars on your card. However, you can't charge gasoline purchases in Mexico at all.

VISA, MasterCard (which is "Carnet" in Mexico), American Express, and their affiliates are the most widely accepted cards. You may not see your card's logo in a shop window or on a travel agency door, but don't worry—the Mexican equivalents such as Bancomer and/or Bancomatico will do just as well.

NEWSLETTERS: The following newsletters may be of interest to readers who want to keep up with Mexico between visits: *AIM,* Apartado Postal 31-70, Guadalajara 45050, Jal. Mexico, is a newsletter on retirement and travel in Mexico. A recent issue provided tips on whether or not to bring a dog, buying versus renting, tipping, medical services, golf courses, adapting to Mexico, and cost of living. It costs $15 to the United States and $18 to Canada. Back issues are $2. **Sanborn's News Bulletin,** Dept. FR, P.O. Box 310, McAllen, TX 78502, is a free newsletter produced by Sanborn's Insurance and it's full of tips on driving conditions, highways, hotels, economy and business, RV information, and fishing and hunting. **Travel Mexico,** Apartado Postal 6-1007, Mexico, DF 06600, is published six times a year by the publishers of *Traveler's Guide to Mexico*—the book frequently found in hotel rooms in Mexico. The newsletter covers a variety of topics from news about archeology, to hotel packages, new resorts and hotels, and the economy. A subscription costs $12.

NEWSPAPERS AND MAGAZINES: For American travelers in Mexico the English-language newspaper *The News* is an excellent buy. It carries many Stateside columnists as well as newsworthy commentaries, and a calendar of the day's events including concerts, art shows, and plays. A Spanish-language paper, *Excelsior,* has a daily partial page in English.

Newspaper kiosks in larger Mexican cities will carry a selection of English-language magazines—*Time, Newsweek,* and the like.

POST OFFICE (SEE "MAIL")

SIESTA: The custom of having a copious, long lunch and taking a rest during the heat of the day is still well entrenched south of the border. You may notice it less in mountainous areas and in the big cities, where life seems to plow onward from morning to evening without a break. But in coastal towns and hot climates, expect banks, offices, consulates, and museums to take a somewhat lengthy break for lunch. You'd be well advised to do the same.

TELEPHONES: Special care is required when calling to, from, or within Mexico in order to reduce the risk of "telephone bill shock." Information on placing calls to Mexico from other countries is included in Chapter I of this book.

Note: Now that *Teléfonos de México* has decided to reduce long-distance rates by 40% while raising local rates, travelers making international calls should see a pleasing difference; but long-distance calls are still high. At the same time, the company, which is government-owned, is also looking for a private buyer or buyers. That could happen by the time you read this; even more changes may be in the offing. Here's what you need to know when you want to make a call from or within Mexico.

Local Calls

Local calls in Mexico are very inexpensive. There are two types of coin phones: in one the slot at the top holds your coin (the smallest coin you can find) in a gentle grip until your party answers, then it drops; if there's no answer or a busy signal you can pluck your coin from the slot. The other type is the sort where you insert a coin that disappears into the bowels of the machine, and drops into the cash-box when your call goes through, or into the return slot if it doesn't (after you hang up). This type of phone is often jammed, and your coin won't drop, so that when your party answers you will hear them but they won't hear you. Try from another pay phone.

Note: The government-owned phone company, *Teléfonos de México,* has decided to reduce long-distance rates by 40% while hiking local rates. This means that hotels *may* begin charging for local calls made from a hotel room phone. Until now these calls were free. So far, most of the inexpensive hotels listed in this book do not have the equipment to track calls made from individual rooms and therefore telephone use charges are not added to the room bill. But hotels with more sophisticated telephone systems are charging around 35¢ per call. To avoid check-out shock, ask during check-in if local calls are extra.

Long Distance

Long-distance calls in Mexico are as expensive as local calls are cheap. And *international long-distance calls tend to be outrageously expensive,* even if you are calling *collect* to the United States, Canada, or Britain.

To call the United States or Canada collect, dial 09, and tell the *operadora* that you want *una llamada por cobrar* (a collect call), *teléfono a teléfono* (station-to-station), or *persona a persona* (person-to-person).

If you don't want to call collect, you'll have to go to a *caseta de larga distancia,* or call from your hotel, as it's impracticable to load hundreds of small coins into a pay phone. Your hotel will levy a service charge—perhaps a percentage!—on top of the already exorbitant rate. Ask in advance what they'll add on. At a caseta you pay just the call charge.

From a caseta or hotel, dial 95 + Area Code + number for the United States and Canada, or 98 + Area Code + number for anywhere else in the world.

To call long distance (abbreviated "lada") within Mexico, dial 91 + Area Code + number. Mexican area codes *(claves)* are listed in the front of the telephone directories, and in the hotel listings for each area in this book.

Calling to Mexico from Abroad

I've included Mexican telephone Area Codes *(claves)* in all important telephone numbers given in this book so that you can call long distance within Mexico, or to Mexico from the United States, Canada, Europe, or anywhere in the world. Mexico's area codes and numbers are sometimes shorter than North American ones, but they work just as well. If you have international direct-dial service from your home telephone exchange in the United States or Canada, here's how you place a call to Mexico: Dial the international service (011), then Mexico's country code (52), then the Mexican area code (for Cancún it's 988), then the local number. Thus, to call the tourist information number in Cancún, you'd dial 011-52-988-4-3238.

If you don't have international direct-dial service, dial "Operator," ask for an international operator, and give that operator the numbers starting with the country code.

Keep in mind that calls to Mexico are quite expensive, even if dialed direct from your home phone. As a rule of thumb, it's usually much cheaper to call Europe or the Middle East than it is to call Mexico!

Ladatel Automatic Phones

As of this writing, some relief is in sight from exorbitant Mexican telephone charges. The national phone company, Teléfonos de México, is installing special **Ladatel** call stations at major transportation termini and other public places of importance. These special telephones have bright blue handsets and liquid-crystal display panels, and they allow you to dial direct long-distance calls to anywhere in Mexico or the world, at reasonable prices.

Here's how to use a Ladatel phone. First, have a good supply of the 100 peso coins, or of special Ladatel tokens. Next, find out the approximate rate per minute for your call. You do this by picking up the blue Ladatel handset and punching in the long distance code (91 for Mexico, 95 for the U.S. and Canada, 98 for the rest of the world), plus the area or country and city codes for the destination of your call. The charge per minute in pesos will appear on the LCD display. For instance, if you press 95-212, you'll get the charge per minute for a call to Manhattan. Normal operator-assisted, caseta, and collect calls can cost 50% to 200% more, so the value of Ladatel phones is obvious.

Once you know the charge per minute, count your coins or tokens, make sure you have as many as you'll need, then dial your number and insert coins. The display will keep you informed of when more coins are needed. Instructions on Ladatel phones are in Spanish, English, and French.

Off-Peak Calling

You can save considerably by calling in off-peak periods. The cheapest times to call are after 11pm and before 8am any day, and all day Saturday and Sunday; the most expensive times are 8am to 5pm weekdays.

TIME: The entire Yucatán peninsula, like most of Mexico, uses Central Standard Time all year round (Daylight Saving Time is not used). That means that it's the same hour in Mérida or Cancún as it is in Chicago, New Orleans, or Houston. But when it's noon in Yucatán, it's 1pm in New York and Miami, or 11am in Sante Fe or Salt Lake City, or 10am in Seattle or Los Angeles.

TIPPING: When it comes to tipping, you should throw out the iron 15% rule right away south of the border, no matter what other travel literature may say. Do as the locals do: For meals costing $2 to $3 or under, leave the loose change; for meals costing around $4 or $5, leave from 6% to 10%, depending on service. Above $10, you're into the 10% to 15% bracket. Some of the more crass high-priced restaurants will actually add a 15% "tip" to your bill. Leave nothing extra if they do.

Bellboys and porters will expect about 15¢ to 50¢ per bag, depending on the quality of hotel. You needn't tip taxi drivers unless they've rendered some special service—carrying bags or trunks, for instance.

TRAIN: By the time you travel, it's possible that the Yucatán will be linked by one of the new first-class *Estrella* trains from Mexico City to Palenque, Campeche, and Mérida. At this writing, the second-class train that serves the Yucatán from Mexico City is slow and the service is erratic. For the latest train itinerary or other questions contact the Commercial Passenger Department, **National Railways of Mexico,** Buenavista Grand Central Station, 06358 Mexico, DF (tel. 5/547-8972). For advance planning using *Estrella* trains, the most secure way is **Mexico by Rail,** Box 3508, Laredo, TX 78044, or call toll free 800/228-3225 in the United States. Given 15 days notice they will pre-purchase your *Estrella* service train ticket and mail it to you. For holiday travel, make plans 45 days ahead. They charge a percentage on top of the regular price of the train ticket.

TRAVELER'S DIARRHEA: This is the doctors' term for diarrhea from which many tourists suffer, although others seem immune. It's not only unclean food or water that's to blame but also the change of eating habits and environment. If your condition becomes serious—fever and chills, stomach pains—do *not* hesitate to call a doctor. Diseases far more serious than traveler's diarrhea are on the loose down here. To neglect a potentially serious ailment, because of the belief that traveler's diarrhea is painful but not dangerous, could be an unhappy mistake. Also, it is advisable, no matter how serious your illness, to consult a doctor before buying or taking any kind of drug. For more information on traveler's diarrhea, refer to Chapter I, under "Health."

TRIPS: With it's concentration of archeology, nature, and history, the Yucatán offers some of Mexico's most diverse travel opportunities. Several tour operators offer special-interest trips in the Yucatán, often led by a specialist in the area covered. Options for such a trip might include rafting the Usumacinta River between Mexico and Guatemala, camping at the Maya ruins of Yaxchilán, indepth expeditions to archeological sites with an archeologist, cave diving in a Yucatán cenote, assisting scientists to study turtle nesting habitats, and jungle birding at Palenque.

Caiman Expeditions, 3449 E. River Rd. Tucson, AZ 85718 (tel. 602/299-1047, or toll free 800/365-2383 in U.S.).
Far Flung Adventures, Box 31, Terlingua, TX 79852 (tel. 915/371-2489, or toll free 800/359-4138 in U.S.).
Far Horizons Cultural Discovery Tours, 16 Fern Lane, San Anselmo, CA 94960 (tel. 415/457-4575).

Jaguar Tours, 1202 Citation Circle, Del Valle, TX 78617 (tel. 512/247-4435).
Wings, Inc., P.O. Box 31930, Tucson, AZ 85751 (tel. 602/749-3175).

VILLAS AND CONDOS

Renting a private villa or condominium home for a vacation is an increasingly popular vacation alternative. The difference between the two, of course, is that villas are usually freestanding and condos may be part of a large or small complex. Often the villas are true private homes, in exclusive neighborhoods and rented seasonally by their owners. Condominiums on the other hand *may* seem more like a hotel, though some are secluded and exclusive in feel. Either type ordinarily comes with private kitchen and dining area, maid service, and pool. Often a full-time cook, maid, or gardener/chauffeur are assigned to an individual property. I've seen prices as low as $80 a night to a high of $500. Prices vary with the season and the best deals are found between May and December 1. Of course, depending on the number of bedrooms, you can get a group together and share the cost. Four companies specializing in this type of vacation rental are:

Casa Cozumel, Apdo. Postal 312, Cozumel, Q. Roo 77600 (tel. 987/2-2259, or Fax 2-2348).
Creative Leisure, 951 Transport Way, Petaluma, CA 94951 (tel. 707/778-1800, or toll free 800/426-6367 in U.S.).
Travel Resources, P.O. Box 1042, Coconut Grove, FL 33133 (tel. 305/444-8583, or toll free 800/327-5039 in U.S., or toll free 800/523-5534 in Florida.
Mexico Condo Reservations, 5151 Soledad Road, San Diego, CA 92109 (tel. toll free 800/262-4500 in U.S., or toll free 800/622-4500 in California or toll free 800/654-5543 in Canada).

All have extensive brochures with photographs of potential properties.

WATER

Most hotels have decanters or bottles of purified water in the rooms and the snazzier hotels have special taps marked *"Aqua Purificada."* Virtually any hotel, restaurant, or bar will bring you purified water if you specifically request it.

WEIGHTS AND MEASURES:

Length

1 millimeter = 0.04 inches (*or* less than ¹⁄₁₆ inch)
1 centimeter = 0.39 inches (*or* just under ½ inch)
1 meter   = 1.09 yards (*or* about 39 inches)
1 kilometer = 0.62 mile (*or* about ⅔ mile)

To convert kilometers to miles, take the number of kilometers and multiply by .62 (for example, 25km × .62 = 15.5 miles).

To convert miles to kilometers, take the number of miles and multiply by 1.61 (for example, 50 miles × 1.61 = 80.5 km).

Capacity
1 liter = 33.92 ounces
       = 1.06 quarts
       = 0.26 gallons

To convert liters to gallons, take the number of liters and multiply by .26 (for example, 50 l × .26 = 13 gal).

To convert gallons to liters, take the number of gallons and multiply by 3.79 (for example, 10 gal × 3.79 = 37.9 l).

Weight
1 gram   = 0.04 ounce (*or* about a paperclip's weight)
1 kilogram = 2.2 pounds

To convert kilograms to pounds, take the number of kilos and multiply by 2.2 (for example, 75kg × 2.2 = 165 lbs).

To convert pounds to kilograms, take the number of pounds and multiply by .45 (for example, 90 lb × .45 = 40.5kg).

Temperature

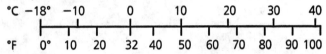

To convert degrees C to degrees F, multiply degrees C by 9, divide by 5, then add 32 (for example 9/5 × 20°C + 32 = 68°F).

To convert degrees F to degrees C, subtract 32 from degrees F, then multiply by 5, and divide by 9 (for example, 85°F − 32 × 5/9 = 29°C).

YOUTH HOSTELS
Mexico has some beautiful government-built and supported hostels, at very low prices. For a list, write to **SETEJ**, Hamburgo 273, in Mexico City (tel. 5/211-0743), or write to Red Nacional de Albergues Turísticos (CREA), Oxtopulco 40, Colonia Oxtopulco, Universidad, México, DF 04310.

SPEAKING SPANISH

A. VOCABULARY
B. MENU TERMS

You'll be surprised at the number of Mexicans you'll meet who are fluent in English. It is, after all, the most important language in Mexican tourism, commerce and industry, science, banking, and diplomacy. English is taught in most Mexican high schools and colleges.

But many people not involved in these fields have no reason to learn English (or to remember the English they learned in school), and so the time will come when you'll need a Spanish word or phrase in order to make yourself understood. This chapter should fill the need nicely, if you're on the average one- or two-week trip.

Should you plan a long trip in Yucatán, I'd suggest picking up a good Spanish phrase book. Berlitz Publications puts out a handy pocket-size phrase guide with copious background notes on cultural matters, social customs, and "body language." In effect, it's a guidebook to the language and culture attuned to regional dialects, as its title, *Latin American Spanish for Travelers,* reveals. It's available in most bookstores.

Bueno. Here's your first lesson in Spanish, the one most visitors find necessary first: the numbers.

A. Vocabulary

NUMBERS

1	**uno** (ooh-noh)	**8**	**ocho**		(tray-say)
2	**dos** (dose)		(oh-choh)	**14**	**catorce**
3	**tres** (trayss)	**9**	**nueve**		(kah-tor-say)
4	**cuatro**		(nway-bay)	**15**	**quince**
	(kwah-troh)	**10**	**diez** (dee-ess)		(keen-say)
5	**cinco**	**11**	**once**	**16**	**dieciseis**
	(seen-koh)		(ohn-say)		(dee-ess-ee
6	**seis** (sayss)	**12**	**doce**		says)
7	**siete**		(doh-say)	**17**	**diecisiete**
	(syeh-tay)	**13**	**trece**		(de-ess-ee

see-ay-tay)

18 dieciocho
(de-ess-ee-oh-choh)

19 diecinueve
(dee-ess-ee-nway-bay)

20 veinte
(bayn-tay)

30 treinta
(trayn-tah)

40 cuarenta
(kwah-ren-tah)

50 cincuenta
(seen-kwen-tah)

60 sesenta
(say-sen-tah)

70 setenta
(say-ten-tah)

80 ochenta
(oh-chen-tah)

90 noventa
(noh-ben-tah)

100 ciento
(see-en-toe)

200 doscientos
(dos-see-en-tos)

500 quinientos
(keen-ee ehn-tos)

1000 mil (meel)

USEFUL PHRASES

Hello	**Buenos días**	bway-nohss dee-ahss
How are you?	**¿Cómo está usted?**	koh-moh ess-tah oo-sted
Very well	**Muy bien**	mwee byen
Thank you	**Gracias**	grah-see-ahss
You're welcome	**De nada**	day nah-dah
Goodbye	**Adiós**	ah-dyohss
Please	**Por favor**	pohr-fah-bohr
Yes	**Sí**	see
No	**No**	noh
Excuse me	**Perdóneme**	pehr-doh-neh-may
Give me	**Déme**	day-may
Where is?	**¿Dónde está?**	dohn-day ess-tah
the station	**la estación**	la ess-tah-see-own
a hotel	**un hotel**	oon oh-tel
a gas station	**una gasolinera**	oon-nuh gah-so-lee-nay-rah
a restaurant	**un restaurante**	oon res-tow-rahn-tay
the toilet	**el baño**	el bahn-yoh
a good doctor	**un buen medico**	oon bwayn may-dee-co
the road to . . .	**el camino a . . .**	el cah-mee-noh ah . . .
To the right	**A la derecha**	ah lah day-ray-chuh
To the left	**A la izquierda**	ah lah ees-ky-ehr-day
Straight head	**Derecho**	day-ray-cho
I would like	**Quisiera**	keyh-see-air-ah
I want	**Quiero**	kyehr-oh
to eat	**comer**	ko-mayr
a room	**una habitación**	oon-nuh hab-bee-tah-see-own
Do you have?	**¿Tiene usted?**	tyah-nay oos-ted
a book	**un libro**	oon lee-bro
a dictionary	**un diccionario**	oon deek-see-own-ar-eo

How much is it?	**¿Cuánto cuesta?**	kwahn-toh kwess-tah
When	**¿Cuándo?**	kwahn-doh
What	**¿Qué?**	kay
There is (Is there?)	**¿Hay . . .**	eye
Yesterday	**Ayer**	ah-yer
Today	**Hoy**	oy
Tomorrow	**Mañana**	mahn-yawn-ah
Good	**Bueno**	bway-no
Bad	**Malo**	mah-lo
Better (best)	**(Lo) Mejor**	meh-hor
More	**Más**	mahs
Less	**Menos**	may-noss
No smoking	**Se prohibe fumar**	seh pro-hee-beh foo-mahr
Postcard	**Tarjeta postal**	tahr-hay-tah pohs-tahl
Insect repellent	**Rapellante contra insectos**	rah-pey-yahn-te cohn-trah een-sehk-tos

Do you speak English?	**¿Habla usted Inglés?**
Is there anyone here who speaks English?	**¿Hay alguien aquí que hable Inglés?**
I speak a little Spanish.	**Hablo un poco de Español.**
I don't understand Spanish very well.	**No lo entiendo muy bien el Español.**
The meal is good.	**Me gusta la comida.**
What time is it?	**¿Qué hora es?**
May I see your menu?	**¿Puedo ver su menú?**
What did you say?	**¿Mande? (colloquial expression for American "Eh?")**
I want (to see) a room	**Quiero (ver) un cuarto (una habitación)**
for two persons	**para dos personas**
with (without) bath	**con (sin) baño**
We are staying here only one night (one week)	**Nos quedaremos aquí solamente una noche (una semana)**
We are leaving tomorrow.	**Partimos mañana.**
Do you accept traveler's checks?	**¿Acepta usted cheques de viajero?**
Is there a laundromat near here?	**¿Hay una lavandería cerca de aquí?**
Please send these clothes to the laundry.	**Hágame el favor de mandar esta ropa a la lavandería.**

B. Menu Terms

GENERAL TERMS

almuerzo lunch
cena supper
comida dinner
desayuno breakfast
el menu the menu
la cuenta the check
tampiqueña thinly sliced meat
cocido boiled

empanado breaded
frito fried
poco cocido rare
asado roast
bien cocido well done
milanesa breaded
veracruzana tomato and green olive sauce
pibil roasted

BREAKFAST (DESAYUNO)

jugo de naranja orange juice
cafe con crema coffee with cream
pan tostado toast
mermelada jam
leche milk
te tea
huevos eggs
huevos rancheros fried eggs on a tortilla, huevos revueltos covered with tomato sauce

huevos cocidos hard-boiled eggs
huevos motuleños egg on ham with tortilla, cheese, and tomato sauce
huevos poches poached eggs
huevos fritos fried eggs
huevos pasados al agua soft-boiled eggs
huevos revueltos scrambled eggs
tocino bacon
jamón ham

LUNCH AND DINNER

antojitos Mexican specialties
caldo broth
sopa soup
sopa de ajo garlic soup with egg
sopa clara consommé
sopa de lentejas lentil soup
sopa de chicaros pea soup
sopa de arroz rice pilaf (not soup!)
pozole meat-hominy stew

caldo de pollo chicken broth
fijoles refritos refried beans
menudo tripe soup
médula bone marrow soup
salchichas knockwurst
taco filled fried tortilla
torta sandwich
tostada crisp fried tortilla
enchilada filled tortilla
tamales russos cabbage rolls

SEAFOOD (MARISCOS)

almejas clams
anchoas anchovies
arenques herring

atún tuna
calamares squid
camarones shrimp

caracoles snails
caviare caviar
corvina bass
huachinango red snapper
jaiba crab
langosta lobster
lenguado sole
merluza hake (type of cod)
ostiones oysters
pescado fish

mojarra perch
pez espada swordfish
robalo sea bass
salmon salmon
salmon ahumada smoked
   salmon
sardinas sardines
solo pike
trucha trout

MEATS (CARNES)

ahumado smoked
alambre shish kebab
albondigas meatballs
aves poultry
bistec steak
cabeza de ternera calf's
   head
cabrito kid (goat)
carne meat
carne fría cold cuts
cerdo pork
chiles rellenos stuffed
   peppers
chicharrón pigskin
   cracklings
chorizo spicy sausage
chuleta chop
chuleta de carnero mutton
   chop
chuletas de cordero lamb
   chops
chuletas de puerco pork
   chops
paloma pigeon
pato duck

pechuga chicken breast
perdiz partridge
pierna leg
callos tripe
venado venison
conejo rabbit
cordero lamb
costillas de cerdo spareribs
faisan pheasant
filete milanesa breaded veal
   chops
filete de ternera filet of
   veal
ganso goose
pavo turkey
higado liver
jamón ham
lengua tongue
lomo loin
mole chicken in spicy
   bitter-chocolate sauce
pollo chicken
res beef
riñones kidneys
ternera veal
tocino bacon

VEGETABLES (LEGUMBRES)

aguacate avocado
aceitunas olives
arroz rice
betabeles beets
cebolla onions
champiñones mushrooms
chicharos peas
col cabbage
col fermentada sauerkraut
coliflor cauliflower

ejotes string beans
elote corn (maize)
entremeses hors d'oeuvres
esparragos asparagus
espinaca spinach
frijoles beans
hongos mushrooms
jicame sweet yellow turnip
lechuga lettuce
lentejas lentils

papas potatoes
pepino cucumber
rabanos radishes

tomate tomato
verdura green
zanahorias carrots

SALADS (ENSALADAS)

ensalada de apio celery
ensalada de frutas fruit
    salad
ensalada mixta mixed salad
ensalada de
    pepinos cucumber
    salad
guacamole avocado salad
lechuga lettuce salad
chavacanos apricots
ciruelas yellow plums
coco coconut
duraznos peaches
frambuesas raspberries
fresas strawberries
   con crema with cream
fruta cocida stewed fruit
tomate tomato

verdura green
zanahorias carrots
granada pomegranate
guanabana green pear-like
    fruit
guayabas guavas
higos figs
himón lime
mamey sweet orange fruit
mango mango
manzanas apples
naranjas oranges
pera pear
piña pineapple
plátanos bananas
tuña prickly pear fruit
uvas grapes
zapote maple-sugary fruit

DESSERTS (POSTRES)

arroz con leche rice
    pudding
brunelos de fruta fruit tart
coctel de aguacate avocado
    cocktail
coctel de frutas fruit
    cocktail
compota stewed fruit
flan custard

galletas crackers or cookies
helado, nieve ice cream
macedonia fruit salad
nieve sherbet
pastel cake or pastry
queso cheese
torta cake
leche tipo bulgar,
    lavin yogurt

BEVERAGES (BEBIDAS)

agua water
brandy brandy
café coffee
café con crema coffee with
    cream
café negro black coffee
cerveza beer
ginebra gin
hielo ice
jerez sherry
jugo de naranja orange
    juice
jugo de tomate tomato
    juice

jugo de toronja grapefruit
    juice
leche milk
licores liqueures
manzanita apple juice
refrescas soft drinks
ron rum
sidra cider
sifon soda
té tea
vaso de leche glass of milk
vino blanco white wine
vino tinto red wine
refresco soft drink

CONDIMENTS AND CUTLERY

aceite oil
azucar sugar
copa goblet
epazote Mexican tea
mantequilla butter
mostaza mustard
pan bread
bolillo roll
pimienta pepper

cilantro coriander leaf
cuchara spoon
cuchillo knife
sal salt
taza cup
tenedor fork
tostada toast
vinagre vinegar
vaso glass

PREPARATION AND SAUCES

asado roasted
cocido cooked
bien cocido well done
poco cocido rare
empanado breaded
frito fried
al horno baked
milanesa Italian breaded
mole poblano hot red peppers and cocoa sauce with raisins and spices
a la parilla grilled
pibil sauce of tomato, onion, red pepper (hot), cilantro, vinegar; wrapped in a banana leaf

poc chuc pork leg cooked with onions, cilantro, sour oranges, and served with black beans
relleno negro stuffed ground pork, pimiento, olives, eggs, epazote, salt, vinegar and tomato stuffing
blanco the above with raisins, cinnamon, and capers
tampiqueño thinly sliced meat
veracruzana tomato and green olive sauce

GENERAL INFORMATION

SIGHTS AND ATTRACTIONS

Palenque

Uxmal & the Puuc Cities

Villahermosa

ACCOMMODATIONS

Campeche

Cancún

KEY TO ABBREVIATIONS: *B* = Budget; *C* = Condominiums; *E* = Expensive; *M* = Moderately priced; *T* = Top hotels; *TC* = Tent Camp

Caribbean Coast

Chichén-Itzá

Cozumel

Mérida

Palenque

Uxmal & the Puuc Cities

Villahermosa

RESTAURANTS

Cancún

Campeche

Caribbean Coast

Chichén-Itzá

Cozumel

Isla Mujeres

Mérida

Palenque

Uxmal & the Puuc Cities

Villahermosa

NOW, SAVE MONEY ON ALL YOUR TRAVELS!
Join Frommer's™ Dollarwise® Travel Club

Saving money while traveling is never a simple matter, which is why the **Dollarwise Travel Club** was formed 31 years ago. Developed in response to requests from Frommer's Travel Guide readers, the Club provides cost-cutting travel strategies, up-to-date travel information, and a sense of community for value-conscious travelers from all over the world.

In keeping with the money-saving concept, the annual membership fee is low—$18 for U.S. residents or $20 for residents of Canada, Mexico, and other countries—and is immediately exceeded by the value of your benefits, which include:

1. Any TWO books listed on the following pages.
2. Plus any ONE Frommer's City Guide.
3. A subscription to our quarterly newspaper, *The Dollarwise Traveler.*
4. A membership card that entitles you to purchase through the Club all Frommer's publications for 33% to 50% off their retail price.

The eight-page *Dollarwise Traveler* tells you about the latest developments in good-value travel worldwide and includes the following columns: **Hospitality Exchange** (for those offering and seeking hospitality in cities all over the world); **Share-a-Trip** (for those looking for travel companions to share costs); and **Readers Ask . . . Readers Reply** (for those with travel questions that other members can answer).

Aside from the Frommer's Guides and the Gault Millau Guides, you can also choose from our Special Editions. These include such titles as *California with Kids* (a compendium of the best of California's accommodations, restaurants, and sightseeing attractions appropriate for those traveling with toddlers through teens); *Candy Apple: New York with Kids* (a spirited guide to the Big Apple by a savvy New York grandmother that's perfect for both visitors and residents); *Caribbean Hideaways* (the 100 most romantic places to stay in the Islands, all rated on ambience, food, sports opportunities, and price); *Honeymoon Destinations* (a guide to planning and choosing just the right destination from hundreds of possibilities in the U.S., Mexico, and the Caribbean); *Marilyn Wood's Wonderful Weekends* (a selection of the best mini-vacations within a 200-mile radius of New York City, including descriptions of country inns and other accommodations, restaurants, picnic spots, sights, and activities); and *Paris Rendez-Vous* (a delightful guide to the best places to meet in Paris whether for power breakfasts or dancing till dawn).

To join this Club, simply send the appropriate membership fee with your name and address to: Frommer's Dollarwise Travel Club, 15 Columbus Circle, New York, NY 10023. Remember to specify which single city guide and which two other guides you wish to receive in your initial package of member's benefits. Or tear out the next page, check off your choices, and send the page to us with your membership fee.

FROMMER BOOKS
PRENTICE HALL PRESS
15 COLUMBUS CIRCLE
NEW YORK, NY 10023
212/373-8125

Date _____

Friends:

Please send me the books checked below.

FROMMER'S™ GUIDES

(Guides to sightseeing and tourist accommodations and facilities from budget to deluxe, with emphasis on the medium-priced.)

☐ Alaska $14.95	☐ Germany $14.95
☐ Australia $14.95	☐ Italy $14.95
☐ Austria & Hungary $14.95	☐ Japan & Hong Kong. $14.95
☐ Belgium, Holland & Lux-	☐ Mid-Atlantic States $14.95
embourg $14.95	☐ New England $14.95
☐ Bermuda & The Bahamas $14.95	☐ New York State. $14.95
☐ Brazil $14.95	☐ Northwest. $14.95
☐ Canada. $14.95	☐ Portugal, Madeira & the Azores. $14.95
☐ Caribbean $14.95	☐ Skiing Europe $14.95
☐ Cruises (incl. Alaska, Carib, Mex, Ha-	☐ South Pacific $14.95
waii, Panama, Canada & US) . .$14.95	☐ Southeast Asia $14.95
☐ California & Las Vegas. $14.95	☐ Southern Atlantic States $14.95
☐ Egypt $14.95	☐ Southwest. $14.95
☐ England & Scotland. $14.95	☐ Switzerland & Liechtenstein $14.95
☐ Florida $14.95	☐ USA $15.95
☐ France. $14.95	

FROMMER'S $-A-DAY® GUIDES

(In-depth guides to sightseeing and low-cost tourist accommodations and facilities.)

☐ Europe on $40 a Day $15.95	☐ New York on $60 a Day $13.95
☐ Australia on $40 a Day $13.95	☐ New Zealand on $45 a Day. $13.95
☐ Eastern Europe on $25 a Day .$13.95	☐ Scandinavia on $60 a Day. $13.95
☐ England on $50 a Day $13.95	☐ Scotland & Wales on $40 a Day $13.95
☐ Greece on $35 a Day. $13.95	☐ South America on $35 a Day. $13.95
☐ Hawaii on $60 a Day $13.95	☐ Spain & Morocco on $40 a Day $13.95
☐ India on $25 a Day $12.95	☐ Turkey on $30 a Day $13.95
☐ Ireland on $35 a Day $13.95	☐ Washington, D.C. & Historic Va. on
☐ Israel on $40 a Day $13.95	$40 a Day $13.95
☐ Mexico on $35 a Day. $13.95	

FROMMER'S TOURING GUIDES

(Color illustrated guides that include walking tours, cultural and historic sites, and other vital travel information.)

☐ Amsterdam $10.95	☐ New York. $10.95
☐ Australia. $9.95	☐ Paris. $8.95
☐ Brazil $10.95	☐ Rome $10.95
☐ Egypt $8.95	☐ Scotland $9.95
☐ Florence $8.95	☐ Thailand $9.95
☐ Hong Kong $10.95	☐ Turkey. $10.95
☐ London. $8.95	☐ Venice. $8.95

TURN PAGE FOR ADDITONAL BOOKS AND ORDER FORM

0690

FROMMER'S CITY GUIDES

(Pocket-size guides to sightseeing and tourist accommodations and facilities in all price ranges.)

☐ Amsterdam/Holland. $8.95		☐ Montréal/Québec City $8.95
☐ Athens $8.95		☐ New Orleans $8.95
☐ Atlanta. $8.95		☐ New York. $8.95
☐ Atlantic City/Cape May $8.95		☐ Orlando. $8.95
☐ Barcelona $7.95		☐ Paris $8.95
☐ Belgium $7.95		☐ Philadelphia $8.95
☐ Boston $8.95		☐ Rio $8.95
☐ Cancún/Cozumel/Yucatán . .$8.95		☐ Rome $8.95
☐ Chicago $8.95		☐ Salt Lake City $8.95
☐ Denver/Boulder/Colorado		☐ San Diego $8.95
Springs $7.95		☐ San Francisco $8.95
☐ Dublin/Ireland. $8.95		☐ Santa Fe/Taos/Albuquerque $8.95
☐ Hawaii $8.95		☐ Seattle/Portland. $7.95
☐ Hong Kong $7.95		☐ Sydney $8.95
☐ Las Vegas $8.95		☐ Tampa/St. Petersburg $8.95
☐ Lisbon/Madrid/Costa del Sol. .$8.95		☐ Tokyo $7.95
☐ London. $8.95		☐ Toronto. $8.95
☐ Los Angeles. $8.95		☐ Vancouver/Victoria. $7.95
☐ Mexico City/Acapulco $8.95		☐ Washington, D.C. $8.95
☐ Minneapolis/St. Paul. $8.95		

SPECIAL EDITIONS

☐ Beat the High Cost of Travel . . .$6.95	☐ Motorist's Phrase Book (Fr/Ger/Sp). . . .$4.95
☐ Bed & Breakfast—N. America $11.95	☐ Paris Rendez-Vous $10.95
☐ California with Kids $14.95	☐ Swap and Go (Home Exchanging) $10.95
☐ Caribbean Hideaways $14.95	☐ The Candy Apple (NY with Kids) $12.95
☐ Manhattan's Outdoor	☐ Travel Diary and Record Book $5.95
Sculpture. $15.95	

☐ Honeymoon Destinations (US, Mex & Carib) $14.95

☐ Where to Stay USA (From $3 to $30 a night) $10.95

☐ Marilyn Wood's Wonderful Weekends (CT, DE, MA, NH, NJ, NY, PA, RI, VT) $11.95

☐ The New World of Travel (Annual sourcebook by Arthur Frommer for savvy travelers) . .$16.95

GAULT MILLAU

(The only guides that distinguish the truly superlative from the merely overrated.)

☐ The Best of Chicago $15.95	☐ The Best of Los Angeles $16.95
☐ The Best of France. $16.95	☐ The Best of New England $15.95
☐ The Best of Hong Kong $16.95	☐ The Best of New York. $16.95
☐ The Best of Italy $16.95	☐ The Best of Paris $16.95
☐ The Best of London. $16.95	☐ The Best of San Francisco $16.95

☐ The Best of Washington, D.C. $16.95

ORDER NOW!

In U.S. include $2 shipping UPS for 1st book; $1 ea. add'l book. Outside U.S. $3 and $1, respectively. Allow four to six weeks for delivery in U.S., longer outside U.S.

Enclosed is my check or money order for $_____

NAME_____

ADDRESS_____

CITY_____ STATE _____ ZIP____

0690